SERIOUS
Cycling

Edmund R. Burke, PhD
University of Colorado

Human Kinetics

Library of Congress Cataloging-in-Publication Data

Burke, Ed, 1949-
    Serious cycling / Edmund R. Burke.
        p.   cm.
    Includes index.
    ISBN 0-87322-759-X
    1. Cycling.   2. Cycling--Training.   I. Title.
GV1041.B77   1995
796.6--dc20   94-17276
                                                                                      CIP

ISBN: 0-87322-759-X

Copyright © 1995 by Edmund R. Burke

Developmental Editor: Rodd Whelpley
Assistant Editors: Julie Marx Ohnemus and Jenny Wilson
Copyeditor: Lisa Sotirelis
Proofreader: Jim Burns
Indexer: Kathy Bennett
Text Designer: Judy Henderson
Typesetters and Layout Artists: Kathy Boudreau-Fuoss and Judy Henderson
Photo Editor: Karen Maier
Cover Designer: Jack Davis
Photographer (cover): F-Stock/John Laptad
Illustrators: Gretchen Walters and Keith Blomberg
Printer: United Graphics

Human Kinetics books are available at special discounts for bulk purchase. Special editions or book excerpts can also be created to specification. For details, contact the Special Sales Manager at Human Kinetics.

Printed in the United States of America   10   9   8   7   6   5   4   3   2

Human Kinetics
P.O. Box 5076, Champaign, IL 61825-5076
1-800-747-4457

Canada: Human Kinetics, Box 24040, Windsor, ON N8Y 4Y9
1-800-465-7301 (in Canada only)

Europe: Human Kinetics, P.O. Box IW14, Leeds LS16 6TR, England
(44) 532 781708

Australia: Human Kinetics, 2 Ingrid Street, Clapham 5062, South Australia
(08) 371 3755

New Zealand: Human Kinetics, P.O. Box 105-231, Auckland 1
(09) 309 2259

Contents

Preface

The heights by great men reached and kept
Were not attained by sudden flight
But they, while their companions slept,
Were toiling upward in the night.
—*Henry Wadsworth Longfellow*

When I mention to cyclists that I have written books and articles on the scientific and technical aspects of cycling, many suggest, with a bit of frustration, "Ed, why not write a book for riders who don't have PhDs?" They need a text that will bridge the gap between scientific observation and cycling performance. The great body of knowledge about the science of cycling lies unused by most cyclists. Trial and error may go a long way, but who knows the potential of a cyclist armed with the knowledge of a thousand dedicated scientists? Knowledge is strong medicine.

Although many books have been written on cycling, few report the cutting-edge data in the depth and manner that I believe will improve performance. This is not a primary goal for many scientists, but it may be one of the most important contributions they can make. Interpreting complex information on physiology, biomechanics, nutrition, injury, and training in a manner that is understandable to all cycling participants is my primary goal for this book.

Serious Cycling provides the basis for a better understanding of the scientific preparation for cycling for all cyclists, whether they are top-level racers or dedicated enthusiasts with a passion for riding. Drawing together the latest research in cycling science and training theory, I have created a framework of training principles for improved performance. The text provides a basis for understanding cycling research, so you can use its discoveries to improve your fitness and excellence in the sport.

Chapters 1 and 2 discuss the physiological aspects of cycling. The best training programs are designed to build up your body in a way that is specific to the demands of your cycling specialty. You need a basic knowledge of what makes a stage racer durable, a match sprinter quick, and a time trialist successful in order to have some idea of what it takes, physically, to improve every element of your riding. In these two chapters I describe the typical body composition of successful cyclists; how the respiratory system works; how the body stores, restores, and uses energy; and how the genetic makeup of muscles may influence speed and endurance. I have tried to keep these topics as uncluttered of "sciencespeak" as possible without watering down the information. Use the knowledge you gain in these early chapters to help understand later discussion on designing sound training programs.

Chapters 3 through 5 use the physiological principles covered in chapters 1 and 2 as the basis for designing endurance-training workouts especially suited for road racers, tempo-training regimens time trialists will value, and sprint workouts not only for sprinters but also for road cyclists (who, after working hard on their bikes for over an hour, often find that the race comes down to a mad dash for the tape). Whatever your cycling goals, you're bound to benefit from several of these workouts.

Chapter 6 discusses many off-the-bike and off-season training modes and explains how to use equipment such as cyclocomputers and heart rate monitors that allow you to gauge what is happening in your body while you work out. Chapter 7 shows you how to put it all together and outlines year-long training programs for serious cyclists. Whether you're a junior competitor, a senior-level competitor, a college student, or a working person who loves nothing more than to cycle like a pro, this chapter has a program that's right for you.

But cycling performance doesn't come exclusively from the power of your lungs and legs. Successful cycling also takes brain power. Feed your mind with chapters 8 through 11 on nutrition, biomechanics, wind and rolling resistance, and health- and injury-related issues. These chapters represent much of the best and most current cycling-specific information available on these subjects. You'll learn ways to make you and your bike work with, not against, each other.

Of course, all this information does little good unless you remain committed to your cycling. Whether you plan to race or you ride "just" to keep yourself in top shape, you need to stay with your program. Commitment combined with correct technique and smart training equal cycling success. I urge you to commit to your sport by using this four-step process:

1. Know yourself. Acknowledge your strengths and weaknesses. If you are a poor sprinter, are you willing to spend time on the track to improve your speed? What keeps you going when the times are tough?
2. Set goals and targets for yourself. What do you want to achieve during this season and the next? How will you get there?
3. Be tough on yourself. What are you willing to give up to become a better cyclist? Will you go out on those long rides in the middle

of winter? If you get dropped, do you chase until you get back to the pack?

4. Have a plan. Do you have a year-long training schedule designed to let you peak for the events that are most important to you? Do you have specific goals for each training ride? Do you keep a training diary? Know where you are going and how to get there.

We all have surprising athletic potential; it waits only for us to understand our bodies, coax our strengths, and meet the special needs that result. If this book offers you inspiration, the empirical basis for making sound training decisions, or the wherewithal to implement the four-step process that enhances your commitment to cycling, it serves its purpose. *Serious Cycling* provides a working base for you to achieve greater performance. Work your hardest; cycle your best; and enjoy the ride.

Acknowledgments

I am indebted to many people for the information, ideas, and concepts that make up this book. First, I would like to express my appreciation to the athletes who have worked with me over the last 18 years and to the sport science and cycling researchers who have shared their information. I particularly want to thank Dave Costill, who first showed me the way of sport science; Chester Kyle, who is always a source of assistance; and Peter VanHandle, who was always there to help not only cyclists but all athletes trying to improve their performance. To the many coaches, especially Eddy Borysewicz, who helped me better understand the sport, my thanks. I must also acknowledge the editors who have helped me: Ed Pavelka, Rich Carlson, Barbara George, Marilee Attley, Marni Basic, and Rodd Whelpley, among others. Michael Parker's careful review of this book was invaluable. To Kathleen, my wife, I owe the greatest debt. She has unselfishly provided the encouragement and support that has allowed me to devote an excessive amount of time to work and to writing.

© F-Stock/John Laptad

Profile of the Serious Cyclist

There seems to be no formula that determines a champion. Champions are born, and then made. This applies to all of us. We all need to work to be our best.

—*Connie Carpenter-Phinney*

Competitive road cycling is more demanding physiologically and psychologically than any sport I know. Criteriums last about an hour, calling upon a cyclist for stamina, gamesmanship, and bursts of all-out speed. Cycling's premier event, the Tour de France, is a 3-week grind that tests and punishes—and sometimes even rewards—cyclists for their endurance, determination, and just plain guts. Cycling may even require you to race city-to-city in weather that reaches all extremes and on terrain that sometimes takes you above the clouds. No wonder afficionados call it the king of sports. No wonder its champions are epic figures.

Champions adopt training procedures that match, as closely as possible, racing situations—procedures that simulate the exertion of the long-distance ride ending in a breakaway that spends the cyclist's reserves. These sessions also test a rider's knowledge of tactics and strategies, mastery of skills, and courage. Strict emulation of your favorite champion, however, may be misguided because individuals possess unique physical, physiological, and psychological potentials.

The first challenge of creating the right training program, then, is understanding a little bit about your physiology. After all, you are the human engine that makes your bike go. This chapter will focus on three specific areas in the profiles of serious cyclists. They are

- body composition,
- the respiratory system, and
- muscles.

The chapter will finish with a brief discussion of physical characteristics unique to female cyclists.

With an appreciation of the correct body composition for cycling, an understanding of how the respiratory system turns oxygen into energy, and a knowledge of why some cyclists' muscles respond faster than others, you will be set to apply the advice in the remainder of this book to your own physiological and biomechanical needs, which are determined by your body type and stage of training. You will also be guided through the demands of your cycling and given guidelines for better developing your yearly training programs.

Body Composition

This discussion of body composition will focus on the relationship of body weight to body fat and how body weight can influence cycling. In cycling, as in most sports, carrying extra weight is a definite disadvantage—especially when climbing a hill. On the other hand, a cyclist needs a specific amount of muscle mass for the power aspects of the sport, such as time trials and sprints. Body weight, then, is probably not the best fitness indicator. Body composition (the amount of fat and muscle) is more important, and it gives a truer indication of how much "extra baggage" you may be carrying on the bicycle.

Your body weight is largely determined by the size of your body frame, sex, and genetics. Determining your *ideal* body weight can be difficult. Charts and articles based on the general population are not always good guides for your body weight because cyclists are typically more muscular than the average person. A fit cyclist weighs more than a less-fit noncyclist of the same age and height because the cyclist has more muscle mass. Avoid comparing yourself with other cyclists you read about. They may feel comfortable and perform well weighing either more or less than you, even if they are your age and height.

Percent body fat is a measure of relative leanness or fatness, and it can be calculated from underwater weighing or skinfold measurements. Because a certain amount of body fat (referred to as *essential fat*) is necessary for proper physiological functioning and because some fat is even located within muscle cells, it is not good for cyclists to lower their body fat percentages too much.

The "gold standard" for determining body fat is underwater weighing. It involves measuring body density by comparing body weight on land and under water. Fat is lighter per unit volume than water, so it floats. Individuals who have more than their fair share of body fat have a low density, and they usually have no problem floating.

Many laboratories and health clubs use instruments called skinfold calipers to give relatively good estimates of a person's body fat. Properly used, these measurements can determine your percent body fat, even showing changes in body composition if you measure on a monthly basis.

Measurements of competitive cyclists have shown the average percent body fat to be between 8% and 12% for male cyclists, between 10% and 15% for female cyclists, and between 8% and 12% for juniors. The average U.S. male has about 18% to 21% body fat, whereas the average female has 20% to 25%.

Remember, there is a normal variation among individuals in percent body fat, just as there is with most physiological variables. Also, because of the errors inherent in the methods of calculating percent body fat, the best way to monitor your own body composition is to record changes in it throughout the season. Your percent body fat calculated during the peak training season, when you feel strong, should be used as your baseline. If that percentage falls within the expected range for fit cyclists, you can use that value to monitor changes in your weight and percent body fat during the off-season or if you are injured for any long period.

Body size and weight have also been shown to have an effect on the energy cost of cycling. When you cycle on level ground at typical training or racing speeds, wind resistance is by far the most important factor in slowing you down and increasing your energy cost (as you will

Weight Loss and Cycling Performance

In road cycling, maintaining a low body weight and having a low percentage of fat is critical. During the initial months of the season many cyclists adhere to strict diets and put in plenty of miles to burn the excess fat they may have stored over the winter.

Although you may use many techniques and diets to lose weight, the bottom line is to balance your calories. Weight loss results only when you withdraw calories either by exercising more (burning calories) or by consuming less calories. One pound of fat is equal to about 3,500 calories, so burning fat from your body can be difficult and can require a lot of time on the bike. Even when you are racing hard, you are only burning about 600 to 900 calories per hour (or possibly more when time trialing). And early in the season you will likely be burning significantly less.

Riding more and eating less is the best way to lose weight in the early season. Fasting and low-calorie diets should be avoided. Severe food restriction, even on a short-term basis, can be detrimental to training and racing and is not recommended. When low-calorie diets are undertaken, it is primarily lean body mass and water, not fat, that is lost. The result is a decrease in muscle glycogen (stored carbohydrates), muscle water content, and endurance as well as impaired cardiovascular function and thermoregulation.

As you will see in chapter 2, a main energy source for cycling is carbohydrate. Carbohydrate is stored as glycogen in your muscles and liver. Food restriction, with or without exercise, depletes your body's glycogen stores. When your body is low on glycogen, it is like a car running on gas fumes. Longer periods of food restriction can slow down your body's metabolic rate, which makes losing weight even more difficult.

Most health professionals recommend slow weight loss as the safest and most effective approach. A sensible weight-loss program allows you to lose weight gradually—about 1 or 2 pounds per week. Remember, to lose 1 pound, you must burn 3,500 calories more than you consume. For example, reducing your caloric intake by 300 to 500 calories per day, along with some long rides to burn more calories, will result in a weight loss of 1-1/2 to 2 pounds per week.

Before beginning a weight-loss program, assess your diet. Find out where your food calories are coming from by keeping a diary of everything you eat and drink in a day. Keep this diary for several days so you can get an idea of what is normal for you.

For optimal performance and training, you should try to achieve your desired weight before the season begins or in your first few weeks back on the bike. It is also essential that you keep your daily carbohydrate intake high (a minimum of 60% of your total caloric intake).

Here are some additional suggestions to help you achieve your ideal weight by the first race of the season:

- Use girth measurements (distance around arms, legs, waist, and chest) or skinfold measurements and body weight to determine changes in your body composition. (The person who takes the skinfold measures for you should be trained and experienced.) Remember, as you lose fat and gain lean body mass you may maintain or gain a little weight because muscle tissue weighs more than fat tissue.

- Keep track of the fat in your diet. Fat has over twice the calories as the same amount of carbohydrate and protein. Products such as butter, salad dressings, sour cream, and mayonnaise are very high in fat.

- Keep track of your morning body weight. Once again, you should be losing only 1 or 2 pounds per week. If you are down several pounds from the previous day, chances are you are just chronically dehydrated. Research has shown that fluid losses in excess of 2% to 3% of your body weight will affect your performance by reducing your blood volume. A reduced blood volume limits your ability to carry oxygen to your working muscles and will also reduce your tolerance to heat. As with carbohydrate depletion, dehydration can make you feel sluggish, weak, and dizzy when riding long distances in hot weather.

Some cyclists can lose weight easily and don't need very much help. For others, losing weight is difficult. If you are having trouble losing weight or even deciding if you *should* lose weight, visit a registered dietitian or someone with an extensive background in exercise physiology and nutrition.

see in chapter 10). Larger cyclists have more body surface for the wind to push against than do smaller cyclists, so they need to use more energy to overcome the higher wind resistance. Energy supply comes from the ability to provide the working muscles with oxygen. By virtue of their size, larger cyclists, while being hampered by wind resistance more than smaller cyclists, also have greater absolute energy supplies. So which factor wins? It turns out that the disadvantage of a little extra wind resistance is more than outweighed by the extra energy supply larger cyclists have when cycling on level ground. This is why the best time trial cyclists tend to be large.

If you're a small cyclist, you may be asking when you are at an advantage. But you probably already know the answer from experience. When the uphills arrive, speed decreases and overcoming wind resistance is no longer the main energy cost. Instead, gravity plays the major role in holding you back. The more you and your bicycle weigh (that is, the more weight you have to push uphill), the higher the energy cost you incur. Just as in cycling on level ground, the energy supply still stems from the ability to supply the working muscles with oxygen. So it might appear that we have the same situation as cycling on level roads: a higher absolute energy cost for larger cyclists, but also a higher absolute energy supply. But in this case the energy cost of being bigger outweighs the advantage of the extra energy supply. So small cyclists will usually be able to get to the top of a hill faster than their competitors.

Research by David Swain of Old Dominion University shows that relative to body mass, smaller cyclists are better able to produce energy aerobically than larger cyclists because they have more surface area in their lungs and blood vessels proportional to their body mass. Consequently, smaller cyclists have a larger relative capacity to deliver oxygen to their working muscles (a larger relative aerobic capacity). This larger relative capacity works to the smaller cyclist's advantage when the energy costs increase, as they do in hill climbing.

Although small cyclists tend to be better hill climbers, recent years have seen Miguel Indurain (not a small cyclist) demonstrate the ability to climb with the best of them over major mountain passes. This ability stems from Miguel's large aerobic capacity, as you'll see later in this chapter. Your ability to climb depends on your ability to process oxygen. A smaller cyclist who happens to have a higher maximal aerobic capacity (relative to size) than you will probably beat you to the top.

The Respiratory System

Oxygen is one of the keys to success in road racing. A steady supply of oxygen allows you to use the more efficient aerobic energy system to produce energy for cycling. Just as oxygen is required for a fire to burn efficiently, it is necessary for your muscles to produce energy efficiently. When your cycling muscles can't get a sufficient supply of oxygen, the body is forced to use inefficient anaerobic energy systems. (Aerobic and anaerobic energy systems will be discussed in greater detail in chapter 2.)

Let's look at how oxygen enters your body and helps produce energy with your muscles. First we'll examine the process of oxygen entering the lungs, getting assimilated into the blood, and being pumped by the heart to the muscles. Then we'll see how energy is produced within the muscle cells.

The Heart and Lungs of a Champion

The lungs of the trained cyclist can process a larger volume of air than an untrained individual's lungs. The *vital capacity* of the lungs is the maximum volume of gas that can be exhaled following maximum inspiration. This capacity reflects the volume of the lung and the strength of the respiratory musculature. As you might expect, cyclists have much greater vital capacities than nonathletes. Nearly 6 liters of air can be processed in a single breath by the average trained cyclist whereas the untrained person has a vital capacity of less than 5 liters.

Just as important to cyclists is the maximum amount of air they can move in and out of their lungs per minute. This is called *minute ventilation*. Minute ventilation for untrained individuals averages between 120 and 170 liters per minute. Figures of more than 200 liters per minute are not uncommon for road cyclists. This capacity is developed over years of training, increasing the strength of their respiratory muscles, and is also due to their slightly larger vital capacities.

Moving large volumes of air into and out of the lungs is pointless unless the blood has a correspondingly greater capacity to extract oxygen from the inhaled air and to transport it to the working muscles. Trained athletes have a large network of capillaries in the lungs that transport the oxygen from the lungs to the red blood cells in the capillaries and pass off the carbon dioxide. In addition, the trained cyclist has more red blood cells than an untrained person has, to help transport the oxygen.

Once the blood is saturated with oxygen, it needs to be pumped through the arteries to the capillaries of the leg muscles. Through training, the cyclist's heart has grown in size and muscular strength. Because the volume and musculature of the heart have increased, you might expect the pumping capacity of the heart to have increased. Such is the case. As Figure 1.1 shows, the volume of blood that can be pumped out of the heart with each beat (stroke volume) is roughly twice the amount in the trained individual (140 to 160 milliliters) as in the untrained individual (80 to 100 milliliters).

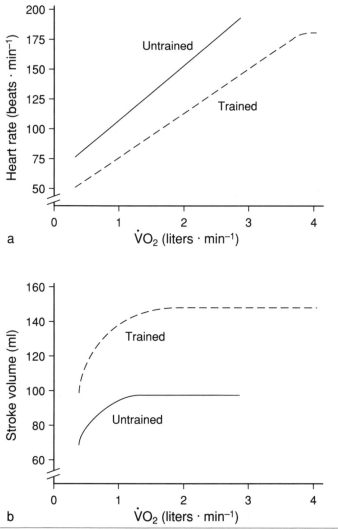

Figure 1.1   Cardiac output = heart rate × stroke volume. These figures show the relationship of exercise intensity (oxygen intake measured as $\dot{V}O_2$, which is the symbol for oxygen consumption in a given amount of time) to the heart rate (a) and the stroke volume (b), before and after training.

Note. From *Training for Cross-Country Ski Racing: A Physiological Guide for Athletes and Coaches* (p. 34) by B.J. Sharkey, 1984, Champaign, IL: Human Kinetics. Copyright 1984 by Brian J. Sharkey. Reprinted by permission.

This explains why highly trained cyclists have lower resting heart rates. If the body requires a certain amount of oxygenated blood per minute and the heart can pump more blood per beat than it could before training, then it stands to reason that the heart has to beat less often per minute to maintain the same output. There is also evidence of decreased sympathetic activity and increased parasympathetic activity on the heart. The sympathetic nervous system, when stimulated, increases heart rate; the parasympathetic nervous system decreases heart rate when stimulated.

The amount of blood pumped per minute is called *cardiac output*. Cardiac output at rest is about 5 to 6 liters per minute. Trained cyclists can pump 30 to 40 liters per minute during intense exercise, whereas untrained individuals pump 20 to 25 liters per minute.

But what good is a large cardiac output if a cyclist cannot maintain this output for long periods of time? It is not uncommon for road cyclists to maintain heart rates in excess of 160 to 170 beats per minute for several hours in a race. This is well over 75% to 85% of their maximum heart rates. Because we have seen in Figure 1.1 that cardiac output, heart rate, and oxygen consumption are closely related, we can assume that these values are correspondingly as high during intense cycling.

In fact, Lance Armstrong rode with his heart rate close to 180 beats per minute during the 59-kilometer Lac de Madine time trial. "I was able to hold my maximum effort for about 80% of the ride, and for about 20% of the time I was riding somewhere between 160 and 180 beats per minute," stated the recent world champion while being tested at the Olympic Training Center in Colorado Springs, Colorado.

Major circulatory changes take place at the muscle level also. Both the number of arterioles running to the working muscles and the number of capillaries within the muscles increase with training, providing more efficient oxygen transport. This increase is proportional to the role the particular muscle plays in training. A cyclist's thigh muscles have been found to double the number of capillaries in response to a long-term aerobic training program.

Cardiorespiratory Fitness

If you were to look at a list of all physiological changes brought about by training, one thing would become immediately apparent. The vast majority of measurable changes are in the oxygen-transport system and at the muscle-cell level, which accounts for the increased utilization of oxygen during cycling. These changes reflect a basic increase in what is called *cardiorespiratory fitness*—your body's ability to take oxygen from the atmosphere and transport it to the muscle cells where energy is produced to pedal the bicycle.

Because the limiting factor of the system is oxygen, scientists can evaluate the functional capacity of the system by measuring how much oxygen is consumed while a person performs maximal work. This measure is referred to as $\dot{V}O_2$max, or maximal oxygen consumption, and is probably the best known and most frequently used laboratory test in fitness evaluation. This test determines the maximal rate at which a cyclist can use oxygen. Because oxygen is needed to convert food (mainly carbohydrates and fat) into energy, the more oxygen you can use, the more energy you can produce. Translated into practical terms, to ride at a pace of 20 miles per hour, your body needs to produce a certain amount of energy. To cycle at 30 miles per hour requires more energy. Therefore, the more energy you can produce, the faster you can pedal the bicycle. Training improves your $\dot{V}O_2$max up to what is your *genetic ceiling*. Reaching your true maximal oxygen consumption will take several years of hard training.

A $\dot{V}O_2$max test is usually conducted using some type of stationary bicycle, either the cyclist's own bike on a trainer or a stationary bicycle (ergometer) that allows the intensity of exercise to be increased in small increments at set time intervals (usually 2 to 3 minutes). Because the body's ability to use oxygen is partly based on the muscles used, an individual's $\dot{V}O_2$max is usually slightly lower when cycling than when running or cross-country skiing. This is because very little of the upper body is used in cycling; most of the power comes from the leg muscles.

During the test, the amount of oxygen used at each exercise intensity is calculated by collecting and analyzing the cyclist's expired air. As the workload increases, so does the body's use of oxygen. When the body reaches its maximum ability to consume oxygen, the amount of oxygen use can no longer increase and it levels off. At this plateau, the cyclist is said to have reached $\dot{V}O_2$max, or maximal oxygen consumption. This is shown as point A in Figure 1.2. The units for $\dot{V}O_2$max are milliliters of oxygen consumed per kilogram of body weight per minute (ml/kg/min).

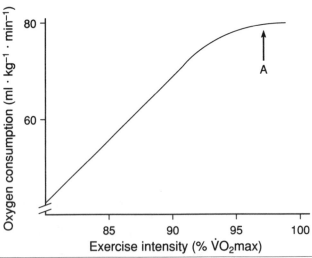

Figure 1.2   Oxygen consumption increases linearly as workload increases.

Lactate Threshold—
A Fitness Predictor That Won't Max You Out

Although most top endurance cyclists have high $\dot{V}O_2$max values, and it *is* a good predictor of performance, coaches and scientists have begun to look at physiological tests that don't push cyclists completely to the maximum to determine fitness and economy of effort.

One submaximal test determines a rider's lactate threshold. Lactic acid is the by-product of anaerobic energy production (energy produced without oxygen). Because it is an acid, it begins to shut down the muscles' contractile mechanisms and may even cause a burning sensation in the muscles. During exercise, a cyclist can perform up to a certain intensity without building up very much lactic acid in the blood. When this intensity is exceeded, lactic acid levels in the muscles rise, and the muscles fatigue rapidly. The critical exercise intensity at which the contractile mechanisms begin to shut down has been referred to as *lactate threshold*.

The best way to determine lactate threshold is to have a cyclist ride a stationary bicycle at a given intensity for 4 to 5 minutes in a laboratory. Then a small sample of blood is taken from the fingertip to be analyzed for lactic acid. The workload (intensity) is increased slightly. This process is repeated for four to five workloads. When lactic acid values are plotted against oxygen consumption and heart rate, an upswing in the graph occurs. The cyclist then has a range of heart rates corresponding to her lactate threshold use to guide training intensity. Most elite cyclists reach their lactate threshold at about 85% to 90% of their $\dot{V}O_2$max, whereas untrained individuals reach theirs at about 50% to 70% of their $\dot{V}O_2$max.

Figure 1.3 graphs a cyclist completing a test on a bicycle ergometer that progresses from an easy to a maximum workload. His lactate threshold is at about 90% of his maximum, and the curve plotting lactic acid shows a distinct break. At this point the body begins to produce lactic acid excessively and/or has a hard time removing it from the muscles and blood.

Being able to compete at your lactate threshold for long periods of time is essential for successful performance. This is the

(continued)

Lactate Threshold   *(continued)*

intensity you need to hold in a 10- to 25-mile time trial or while going hard in a breakaway. In later chapters guidelines will be given to help improve your lactate threshold.

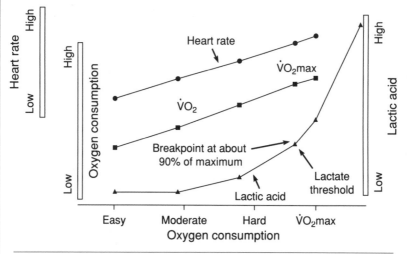

Figure 1.3   Physiological characteristics and the lactate threshold of a road cyclist.

To repeat the most popular of all sports metaphors, imagine your body as an automobile: Your $\dot{V}O_2$max represents your engine, and your heart and lungs are what pump fuel throughout your body. So having a high $\dot{V}O_2$max is like having a powerful engine—you have the potential to go long distances.

Elite road cyclists' average values for maximal oxygen uptake are among the highest levels recorded. Male and female cyclists range between 75 and 90 ml/kg/min and between 60 and 70 ml/kg/min, respectively. For comparison, Swedish elite male cross-country skiers seldom show $\dot{V}O_2$max below 80 ml/kg/min and range between 80 and 94 ml/kg/min, and female counterparts' values range from 70 to 75 ml/kg/min. In healthy, nonathletic males, $\dot{V}O_2$max values range between 45 and 55 ml/kg/min; in untrained females, between 35 and 45 ml/kg/min.

The tremendous endurance capacity and recuperation ability of Miguel Indurain, a several-time winner of the Tour de France, are well known in the peleton. But only recently in the *Penn State Sports Medicine Newsletter* did the University of Navarra reveal the Spaniard to be so remarkable. His resting heart rate is 28 beats per minute; during moderate mountain climbs, it registers 150 beats per minute, but within 30 seconds of beginning the descent it drops to around 60. His $\dot{V}O_2$max is 88 ml/kg/min, the highest recorded for a cyclist. During an all-out maximum effort, Indurain's heart is reportedly capable of circulating 50 liters of blood per minute, which is double that of a sedentary individual's.

The data for elite cyclists suggest that high oxygen uptake is required for successful competition at the national and international levels. But even though high aerobic consumption is necessary for success in road cycling, it is not the only determinant for success.

Cycling Economy: Using Your Aerobic Capacity Wisely

Economy to a cyclist is like economy to an automobile driver: the ability to do a certain amount of work using as little energy as possible. You want to conserve gas in your car. You want to use a low percentage of your $\dot{V}O_2$max in your body at a given cycling speed. Both examples represent economy.

"I would say that economy is one of the single most important determinants of success at the elite level of cycling," says Jay T. Kearney, PhD, senior exercise physiologist for the U.S. Olympic Committee. "If two cyclists have similar $\dot{V}O_2$max profiles, the more economical cyclist will win most races. Even if a cyclist has a relatively low $\dot{V}O_2$max, he often can defeat other cyclists, because he may ride at a lower percentage of his maximum at any given speed."

An uneconomical cyclist may need to use 5% to 10% more energy than an economical cyclist to cycle at a given pace. This means that if the two cyclists have comparable $\dot{V}O_2$max values, the uneconomical cyclist will work closer to his maximal capacity than the economical cyclist. Because the physiological strain the body feels is directly related to the percentage of $\dot{V}O_2$max, the economical cyclist will have an advantage. In other words, she will be able to ride faster while experiencing less fatigue.

Here is another example of the power of economy: Two cyclists enter a time trial. They have the same $\dot{V}O_2$max profiles, but Cyclist A is more economical. Both ride at a high speed. However, to reach and maintain this speed, Cyclist B must ride at a pace equal to 95% of her $\dot{V}O_2$max. Cyclist A, on the other hand, can ride at the same speed, yet only be at 90% of his max. Should he increase his effort to 95%, he would outride B and win.

Economy can be determined by measuring the amount of oxygen needed to perform at several submaximal intensities. To measure economy this way, a cyclist rides on a stationary bicycle for 5- to 10-minute bouts. Training has been shown to improve economy. If economy really has improved after training, the oxygen cost for each intensity should be less.

Figure 1.4 shows the oxygen consumption of two cyclists at different workloads who have similar $\dot{V}O_2$max measurements. Cyclist A is more economical. At any workload she consumes less oxygen than Cyclist B. At a workload of 300 watts, Cyclist B uses about 70 ml/kg/min while Cyclist A uses about 15% less. Cyclist A achieves a higher work output at her $\dot{V}O_2$max.

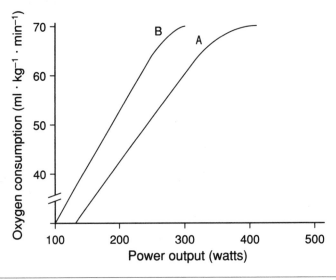

Figure 1.4   Economy curves for two cyclists.

Tempo and interval training (see chapters 4 and 5) can improve your economy. The theory is that by practicing fast cycling you naturally become more economical. You have to be economical to ride at 30-plus miles per hour. Once you've trained your body to respond economically at these speeds, it will most likely do so at the slower speeds of distance cycling.

Another way to improve economy is through biomechanical assessments. A film analysis of a cyclist riding is often used for this. From high-speed film, joint angles and forces can be calculated.

And you can improve your economy by improving your performance. First, improve your pedaling mechanics. Learn to pedal smoothly and correctly so your movements are more effective. In other words, improve your pedal stroke from top dead center all the way through the bottom, and learn how to spin instead of pushing big gears.

Other factors that waste energy without propelling the bicycle forward will affect economy. Fighting the bicycle, holding the handlebars too tightly, and riding in an unaerodynamic position will affect your economy. We'll get into the specifics of biomechanically correct riding technique in chapter 9.

Muscles

In addition to having a high $\dot{V}O_2$max, being able to race at a high percentage of your $\dot{V}O_2$max, and being economical, your endurance and speed during competition depend largely on your muscles' ability to produce energy and force.

Thanks to technological advances it is now possible to obtain samples of muscle tissue from cyclists before, during, and after exercise. This has allowed us to study the makeup of muscles and to gauge the effects of exercise and training. Let's look at what the procedure has taught us about the muscle composition of competitive cyclists.

A muscle biopsy is performed using a needle 3 to 5 millimeters in diameter. The subject is given a local anesthetic, and a small incision is made into the muscle being studied. Because muscle tissue has no pain receptors, the feeling is usually described only as "weird." The needle extracts 20 to 40 milligrams of muscle, which is enough for several biochemical tests, including fiber typing. Figure 1.5 is a depiction of the two types of fibers found in muscle biopsies.

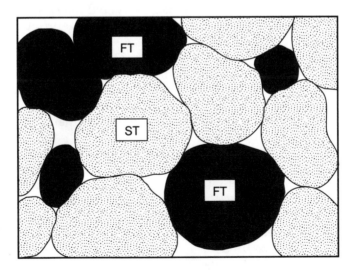

Figure 1.5 Slow- and fast-twitch muscle fibers intermingle in a cross-section of human muscle.

Note. From *Training for Cross-Country Ski Racing: A Physiological Guide for Athletes and Coaches* (p. 11) by B.J. Sharkey, 1984, Champaign, IL: Human Kinetics. Copyright 1984 by Brian J. Sharkey. Reprinted by permission.

Muscle contains bundles of fibers (cells), all of which function basically the same way. That is, when stimulated they contract to maximal tension. Nevertheless, muscle fibers do differ, and the difference is important to cyclists.

Muscle-Fiber Types

Certain muscle fibers are able to contract repeatedly without much fatigue. This type is called Type I, or slow-twitch (ST), fiber because of its high content of myoglobin (an oxygen-storing protein) and enzymes that favor aerobic energy production. Type I fiber has a high aerobic capacity, which means it can produce energy for a long time when sufficient oxygen is available.

The other major type of muscle fiber has a lower aerobic capacity but a high anaerobic capacity (meaning it can produce energy without oxygen) and is known as a Type II, or fast-twitch (FT), fiber. This fiber is normally found in high percentages in sprint and power athletes. Type II fibers can be further broken down into Type IIA and Type IIB fibers. Type IIA fibers are generally described as being a bit more aerobic than Type IIB fibers.

Type I and II fibers have different capacities for breaking down glycogen (stored carbohydrate) and accumulating lactic acid. That is, they have different aerobic and anaerobic capacities. Type I fibers are superior in producing energy aerobically. Type II fibers have a higher anaerobic capacity: they can perform short-term, very intense work when sufficient oxygen is not available.

This isn't the whole story, however. There is a spectrum of aerobic and anaerobic potential within Type I and II fibers. One person's Type II fibers, especially if he has more Type IIA fibers, may have a greater aerobic capacity than another person's. But within an individual, Type I fibers will usually have a higher aerobic capacity than Type II fibers. The reverse is true for anaerobic capacity.

For long-distance cycling, you begin cycling at a submaximal or slow speed, and during this time you recruit primarily the muscle fibers best adapted for endurance activity: Type I fibers and some Type IIA fibers. Gradually, as you become fatigued, you need to call upon other fibers to maintain muscle force and cycling speed. You begin to recruit more Type IIB fibers. As more and more Type I and Type IIA fibers become fatigued (run out of fuel), Type IIB fibers are called upon. This may explain why fatigue seems to come in stages during long road races.

In an average population, muscle-fiber composition is 40% to 50% Type I and 50% to 60% Type II. Within an individual, only very small variations exist from one muscle to another. The lone exception is the soleus muscle (a calf muscle), which is mainly composed of Type I fibers.

Muscle-Fiber Composition and Cycling

Do cyclists need a specific muscle-fiber ratio? Do certain events favor cyclists who are basically Type I or Type II? Table 1.1 provides some answers. Cyclists A and B are both road racers. Cyclist A is especially good in time trials and stage races, but she is usually poor in the sprint at the end of the race. Cyclist B, on the other hand, has an excellent sprint and is a threat to win if he can make it to the last 200 to 300 meters with the lead group. Now look at the biopsy data: Cyclist A has a very high amount of Type I fibers (75%); cyclist B has about an equal number of Type I and II fibers.

Table 1.1 Muscle-Fiber Composition of Three Cyclists			
Cyclist	Type I fiber (%)	Type II fiber (%)	$\dot{V}O_2$max (ml/kg/min)
A	75	25	79
B	52	48	75
C	68	32	72

Cyclist C has 68% Type I fibers and a correspondingly high amount of aerobic enzyme activity. Enzymes are catalysts within the muscle cells that help speed up reactions—in this case, the ability to produce energy aerobically. This explains why she is able to excel in long-distance road races. Similarities have been found in marathon runners: Those who excel in longer distances have a higher percentage of Type I fibers. Some world-class marathoners, for example, have more than 80% Type I fibers. Such runners are usually poor sprinters.

Now we can speculate about the ideal muscle-fiber composition for cyclists. For a sprinter it is easy: Ideal would mean possessing a very high percentage of Type IIA or Type IIB fibers. With weight training and sprint workouts, the strength and anaerobic capacities of these fibers can be developed.

It is more difficult to determine an ideal fiber type for criterium riders, time trialists, and road racers. Due to the strategies available to them, these cyclists can more easily overcome any unfortunate consequences associated with having less desirable fast- to slow-twitch muscle-fiber ratios. For example, thanks to drafting, a cyclist with a mediocre aerobic capacity and a low percentage of Type I fibers can keep pace with good road cyclists. This is especially true on flat-road courses or criteriums.

Nevertheless, Table 1.2 speculates as to what may be the ideal fiber types for various disciplines within the sport of cycling. However, I must caution you, this table is a broad outline, and there may be very successful road cyclists out there who have 50% Type II fibers, with most of them being Type IIA.

Table 1.2 Ideal Muscle-Fiber Types for Specific Cycling Events			
Event and performance time	Type I fiber (%)	Type II fiber (%)	$\dot{V}O_2$max (ml/kg/min)
Kilometer 1000 meters: 1 minute, 6 seconds	25	75	55
Criterium specialist* 50 miles: 2 hours	50	50	72
Criterium specialist** 50 miles: 2 hours	65	35	75
Stage racer 120 miles: 4 hours, 30 minutes	60	40	80
Time trialist 25 miles: 58 minutes	70	30	75
*Excellent sprinter **Poor sprinter			

Several studies have investigated what physiological variables may predict bicycle performance. Work completed by Ed Coyle and others from the University of Texas found that, in addition to needing a high maximal oxygen consumption for success in competition, elite national-class road cyclists (Group 1) possessed a higher percentage of Type I fibers and a greater amount of capillaries supplying oxygen to the muscles than did a group of good state-class cyclists (Group 2). Actual 40-kilometer time-trial performance also correlated highly with average power output during a 1-hour laboratory performance test.

What factors allowed Group 1 to produce more force and perform better in competition? This is an interesting question because it begins to specifically and directly explain the superior performance of elite national-class cyclists. It is likely there is no single factor, but numerous factors, that may vary in magnitude from one cyclist to another. Coyle thinks that cyclists with a high percentage of Type I fibers have a distinct advantage because at the same level of energy expenditure (oxygen consumption) their muscles produce more force and power.

It also appears that the thigh muscles of the cyclists in Group 1 were less fatigable than those in Group 2; this allowed Group 1 cyclists to maintain higher intensities and to continually push the pedals with more force. As mentioned, Group 1 possessed more capillaries around each muscle fiber; these capillaries serve to flush lactic acid away from the exercising muscle, thereby reducing fatigue.

So, a high percentage of Type II fibers may be a must for a sprinter and a kilometer rider who must accelerate with big gears at slow speeds, and too many Type I fibers may be a disadvantage for a road racer in certain races. Even though a composition of 60% to 80% Type I fiber is ideal for endurance and muscular efficiency, the road racer will have a hard time chasing down breakaways and sprinting at the finish and may have to stick to time trials or stage races to be successful.

The Benefits of Training

One purpose of training is to develop and improve the capacities of your various types of muscle fiber. It only makes sense to pattern workouts so they will consolidate your strengths and improve your weaknesses. A cyclist who has predominantly Type II fibers will already have the edge in anaerobic capacity and sprinting. What she needs is to develop her aerobic ability. The reverse holds true for a cyclist who has mostly Type I fibers.

The subtypes of Type II fibers do show some modification to training. With training, Type IIB fibers can take on the characteristics of Type IIA fibers. This suggests that through training these fibers can change their metabolic capacity and gain endurance capacity. Though the full significance of these changes is not known, it may explain why scientists do not find a high percentage of Type IIB fibers in highly trained endurance cyclists.

How can you tell what your muscle-fiber composition is? A biopsy is the precise way to find out, but science doesn't always tell us something new: More often it explains something we already know. If you've had a variety of racing experiences and have kept a training diary, you have a pretty good idea where your strengths and weaknesses lie. You know if you are very fast, very enduring, or have a certain mixture of these qualities.

Almost every serious cyclist already knows whether to do more endurance work to develop aerobic capacity or more speed work to develop anaerobic and sprinting ability. But if no amount of training ever pays off, you can blame your parents—heredity determines your muscle-fiber type for the most part. You are born with a certain percentage, and it will vary little with age or training.

The Female Cyclist

Research and available evidence provides no support for treating men's and women's training programs differently. Although males and females do differ in their responses to vigorous exercise, there are probably more differences within each sex than between them. Studies have found that the level of physical fitness makes more difference than gender does. Further, when differences are observed in trained male and female athletes, in most cases the response is one of adapting and conditioning to chronic exercise. Because of these similarities, and because their needs are basically the same, there seems to be no physiological reason to keep women's road races as short as they traditionally have been. Although the international governing body of the sport of cycling has begun to increase women's distances, there is still room for improvement.

Research shows that females respond to endurance training in the same manner as males; therefore, restrictions should not be placed on women in endurance events. Although it is generally true that a female has a smaller heart mass, less cardiac output (amount of blood pumped by the heart per minute), and less blood volume and hemoglobin, training can increase the efficiency of her oxygen transport system. When maximal oxygen consumption is expressed in terms of lean body mass (total weight – fat weight), the highly trained female is nearly identical to the male. However, generally speaking, women will have a higher percentage of body fat than men will.

The biggest problem for a female cyclist is that she cannot leave her higher percentage of fat on the starting line; she must carry it on the bike along with her muscle mass, and it will cost her more oxygen to cycle at the same speed as someone with a lower fat percentage. Again, training can help. Several years ago, a study of lean female distance runners found that their maximal oxygen consumption was only 4.1% lower than that of a comparative group of male marathoners when compared by lean body mass.

For many years women were kept from endurance events on the grounds that they could not tolerate heat or the race distance for extended periods of time. It was not until the 1984 Olympic Games that the women's road race was added to the event schedule. Many of these misconceptions were fostered by poorly designed studies. Researchers compared trained males and sedentary females and used standardized work tasks that might be considered moderate for males but significantly harder for females.

Again, the fitness level of the female dictates how well she will adapt and respond to heat stress. A trained female cyclist will be able to elevate her cardiac output to a level sufficient to prevent a drop in blood pressure and loss of blood flow to the working muscles when blood is redistributed to the skin in temperature regulation. Acclimatization to environmental heat stress also adds to heat tolerance. So someday we may see women contest the same distance as men in the individual 4,000-meter pursuit.

One of the great debates about women's performance in athletics concerns menstruation. There seem to be differences among females with regard to exercise and competition during menstruation. Many have few or no menstrual difficulties under any conditions, active or sedentary. On the other hand, a significant number of females have oligomenorrhea (infrequent menstrual flow) or other menstrual difficulties that apparently are neither helped nor aggravated by vigorous activity.

Several female cyclists have reported a total absence of menstruation when training for long distances. This phenomenon may be related to low body weight and reduced levels of body fat: Several studies have reported no menstruation (secondary amenorrhea) in chronically underweight females.

For a survey conducted at a major women's stage race, 33 women were questioned on the mileage ridden each week and the incidence of secondary amenorrhea. Approximately 12% of the women experienced this condition. These women were training between 200 and 300 miles per week.

Many factors may contribute to amenorrhea in cyclists, but it is primarily characterized by loss of body weight and many miles of training on the bicycle each week. Besides loss of body fat, cycling long distances may lead to decreased levels of certain hormones that control various phases of the menstrual cycle, which may lead directly or indirectly to amenorrhea. The role of cycling and the causes of these menstrual irregularities remain unknown.

It is well recognized that the average male is considerably stronger than the average female. Scores from several different studies suggest that men are approximately 30% to 40% stronger than women. However, for males and females of comparable body weight and lean body weight, lower body strength is similar, although the males maintain a clear superiority in upper body strength. Strength training, formerly condemned as a form of training for women because of its supposed masculinizing effects, is now recognized as valuable in building up the physiological profile of the female cyclist.

The Final Spin

This chapter may have led you to think that to be a successful road cyclist you will have to have selected your parents wisely based on their genetic offerings. Obviously, this is not true, because with proper training your body has a tremendous capacity to improve. The current champion cyclists have improved their physiological talent by putting in weeks, months, and years of hard training to develop superior cardiorespiratory and muscular systems.

By training hard, using proper nutrition, learning smart strategies, and building the right psychological frame of mind, you can improve your racing performance. This book will give you the scientific and practical knowledge that will guide you in making the right choices to become the best cyclist you can be.

2

© Graham Watson

Energy Sources for Cycling

Those who are enamored of the practice without the science, are like a pilot who goes into a ship without a rudder or compass and never has any certainty of where he is going.

—*Leonardo Da Vinci*

Have you ever wondered how your muscles produce the energy needed to ride your bike? On the surface it may seem simple: Breathe in oxygen and transport it to your working muscles, where it combines with food fuels and the muscles contract to produce force. Do this for a few months, and your fellow cyclists start to say things like "You're getting stronger," "You're riding longer," and "You're sprinting better at the end of races, aren't you?"

"Yes," you reply modestly. "I am." The miles of training that have allowed you to enjoy racing have also produced noticeable changes. You can ride faster with less effort. It takes less time for your heart rate to return to normal after a ride. You feel more energetic and have a greater facility to perform more work, both on and off the bicycle.

By challenging your muscles, you've forced them to retool and become more efficient. Muscle fibers, like all the cells in your body, run on a molecular fuel called adenosine triphosphate (ATP), which your body makes naturally from the foods you eat. Muscles cannot contract without it. In fact, almost all the metabolic functions in your body depend on it.

Your muscles make and store ATP in several different ways. In this chapter we will explore the ways your body produces, stores, and restores ATP during exercise. This information is important groundwork for later chapters where we discuss training programs, which really boil down to ways to increase your ATP stores for improved cycling.

Aerobic and Anaerobic Energy Systems

Your cycling muscles get ATP from any of three sources, depending on the situation. But before discussing the specifics of ATP production, let's review the two ways your body produces ATP: aerobically and anaerobically.

During cycling the delivery of oxygen to the exercising muscles takes on a special significance. Oxygen is essential for the everyday production of most of the body's ATP needs. In fact, *aerobic* means "with oxygen." Aerobic energy is simply energy produced in the presence of adequate oxygen. When you are cycling easily and performing your daily activities, the vast majority of your ATP for muscular work is being produced aerobically. A good example of cycling aerobically is riding in a group when the pace is slow enough that it is easy to converse.

But what happens when you start chasing down a breakaway, climb a steep hill, or time-trial hard enough that your breathing becomes labored? During high-intensity exercise, your muscles have the unique capability to produce energy when the cardiovascular system is unable to deliver enough oxygen to the muscle cells to meet your energy needs.

This is when the anaerobic energy system in an exercising muscle takes over. *Anaerobic* means "without oxygen."

The aerobic system produces a great deal of energy for your muscles to pedal efficiently compared with the anaerobic system. Carbon dioxide and water, the primary waste products of the aerobic system, are easily eliminated by breathing and sweating. Anaerobic metabolism produces a waste product called *lactic acid*. As lactic acid builds up, it leads to an immediate sense of discomfort—that burning sensation you feel in your muscles—and quickly then to fatigue.

Harnessing Energy

As we have seen, the immediate source of muscular energy is ATP. Now let's look at the three sources of ATP for muscle contraction and how ATP is produced in both your aerobic and anaerobic systems.

A little ATP is always present in well-rested muscles. When you start to exercise, it starts to break down. During ATP breakdown, energy is released for muscular contraction. The problem is that all the ATP stored in your muscles will last only about 2 seconds. ATP needs to be constantly restored during exercise, and this involves a number of carefully coordinated and quickly responding metabolic reactions within your muscle cells. ATP is resynthesized in these three ways:

1. Adenosine–triphosphate–phosphocreatine (ATP-PC) system
2. Lactic acid system
3. With oxygen, in the natural course of the aerobic system

The first two ways are functions of the anaerobic system. The third is obviously a function of the aerobic system. Figure 2.1 gives an overview of the three energy sources for ATP production.

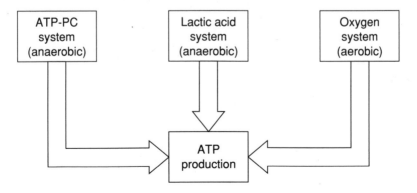

Figure 2.1   The chemical systems that produce ATP.

Restoring Muscle ATP Through the ATP-PC System

As your initial muscular contractions continue, the stores of the ATP compound are broken down to produce the following compounds: Adenosine diphosphate + phosphate + energy (ADP + Pi + energy). This energy (which was used to hold ATP together) can now be used for muscular contraction. However, your ATP stores are quickly depleted, and another compound called phosphocreatine (PC) is broken down, so that the energy released in its breakdown can combine with the ADP to resynthesize ATP for additional energy for muscular contraction. Figure 2.2 shows that during short-term, high-intensity exercise the ATP-PC system contributes significantly to energy production.

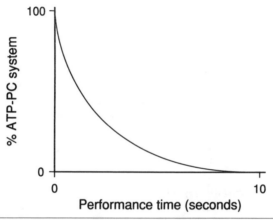

Figure 2.2 The percentage of energy (in the form of ATP) contributed by the ATP-PC system for exercise activities. You can see that as time goes by the ATP-PC system is able to deliver less of the energy required to continue the activity.

PC is stored in the muscles. Almost instantaneously, PC and ADP can manufacture the prime energy substance, ATP, which is also stored in the muscles. The supply of PC is limited, however, and these stores are depleted in 5 to 10 seconds. The ATP-PC source is the primary energy system for short-term, high-intensity exercise like the demanding events in a criterium. After it is depleted, ATP from the other energy sources will eventually replenish it.

The first few seconds of high-intensity work intervals—sprints and racing starts—will probably afford the best stimulus for this system. If you want to train the ATP-PC system, perform multiple intermittent work bouts of 5 to 15 seconds, with recovery periods of 15 to 60 seconds between. Most coaches recommend work-to-rest intervals of 1:3 or more for training the ATP-PC system. This means, for example, if you are doing 10-second sprints, you leave 30 to 40 seconds between sprints to allow the muscles to restore the ATP levels.

Creatine Supplementation—It's PC

A revolutionary new food compound is on the verge of becoming the next "natural" performance-enhancing supplement. No, it's not a new form of anabolic steroid or other banned substance. The product, creatine, is a muscle fuel that is extracted naturally from meat and fish or created in chemical laboratories.

Among those to already use creatine and make public statements in the *London Times* are British athletes Linford Christie and Sally Gunnell, who won gold medals at the Olympic Games in Barcelona. Several newspapers also reported that during this Olympics many athletes—from Bulgarian weight lifters to Russian soccer players—may have been supplementing their diets with creatine. But scientific studies, not just athlete testimonials, are showing coaches, athletes, and scientists that creatine is a powerful erogenic aid. Several studies with humans and with horses (thoroughbred racers and harness racers) have shown that creatine supplements increased performance and decreased recovery time.

Recent studies in human sports science have shown that supplementing a normal diet with creatine will increase the content of PC in the muscles. One study by Dr. Eric Hultman showed that when individuals' diets were supplemented several times a day, creatine concentrations in exercising muscles were increased by over 35%. In the early 1960s Hultman produced the original research on the importance of carbohydrate loading for increasing the time before fatigue sets in during endurance exercise. Today he is showing that creatine supplementation can help decrease an athlete's performance times in sprint events.

In a similar study reported at a recent scientific conference, Hultman and other researchers supplemented five middle-distance runners with creatine over a 6-day period while another group received a placebo supplement. Prior to and following the 6 days of supplementation, the runners ran four 1,000-meter intervals on one day and four 300-meter sprints on another day. After supplementation, the creatine group's times to run four 1,000-meter intervals decreased from 769.8 seconds to 757 seconds; the placebo group's times actually slowed from 774.1 seconds to 775.3 seconds. In the 300-meter sprints, the times for the placebo group decreased from 41.7 to 41.4 seconds and for the

(continued)

Creatine Supplementation   *(continued)*

creatine-supplemented group from 38.4 to 37.7 seconds in the last sprint. The creatine-supplemented group had statistically significant decreases in times at both distances.

In addition, subjective, but scientifically unsubstantiated, reports indicate that recovery from intense activity may be faster following creatine supplementation and that in trained subjects, the incidence of postexercise muscle stiffness is reduced.

Vegetarians have much to gain from creatine supplementation. Their diets are void of creatine, and they tend to have lower levels of creatine in their blood and urine. In fact, in Hultman's first study, one runner who was a vegetarian increased his creatine muscle content by approximately 60% (the group mean was 35%).

How much food would you need to eat to increase your muscles' creatine levels enough to have an erogenic affect? You would probably have to eat 5 to 6 pounds of beef a day. This is highly unlikely, so creatine supplements in tablet form are the only reasonable way to accomplish the levels needed for improved performance.

Many sports scientists suggest a maintenance dose of creatine of 2 to 3 grams per day and a loading regimen of 9 grams per day during the last week before a major competition. Just as with carbohydrate loading (see chapter 8), you would only follow the loading regimen three to four times a year. Several companies are currently marketing this product as a food supplement.

Creatine supplementation is a new concept in sport nutrition. The aim is to meet the specific nutritional needs of muscles in the quest to raise an athlete's performance potential. From scientific research and anecdotal evidence, it appears that creatine is a legal erogenic aid that works.

High-intensity work activates the ATP-PC system and quickly depletes the store. The relatively long recovery allows the aerobic system to replenish the stores. The work bouts must be short enough to minimize the lactic acid system's contribution to the work.

Although some cyclists appear to be endowed with more powerful ATP-PC systems, the quickness and explosiveness of cyclists are determined by many factors, including muscle-fiber type and complex neuromuscular relationships. There is no difference in the biochemical machinery of this system between men and women. Still, higher absolute energy outputs are possible in male cyclists because of their larger muscle mass.

There is no doubt that cyclists training for road or criterium races spend some time training the ATP-PC system. Guidelines for training this system will be given in chapter 5.

Restoring Muscle ATP Through the Lactic Acid System

The other type of anaerobic system that can restore spent ATP is the lactic acid system, which is also known as *glycolysis*. Once the ATP-PC system has been exhausted, muscles can continue to produce ATP anaerobically through the breakdown of muscle glycogen (stored carbohydrate) and the release of food energy (blood glucose). When carbohydrates are broken down without oxygen, one end product is lactic acid; this system derives its name from the accumulation of lactic acid in the exercising muscles. The lactic acid system accounts for most of the energy generated in all-out efforts lasting from 10 to 15 seconds to several minutes. Figure 2.3 shows that activities of high intensity and moderate duration call upon the lactic acid system for energy production.

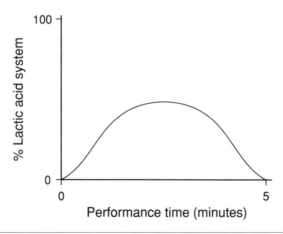

Figure 2.3 The percentage of energy (in the form of ATP) contributed by the lactic acid system for exercise activities. After the ATP-PC system can no longer sustain an intense physical activity, the lactic acid system can prolong the exertion for a few minutes.

The increase in lactic acid is associated with a proportionate increase in the production of hydrogen ions, which make the environment of your muscle cells more acidic. This results in temporary muscle fatigue: Increased hydrogen ion concentration has been shown to limit the force-generating capacity of the muscle as well as decrease the rate of ATP production. The burning sensation in your quadriceps as you climb a steep hill is an excellent example of the accumulation of lactic acid.

When you train with intervals of up to 5 minutes at time-trial pace (or, in physiological terms, when you train at your lactate threshold), you are training your body to break down carbohydrate (glucose) more efficiently without oxygen. In addition, you are training your muscles to tolerate increased buildup of lactic acid before they fatigue.

Thus, the capacity to produce and tolerate large quantities of lactic acid is essential for success in high-intensity events of moderate duration. A cyclist must be able to produce large quantities of lactic acid and resist its effects. As Dave Martin, exercise physiologist with the Olympic Training Center, says, "Without fatigue there is no stimulus for adaptation."

Research that I conducted at the National Championships showed that track events that require this capacity include the kilometer, individual, and team pursuit. Table 2.1 presents the data collected at the National Championships. Values in excess of 10 millimoles are considered indicative of high use of the lactic acid system. This shows that efforts lasting for several minutes at high intensity stress the lactic acid system to produce energy for muscular contraction.

Table 2.1 Postrace Blood Lactic Acid Levels of 19 Cyclists at the National Championships			
	Lactic acid (mM)	Range (mM)	Average time (s)
Rest	1.95	1.80-2.23	
Team pursuit	12.0	9.79-15.25	288
Matched sprints	13.7	11.40-15.11	11
Individual pursuit	15.2	13.55-17.31	303
Kilometer	16.9	15.69-18.22	71
mM = millimoles/L			

You can also expect production of lactic acid when you try to break away from the group, charge up a hill, or compete in a long sprint at the end of a road race. Road racing is a fast, continuous activity that requires intermittent periods of great effort—a double challenge that interval training can help you meet. Guidelines on training this system will be given in chapters 4 and 5.

Lactic Acid—Is It the Bad Boy of Exercise?

As we have seen, one result of the breakdown of glucose in the absence of oxygen (glycolysis) is lactic acid. Early work by scientists like Dr. A.V. Hill from the Harvard Fatigue Laboratory theorized that lactic acid production during intense exercise was due to the lack of oxygen at the cellular level and was an indicator that anaerobic energy production had begun.

Today there is much evidence in the scientific literature showing that lactic acid is always being produced, even when you are at rest. A constant concentration of lactic acid in your bloodstream does not mean that no further lactic acid is being produced, only that it is being removed as fast as you are producing it. There may also be several reasons why lactic acid accumulates in your blood: Insufficient oxygen may be only part of the story. We now know that glycolysis becomes very active during high-intensity exercise even when there is an adequate supply of oxygen being delivered to your muscles.

But when glycolysis becomes significant and not enough oxygen is being supplied to your muscles, the amount of lactic acid being formed becomes greater than what can be removed by your body and the concentration begins to rise in your muscles and blood. At high lactic acid concentrations, your muscles' ability to contract properly is inhibited, and you must either slow down your effort or come to a complete stop. Although anaerobic energy production may not be significant during long road races, you must possess both the aerobic for prolonged energy production and the anaerobic necessary for shorter but more intense strategic efforts. For this reason, both energy systems must be trained to their fullest if you want to be successful.

The point at which lactic acid begins to rise in your blood depends on your $\dot{V}O_2$max and on your lactic threshold. This is the point at which lactic acid production exceeds removal, and the effort becomes debilitating. At race pace, many competitive cyclists stay just below lactic threshold, which allows them to use both aerobic and anaerobic energy. An important part of training is to try to shift the lactic threshold so that it corresponds to a higher percentage of your $\dot{V}O_2$max.

Two basic strategies have been used to train this system. The first requires you to drive the production of lactic acid very high by completing relatively short but intense intervals of 1 to 5 minutes. Rests vary with the intensity and duration of the work. Most coaches recommend a work-to-rest ratio of 1:2. For example, after completing a 90-second work bout, you should rest for 180 seconds. Simply put, higher intensities produce larger amounts of lactic acid. During a specific training session you may complete several such intervals with several minutes of rest between each interval.

The second strategy is to work at a less intense level but increase the duration and shorten the rest intervals. The purpose is to sustain or tolerate the lactic acid for long periods of time. This method ensures that you will begin each work interval with a higher level of lactic acid, because a decrease in the recovery interval reduces the time available for the removal of lactic acid. This means you will be able to train at increasing levels of lactic acid and thus gradually acclimate your body to the challenge of pushing through the fatigue associated with lactic acid buildup.

Restoring ATP Through the Aerobic System

The aerobic system (sometimes called the O_2 system) makes the most significant contribution to energy production during long-distance events such as road races and long time trials. Like the lactic acid system, it uses muscle glycogen as fuel. During events that last more than 20 minutes, it also calls upon fat. This system requires oxygen to function and goes through more than 20 steps within the muscle cell before ATP is produced. For this reason, the aerobic system is a slower producer of ATP during exercise although it produces a greater amount. Figure 2.4 shows that as performance time increases, a greater share of ATP production comes from the aerobic system.

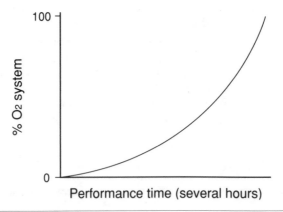

Figure 2.4   The percentage of energy (in the form of ATP) contributed by the aerobic (O_2) system for exercise activities. The longer the activity, the greater the percentage of total energy that comes from the aerobic system.

Because of its continual need for oxygen, the aerobic system is strongly linked to your cardiorespiratory system. As we saw in chapter 1, vigorous training can improve the delivery of oxygen to the muscles. Each heartbeat can pump more oxygenated blood, and your muscles, via their network of capillaries, can extract more oxygen from the blood cells.

Generally, efforts lasting more than 5 minutes receive most of their energy from the aerobic system. The most effective strategy for improving aerobic capacity has been to ride plenty of "steady-state" miles and to perform several endurance workouts each week. Rides should be of moderate, continuous intensity and should become less frequent and of shorter duration as you move into the racing season. Chapter 3 will provide more details on improving your aerobic system.

The Coordination of Energy Systems During Various Cycling Events

No one energy system operates entirely by itself during exercise; there is always a combination of aerobic and anaerobic energy production taking place. Table 2.2 and Figure 2.5 summarize the aerobic and anaerobic energy systems that produce ATP during exercise.

The relationship between various cycling events and energy systems is shown in Table 2.3 As we have seen, for sprinters the most important energy source is the breakdown of ATP-PC, the most available source of energy in the muscle. Kilometer cyclists and pursuiters, after using the immediate high-energy sources, obtain energy from the anaerobic breakdown of carbohydrates. Long-distance cyclists rely on the aerobic breakdown of carbohydrates and fats for energy. The energy systems are linked to the particular distance, time, and intensity the cyclist rides.

			Table 2.2 Relative Contribution of Total Energy Yield From Aerobic and Anaerobic Energy Processes During Maximal Efforts Up to 120 min				
				Exercise time/maximal effort			
Energy source	**10 s**	**1 min**	**2 min**	**4 min**	**10 min**	**30 min**	**60 min**	**120 min**
Anaerobic	85	65-70	50	30	10-15	5	2	1
Aerobic	15	30-35	50	70	85-90	95	98	99

Note. From "The Physiology of Cycling" by E. Burke. In *Science of Cycling* (p. 3) by E.R. Burke (Ed.), 1986, Champaign, IL: Human Kinetics. Copyright 1986 by Edmund Burke. Reprinted by permission.

Table 2.3   Various Cycling Events and Their Predominant Energy Sources

Event	Performance time	Speed (ATP-PC strength) (%)	Anaerobic capacity (ATP-PC and lactic acid systems) (%)	Aerobic capacity (%)
	Hours and minutes			
100-mile road race	3:55-4:10	—	5	95
100K criterium	2:05-2:15	5	10	85
100K team time trial	2:10-2:20	—	15	85
25-mile time trial	0:52-0:60	—	10	90
25-mile criterium	0:50-0:60	5	15	80
	Minutes and seconds			
10-mile points race (track)	20:00-25:00	10	20	70
4,000-meter individual pursuit	4:45-5:05	20	55	25
Kilometer	1:07-1:13	80	15	5
Match sprints	0:11-0:13	98	2	—

Note. From "The Physiology of Cycling" by E. Burke. In *Science of Cycling* (p. 2) by E.R. Burke (Ed.), 1986, Champaign, IL: Human Kinetics. Copyright 1986 by Edmund Burke. Adapted by permission.

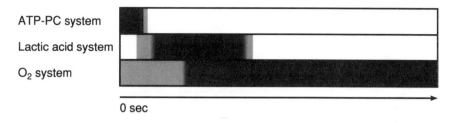

Figure 2.5 The bars on this graph depict the coordination of energy sources during cycling. The darkness of the bar relates to the relative percentage of the total energy output that its corresponding system contributes to the effort. You can see that at the beginning of activity—especially high-intensity anaerobic activity that cannot be sustained for a long time—the ATP-PC is initially the primary source of energy. When that system gives out, the lactic acid system picks up the slack. For activities lasting more than a few minutes, the aerobic (or O_2) system must provide the majority of the energy.

Some of the percentages in the longer events may seem out of proportion at first. In a 100-mile road race of 4 hours and 10 minutes, however, 5% of the total work energy is a considerable amount to be derived from anaerobic energy sources. Though the percentage is low, the anaerobic energy system must be developed to its optimum to work in breakaways, steep climbs, and end-of-race sprints. Table 2.2 gives the approximate total energy yield from both aerobic and anaerobic processes during maximal efforts of up to 120 minutes for a cyclist with high maximal aerobic power. Up to 2 minutes, anaerobic power is most important; at about 2 minutes, a 50:50 ratio exists; and as the length or time of the ride increases, aerobic energy becomes more important.

The Final Spin

In reality, every muscle fiber relies on aerobic and anaerobic energy sources at the same time during any one cycling session; it's just the proportion that changes, depending on the intensity and duration of the effort. Road cyclists will be most interested in restoring muscle ATP by training the aerobic system. However, because road races involve bursts of anaerobic effort, you cannot afford to ignore the ATP-PC and lactic acid systems.

Knowing the basic energy systems of ATP production, you can more easily understand the basis of designing training programs for improved performance. The next three chapters will detail methods of training for endurance (aerobic training) and tempo and speed (anaerobic training).

3

© Graham Watson

Endurance Training

The individual rider makes or breaks himself. There is no magic formula or secret to success.

—*Paul Köchli*

If you want to be successful at road cycling, just about any discussion on training leads to the need to build up your weekly mileage. "You need miles on the bike," says Jiri Mainus, U.S. National Team Operations Manager. How many miles do you need to ride every week? It depends on the time of the season, your goals, your ability, and your schedule—and in some cases, what cyclists you listen to.

Endurance training is the basic training that allows you to feel comfortable on the bike for longer periods without pushing yourself to exhaustion. You achieve this slow buildup of stamina by increasing your aerobic fitness. You must habitually stress the aerobic energy system by staying on the bike longer and longer. After a while, the system acclimates itself to working more efficiently for longer periods.

Contrary to popular belief, endurance training is not used specifically to increase your maximal aerobic capacity. The intensity of the effort is probably too low to have much effect on $\dot{V}O_2$max. One of the greatest disservices perpetuated on endurance cyclists was the concept of long, slow distance (LSD) training, which implied that extensive training with high mileage and low effort would improve aerobic capacity and allow you to race effectively at shorter distances, such as criteriums. Long, easy rides provide a base of endurance that you can sharpen for races with speed work and intervals.

If you only do endurance training, you will not possess the speed to race criteriums, chase down breakaways, or sprint to the end. To the contrary, endurance workouts are aerobic because they are conducted at a pace below the point at which lactic acid begins to accumulate in the blood, a sign that you are starting to use anaerobic metabolism to produce energy.

The purpose of the endurance ride is not only to stress the aerobic system but to give you the experience of being on the bicycle for long periods and to increase your ability to burn fats as fuel. Mileage helps your body adapt to the extended hours of sitting in the saddle during long road races—in ways that only your posterior will appreciate.

Generally, the maximum time spent on the bicycle will be from 90 minutes to 3 hours for juniors, and from 5 to 6 hours for senior male amateurs and professionals. Rides should be conducted at a reasonably comfortable pace; you should be able to conduct a conversation with teammates while riding. However, if you are incorporating sprints or intervals into these rides, conversation will intermittently turn into heavy breathing.

The Physiology of Endurance

Endurance cycling stimulates primarily the Type I (slow-twitch) muscle fibers because they are more responsive than the Type II (fast-twitch) fibers to the lower intensity. The adaptations of the muscle cells and the cardiovascular system that occur with endurance training allow each Type I fiber to work at lower intensities with less fatigability.

In his recent work with trained cyclists at the University of Texas, Ed Coyle has shown Type I fibers to be more efficient in converting chemical energy within the muscle into the mechanical work of pedaling. Thus, fewer muscle fibers are needed to maintain a given pace, or those that are activated do not need to work as hard as before. This helps improve cycling economy because less muscle activity is involved (and less oxygen is needed) for pedaling. Cyclists perceive this, often remarking that they "feel smoother and are pedaling in circles and not in squares."

Work completed by Dr. David Costill and co-workers at Ball State University has shown that when national-class cyclists significantly increase their mileage, they often see little change in $\dot{V}O_2$max. Costill's work shows that the muscle fibers are becoming more economical, which causes improved performance.

Costill's work has also shown that endurance training helps cyclists better utilize stored carbohydrate (glycogen) in their muscles and liver, which can be converted rapidly to simple glucose as it is needed during exercise. Glycogen is the preferred fuel for muscles during cycling, but glycogen stores can become depleted within 90 minutes of riding at a moderate to high intensity. A well-trained cyclist can store from 400 to 500 grams worth (1,600 to 2,000 calories) of carbohydrate. Depleting this supply is often referred to as "bonking" or "hitting the wall." Therefore, cyclists have learned to eat and drink more carbohydrates during long road races (more on this in chapter 8), or they use more of their fat stores for fuel.

Endurance cycling also teaches your body to burn other types of fuel along with stored glycogen, stretching the duration of your reserves from 90 minutes to 2 hours or more. Top professional road riders are probably so efficient in metabolizing fats and glycogen throughout a road race because of the many miles they put in during training and racing, that they probably rarely deplete their glycogen stores. Simply stated, endurance training teaches your body to be more efficient, "sparing" glycogen and teaching your body to burn larger stores of fat.

Some cyclists refer to endurance training in the early season as base training. During this time they are also improving ligament and tendon strength, which will prepare their bodies for harder sessions of intervals and sprints. During the racing season your program should include endurance rides as well as tempo and speed work and races. The faster-paced miles put a lot of stress on your body; slower miles on the bike allow you to recover from hard efforts and to build up your body for even more hard efforts. Putting miles on the bike builds your foundation in the early season and the physiological experience of those miles is used during the season to help maintain fitness. Endurance training is a must for all cyclists because it

- increases the potential to store carbohydrates within the muscles and liver;
- improves your respiratory system, bringing more oxygen to the circulatory system;
- increases the pumping efficiency of your heart, so you can pump more blood per minute to the working muscles;
- helps your thermoregulatory system by increasing blood flow to the skin while cycling;
- brings about increased neuromuscular efficiency of pedaling technique;
- increases your ability to burn more fat during long road races; and
- improves the endurance of your cycling muscles by increasing the number of mitochondria, the subcellular structures in your muscles that produce aerobic energy.

Endurance-Training Guidelines

As a general rule, the longest of these sessions should be no more than 20% to 25% greater than the distance at which you intend to compete. You may need to adjust the distance and effort for environmental (wind or temperature) conditions so that the effort is not too intense. Your heart rate intensity should be between 60% and 80% of your maximum.

At the lower intensities, you should be able to carry on a conversation. It would be interesting to see a study that would show the maximum intensity that would still permit conversation. In the absence of a friend (and not wishing to be caught talking to yourself), pulse rate is another good governor. Maintaining a pulse rate of about 60% of your maximum heart rate is sufficient to produce the desired effects. This is where a heart rate monitor may be helpful in keeping you from going too hard up a hill or from riding with a group that wants to go faster. A pulse rate of closer to 70% will produce similar effects if you have less time to train.

Riding for shorter durations, as little as 30 minutes, at the same effort or pace (or at less than 60% of your maximum heart rate) serves as a recovery session or a warm-up but does little for your overall conditioning. Although various names can be applied to this training, it is essentially *active recovery*. It is too low an intensity and volume for long-term training changes in a serious athlete and is used to help recover from previous intense training or races or to prepare for future races.

Beginning cyclists often want to know at what speed they should be riding during endurance training. Speed is not the important consideration; it is intensity of effort and time on the bike that are important. Remember, speed will be dependent upon the terrain you are riding and on environmental conditions. If it is very hot and windy, your miles per hour may be reduced. Also, these average speeds are easier to maintain if riding in a group of five to eight cyclists.

One of the more enjoyable ways to get in your endurance rides is to join the local cycling club on their weekend ride. This will give you time to ride with other cyclists and to share your knowledge with up-and-comers.

Average cyclists who try to copy the high mileage of professional or elite amateur cyclists may actually spend significantly more time than their mentors on the road. Be cautious when comparing your mileage to other cyclists'. The slower you ride (compared to cyclists of better ability), the more you should consider time, not mileage, in setting your weekly and monthly training goals. Some cyclists prefer to record their hours and minutes in their diaries, because it more accurately represents their training. That makes sense for this group of cyclists, but in this book we will report training programs in miles because we are looking at a total training program of endurance, tempo, and speed.

Increasing Your Mileage

Don't continuously increase your mileage. Every few weeks level off your mileage before adding more to your program. Occasionally, when you have reached a level that you are comfortable with, such as 200 to 250 miles per week, stay there for several weeks. These periodic plateaus help you regenerate physically and mentally before the next mileage increase. These plateaus may last several months and are determined by your age, your ability and past training, and your competition goals. Periods of steady mileage, or even decreased mileage, will help you recover or get physically stronger. You do not have to increase your mileage every week.

Determine the upper limit to the number of miles you can handle, mentally and physically, at this stage in your competitive career. If you are not careful and do not set realistic goals, you may become overtrained or experience an overuse injury. Don't compare your program to a cyclist you read about in a popular magazine. After several years of cycling, you may know that your upper limit is about 300 miles per week. However, the next year, because of a different off-season training program and/or increased experience, you may be able to safely handle

325 miles per week—mileage that would have been too much to handle previously.

Factors That Affect Your Endurance Miles

When you are riding long distances to develop aerobic capacity, you will find it harder to keep up your mileage if you

- are working during the day and are running out of daylight in the morning or evenings,
- are carrying a few extra pounds,
- ride mostly by yourself,
- live in hilly terrain,
- live in a climate that is either too cold or too hot several months of the year, or
- don't have a coach, team, or family to support you.

And you should reduce your training mileage if you

- are recovering from an injury,
- are racing often,
- are tapering for a race,
- are adding speed work to your program,
- are feeling fatigued, or
- have reached the off-season, when it is time to cut back on your mileage.

Year-Round Training

During the off-season and early season, many cyclists refer to endurance training as base building, or the foundation phase that will allow for longer and harder training as the season progresses. During this time, almost all your miles or time on the bike should be spent on endurance rides in smaller gears. You should be spinning, with your revolutions per minute in the 90-plus range.

As you firm up your early-season training base, you can add speed work, intervals, hill training, and race-pace work to your program. You will find out how in later chapters. You can add long intervals and long, gradual climbs to your program as well as a few jumps and short sprints.

During the peak racing season make sure you include one long ride each week. Avoid the temptation to do one every day, or you will get exhausted and your speed will suffer. Instead, ride once a week for as many hours as your longest race or stage in an upcoming race. Getting ready for a 75-mile road race? About 3-1/2 to 4 hours will do.

You will have to eat often on your long rides. Don't make the mistake of riding 3 to 5 hours with only two bottles of water. By the end, you will

Tips for Managing Your Mileage

Many of the cyclists I have worked with have found that by applying these simple rules to their training programs they can safely manage their mileage or time on the bicycle.

- If you are injured or sick for several days or weeks, don't try to make up the mileage. Gradually build back up over a period of weeks, and get back up to your mileage over time.
- Measure your training in miles or time. If you do not know the distance you are riding, purchase an odometer. If you are riding for time, use a watch.
- Some cyclists have more energy if they can alternate longer weeks with shorter weeks (for example, 200-250-200-250 for an average of 225 miles per week for the month). By setting monthly goals you can be more flexible with your training mileage.
- Never be a slave to your training program or diary. If you become ill or have to work late, do not try to make up excessive mileage on the last day of the week. Remember, your success in competition will come from a proper blend of training, mileage, and rest, not by how many miles you record in your diary.

Skip Hamilton, an accomplished masters cyclist and a coach at the Connie Carpenter–Davis Phinney training camps, has these recommendations for increasing your mileage or time on the bike. He says, "Early in the season do not increase your time on the bike or miles covered by more than 20 to 25% from one week to the next. For example, if you have been training for 12 hours a week, then the next week should be in the 14- to 15-hour range. In fact, you should never increase your time by more than 2 or 3 hours per week."

Skip gives this advice to many of the cyclists he works with who are in their early years of training. He recommends, "It takes several weeks to adapt, but it may take several months to adjust." Skip is cautioning his riders to not make too many large jumps in their training programs; he wants their bodies to have time to adjust gradually to the increasing stress.

be seeing stars and pedaling in squares—classic symptoms of the "bonk" or "hitting the wall." Carry plenty of food and drink with you, or, if need be, stop at a convenient store to stock up.

The Final Spin

The endurance phase of training is intended for the optimal development of your Type I (slow-twitch) muscle fibers. It stimulates increased efficiency of these fibers, improves oxygen delivery, increases the number of mitochondria, and improves fat metabolism. This is the foundation upon which all future training and performances are based. Prepare well and you should find the season a success. Neglect this foundation and you will lack the stamina for more intense training and competition as the season progresses.

Peter Snell is one of the greatest middle-distance runners of all time. He trained with the great running coach Arthur Lydiard, who is a proponent of large volumes of endurance training. Peter once said, "What people didn't understand about Lydiard's program was that it wasn't the high mileage that made the runners great. What made his runners great was the training they were able to do because they had done the mileage."

Look at endurance and base training as a multiseason progression. Think of your gains as cumulative: The more years you spend at it, the better you will be. With proper endurance training, you can reap bigger benefits over a longer period of time.

© Graham Watson

Tempo Training

If you're going to be in a race, pick a fast horse.

—Finis Conner

If you were to train a couple of days a week for road racing or time trialing, the best advice would be to spend those days doing lactate-threshold, or tempo, training. This intensity is often referred to as the point of pushing "hard" on the ride. It is the intensity that you can maintain during a long climb, a breakaway, or a time trial.

At this point you are riding in the threshold between when the ATP for muscular contraction is coming primarily from aerobic metabolism and when anaerobic metabolism begins to kick in at a high rate. Once you pass the threshold, excessive amounts of lactic acid produced by the muscles begin to accumulate. Lactic acid begins to shut down the metabolic mechanisms within your muscle cells, and, because it is an acid, you experience that burning sensation in your muscles.

For most fit cyclists this phenomenon will occur when riding at an effort requiring between 80% and 90% of their maximum heart rate. Training in this zone allows you to increase the speed or effort that you can work at before you cross over into the pain of lactic acid accumulation. Provided you have the proper aerobic base, built primarily from endurance work, this could be the level of training your cycling has been missing.

When you are riding at this intensity you will experience heavy breathing, tired muscles, and fatigue. And when you train at this effort, you will experience an effect that will allow you to sustain more work at higher intensities and at a lower heart rate. Of all athletes, competitive road cyclists have some of the highest $\dot{V}O_2$max values recorded. Some coaches and scientists claim the fastest cyclists are those with the highest $\dot{V}O_2$max measures; others claim the fastest cyclists are those whose lactate thresholds are at the highest percentage of their $\dot{V}O_2$max. Many coaches say the best athlete is one blessed with both a high $\dot{V}O_2$max and a high lactate threshold.

Even though many cyclists use lactate-threshold training in their programs, it is still a nebulous term. Ask any group of scientists and coaches to define it and you are likely to get 10 different answers. "The point is that we are defining a small range where an athlete can train and compete optimally," says J.T. Kearney, a sports physiologist at the Olympic Training Center, "and *lactate threshold* is a term used to define that range." Other terms, such as *anaerobic threshold, lactate turnpoint, OBLA* (onset of blood lactate accumulation), and *heart rate deflection point*, are often used in the literature to define the point Dr. Kearney is referring to. When you read other books or magazine articles, realize that all are talking about the same physiological phenomenon.

Training at Lactate Threshold

Training at lactate threshold is significant for several reasons. If everything else were equal, the higher your lactate threshold, the faster the pace or speed you could hold over long distances or steep climbs. Although success in road events is in part related to high maximal aerobic capacity and the ability to sprint, it also requires the cyclist to compete at a pace that is at a high percentage of his maximal capacity. Scientists often refer to this ability as meaning that a cyclist can effectively use a high percentage of maximal oxygen consumption for long periods while training or racing.

Training at the lactate threshold is used to shift to the right the point at which lactate accumulates—that is, at a faster pace or higher percentage of $\dot{V}O_2max$ (see Figure 4.1). Everything else being equal, the higher the lactate threshold, the faster the pace that can be held over long distances.

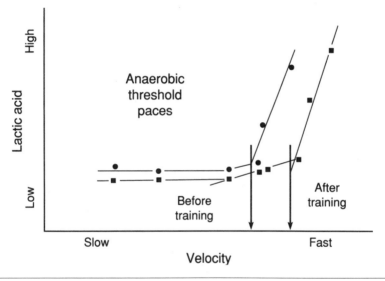

Figure 4.1 Training at your lactate threshold will shift your threshold to the right, as shown on the curves above. A higher lactate threshold allows you to compete at higher intensities and/or speeds.

Note. From "Science of Sport Training for Cycling: Part II" by Peter van Handel, 1991, *Conditioning for Cycling*, **1**(2), p. 22. Copyright 1991 by the National Strength and Conditioning Association. Reprinted by permission.

The training programs listed in this chapter will help you raise your threshold from the 75% or 80% level to the 90% level of elite cyclists. This means that you will be able to ride at a pace closer to your maximal oxygen consumption. For example, you will be able to raise your speed in a time trial from 26 to 29 miles per hour. You will also be able to break away with fitter cyclists, climb hills better, and attack with more speed.

Conconi Testing

Identifying this pace without actually monitoring lactic acid levels in the blood may be difficult. Not many of us are able to be tested in laboratories and have our lactate thresholds determined by lactic acid measurements in relation to our intensity of effort.

Much attention has been given to the Conconi test, which purports to associate a deflection in the heart rate's response to a certain level of cycling speed with the sudden increase in lactic acid that characterizes the lactate threshold. A graphed result is shown in Figure 4.2. A Conconi test requires monitoring a ride that gets progressively more difficult at regular intervals. Heart rate is monitored during each stage and is plotted against cycling speed squared. According to Dr. Francesco Conconi's research, the heart rate's response will, at some point, begin to flatten out. In other words, it no longer increases in direct proportion to increased speed, as it had at less intense work levels. The pace at which this occurs is stated to be the same as the pace where lactic acid suddenly increases in the blood. This pace, effort, or speed is defined as the heart rate deflection point, or velocity of deflection.

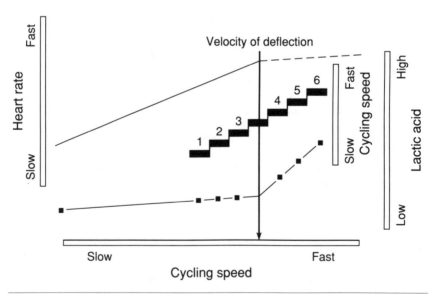

Figure 4.2 The Conconi test showing six progressively harder workloads. Heart rate is plotted against cycling speed squared and lactic acid accumulation.

Note. From "Science of Sport Training for Cycling: Part II" by Peter van Handel, 1991, *Conditioning for Cycling*, 1(2), p. 22. Copyright 1991 by the National Strength and Conditioning Association. Reprinted by permission.

The problem with the Conconi test is that the heart rate deflection point is not always clearly identifiable. In addition, many scientists have recently challenged this test and have learned that it may be a poor indicator of anaerobic or lactate threshold. In fact, several studies have shown that as cycling speed increases during the test, lactic acid begins to rise precipitously long before a heart rate deflection point.

Dave Martin, author of *Training Distance Runners,* is one who has a hard time replicating heart rate deflection point at lactate threshold. Testing a group of runners in his laboratory at Georgia State University, he found that less than half of the runners experienced the flattening out of their heart rates at lactate threshold as measured by oxygen consumption and actual levels of lactic acid in the blood. I have found similar problems in cyclists I have tested at the Olympic Training Center in Colorado Springs.

Time-Trial Testing

An alternative to the Conconi test was developed by Rob Shoemaker, author of *Serious Training for the Serious Athlete.* His method of estimating your lactate threshold and its associated heart rate is for you to complete a 10-mile time trial or a long climb at a steady, moderately hard pace. Perform the ride at the fastest pace you can sustain at a steady effort with no loss of speed. Be sure to warm up properly before the test.

A reliable heart rate monitor (for more on heart rate monitors, see chapter 6), a stopwatch, and a record sheet to record date, distance, time, and your average heart rate are needed. Heart rate should stabilize in about 5 minutes. Start your stopwatch, or use a cyclocomputer with a stopwatch mode, as you begin the test and record your finishing time when you finish. Assume the heart rate you achieved and sustained is your lactate threshold. Make sure you complete a cool-down after this hard effort.

Complete this test every 4 to 6 weeks during the year. You can use this test in place of a scheduled interval, hill, or race-pace workout. Use the results of heart rate and pace per mile to help you plan your workouts for the coming weeks.

As you become more fit, you will reach the point where lactic acid accumulation becomes delayed or shifts to the right (see Figure 4.1) and your lactate threshold coincides with a harder physical effort. Your lactate threshold will improve as your season progresses. Most elite athletes reach peaks in lactate threshold at about 85% to 90% of their $\dot{V}O_2max$.

The heart rate that you can maintain at this pace is indicative of your lactate threshold. Once again, it is important to consider environmental conditions because oxygen use, the level of lactic acid in the blood, and heart rate responses are markedly affected by wind and temperature conditions.

But an experienced cyclist learns to monitor lactate threshold by listening to specific physiological and psychological cues other than heart rate. Lance Armstrong points out his feelings this way: "You are usually at your lactate threshold heart rate when you are breathing hard and it is difficult to carry on a conversation with the other cyclists. In addition to heart rate and respiratory intensity, I try to monitor the feeling in my leg muscles and overall amount of effort."

Every year more cyclists are using wireless heart rate monitors in conjunction with these physiological and subjective measures to determine proper training intensity. A heart rate monitor helps you accurately determine your heart rate while you are riding.

The Right Dose of Lactate-Threshold Training

Lactate-threshold training can give you that extra boost to make those long climbs, breakaways, and time trials easier—but only after you have the proper base of endurance conditioning. If you do not have the proper aerobic conditioning, these workouts will tear you down rather than build you up.

Generally, lactate-threshold workouts take two forms: longer intervals and pace rides. Steady-paced threshold training is often referred to as tempo training; intermittent threshold training is sometimes referred to as tempo intervals, or cruise intervals. Because work at this intensity is difficult to sustain, interval training is the best way to begin. Naturally, warm-up and cool-down rides should be included before and after each workout.

The following paragraphs describe several lactate-threshold workouts. If you're not already using lactate-threshold training, try adding a little to your weekly program. Start off with one session per week, gradually increase the intensity and length of these sessions (but not the frequency—once or twice a week is plenty), and continue your threshold training as you sharpen for big races. Your time-trial times should come down and race performances improve as your lactate threshold shifts to the right.

You do not have to limit yourself to one or two of the following workouts. Feel free to mix several of the workouts—variety will help make the intense efforts of threshold training more tolerable. Whatever you do, do it with commitment: Intensity is the key to getting the most out of threshold training.

Threshold training is hard work and requires recovery, so be sure to spend a day of easy training after such workouts. You must occasionally train easy to give your harder sessions extra power and energy.

Family Affair: Kent and Carol Ann Bostick

In addition to being on the national road team for many years and becoming the senior national champion in the 40-kilometer and 100-kilometer time trials many times, Kent Bostick, at the age of 40, rode 4:38 in the 4,000-meter individual pursuit at the Senior National Championships in 1993, becoming the champion in the individual pursuit. He accomplished this after only one day of training on the track! He then went to the Master's Nationals several weeks later and rode a 3:26 at the 3,000-meter distance. His wife Carol Ann rode a 3:59 for 3,000 meters at the age of 36. During the same championships she turned a 1:14 .7-kilometer to break both the 30-34 and 35-39 national records.

According to Carol Ann, Kent attributes his ability to still compete at such a high level "to his continued sponsorship even at the masters level, which supplies his equipment, nutritional supplements, and travel support, and, after 15 years of racing, to finally knowing how to train and eat properly. We know it is important to follow a strict diet and keep our weight under control if we hope to compete at a top level of competition. As you get older you cannot take anything for granted if you expect to stay in top form." In addition, both Bosticks support and rely on each other as training partners.

Kent tries to ride as much as 300 to 350 miles a week during the season, much of it at what he describes as high-tempo work at 75% to 90% of his maximum heart rate. He rides to work in 1 hour in the morning and will take a longer route to return, trying to get in 2 to 3 hours on the bike before reaching home. On the weekends he tries to get in two 100-mile rides that average around 23 miles per hour. Carol Ann will try to cover at least three quarters of his distance at the same intensity during the week.

"Consistency in our yearly training is what leads to our continued success. We find it's better to train at moderately high levels throughout the year than to try to embark suddenly in the summer months on a high-intensity program; we feel this would lead to increased risk of injury and overtraining," says Kent.

What intense training has given the Bosticks and countless other masters cyclists is a sense of excitement about the future. It's not about how much money they will put in the bank, but about how they are discovering new challenges and setting

(continued)

Family Affair   *(continued)*

records. As Carol Ann puts it, "Cycling has opened up many new doors for me; hard training has got me so excited about what records I [can] set once I really learn this sport." She has only cycled seriously for 3 years, having participated previously in tennis and aerobics.

Long Intervals

These intervals range from 5 to 12 minutes long. Start with shorter intervals; as you become more fit, lengthen the intervals. Many cyclists consider 3- to 4-minute intervals short and 10- to 12-minute intervals long. Gradually raise your heart rate to lactate-threshold level and maintain it to the end of the interval.

The rest intervals between the long intervals at lactate threshold should be in the 2- to 5-minute range, or to when your heart rate returns to about 120 beats per minute, although the length of recovery will vary with the length and intensity of the interval. Ride easily until you feel you have recovered for the next interval.

Start with three or four intervals of up to 5 minutes. Then gradually increase the number of intervals (five is plenty), increasing the length of each interval until, after several months, you can complete two sets of five intervals. In the early part of the season use your small chainring; once you are into heavy racing, use the big chainring.

Timed-Distance Intervals

Mark off a known distance that will require about 5 to 7 minutes to ride at your lactate-threshold heart rate. Then ride the distance and record your time and ending heart rate. Come back to this test every few weeks. Over time your goal is to lower your time, while not going over your lactate-threshold heart rate for extended periods during the ride.

Lactate Criss-Cross Training

Owen Anderson, editor of *Running Research News*, recommends the following workout to stimulate your lactate-threshold training. You need a heart rate monitor with high and low alarms. Simply set the lower alarm about 8 beats below your lactate-threshold heart rate and the upper alarm about 5 or 6 beats above your lactate-threshold heart rate.

After a good warm-up, increase your speed or intensity steadily until the upper alarm goes off, then gradually slow your pace until the lower alarm sounds. Travel back and forth between the upper and lower alarms, taking about 2 minutes to make each ascent and descent. Again, add length to each interval and repetitions to your workout as your fitness progresses during the season.

Fartlek

Fartlek, or speed play, can be another form of lactate-threshold training. This less formal approach to long intervals is performed on a course that contains hills for work and downhills for active rest. Fartlek training can be performed with a small, well-matched group of cyclists. Cyclists should take turns leading up the hills setting the pace; the stronger riders can try to push the pace even harder when about half the hill is completed. Make sure that everyone recovers adequately on the downhills. It is important to learn to go hard on all types of terrain. Fartlek is supposed to be unsystematic and spontaneous, a style of training that lets you tune into your power and rhythm.

Paced Training

This type of training calls for maintaining your riding pace or tempo for longer periods of time or distances. You'll find these longer tempo rides will help you measure your fitness, improve your pedaling technique while pushing larger gears, and keep you motivated. Most cyclists will train on a known course that replicates a time-trial course or short, rolling road circuit. Using the same course will help you gauge your progress and keep you motivated as the season progresses.

Paced training is completed at a specific intensity (use a heart rate monitor), and the course should be from 5 to 10 miles long. The major difference between paced training and long intervals is the length of the workout and the emphasis on maintaining the pace throughout the ride. As your lactate threshold goes up, your times for the course will come down. Remember to take into account wind, temperature, and equipment when riding the set course. Paced training is great for working on your racing technique and for testing your time-trial fitness.

Anaerobic Training—Training Above Your Lactate Threshold

Occasionally you will be called upon for short efforts that exceed your lactate threshold. Attacks lasting a few minutes; starts of criteriums; short, steep climbs; and efforts to close a gap require you to work anaerobically for a few minutes. Training above lactate threshold enhances your muscles' ability to produce ATP. This type of training involves mostly the Type II (fast-twitch) muscle fibers. The prescription to improve your anaerobic capacity is relatively simple: work at a higher intensity (90% to 95% of your maximum heart rate) for a short duration, take an active rest of easy riding, and do another repeat of the interval. The primary method of anaerobic training is interval training.

Most cyclists and coaches find that 6 to 8 weeks of high-intensity work of this nature before the peak of the season is adequate. Most cyclists cannot tolerate more than one or two sessions per week. Be sure to count short time trials as tough sessions.

Hill Intervals

Complete these intervals up a moderately steep hill. Gradually pick up your speed as you enter the hill, then shift to a larger gear and "jump" until you reach maximum speed. Hold it for no more than 1 minute. Ride easily down the hill until your heart rate returns to below 60% of maximum, and repeat three to eight times. These intervals should be done early in the week and not until late spring, after establishing a good base of endurance work and some lactate-threshold training.

Medium Intervals

Work intervals on the flat roads (and hill intervals) lasting from 1 to 2 minutes at 90% to 95% of your maximum heart rate will overload your anaerobic capacity, leading to the increased capacity of your anaerobic system to tolerate more lactic acid and produce more ATP through glycolosis. Eight to 10 intervals with recovery rides of twice the time of the work intervals make for a hard training session.

The Final Spin

From this discussion we can see that having a high $\dot{V}O_2$max, and only testing for a high max, is not the only key to your success in cycling. Again, all other variables being equal, a cyclist who can maintain a pace requiring 90% of his maximum capacity of 70 milliliters of oxygen is far better off in a race than a cyclist who has a maximal oxygen consumption of 75 milliliters but who can only sustain a lactate-threshold pace of 75%. This shows the importance of knowing not only your $\dot{V}O_2$max but also your lactate threshold.

Training at your lactate threshold is the most effective way to induce a shift to the right in the lactic acid curve (Figure 4.1). After proper training, the shift occurs at a faster speed and a higher percentage of maximal aerobic capacity.

Training too far below your lactate threshold does not stimulate your anaerobic systems for lactic acid production within the muscle. You are basically training your aerobic energy system. On the other hand, too intense a pace will rapidly produce lactic acid, which will accumulate, resulting in early fatigue and a reduction in work intensity.

The benefits of training to increase lactate threshold and anaerobic power are primarily for cyclists who are interested in high-performance training. If you just want to improve your fitness, you probably do not need to spend much time training at these intensities. If, however, your goal is to win races and perform well in time trials, you need to spend one or two workouts a week training at your lactate threshold.

5

© Coco McCoy/Rainbow

Sprint Training

Road riders . . . neglect that one weapon—acceleration, or the ability to sprint when it counts in a race.

—*Roger Young,*
U.S. Cycling Federation
Athlete Development Director

Being able to sprint is crucial to your cycling success. Many races come down to a sprint—be it a breakaway with a few riders or a mass sprint at the end of a criterium or road race.

There are many ways to improve your speed and sprinting ability. If you're like professional cyclists Inga Thompson and Lance Armstrong, you've got a mind that's constantly searching for more speed, always squeezing a little more out of your body, your bike, and the course you are training on. Later I will describe some workouts that you can insert into your training program to help you ride faster. First, let's review some of the physiological characteristics of speed that will help you understand it, so you can create methods for increasing your own cycling speed and sprinting ability.

The Physiology of Speed

Speed training is not interval training. Interval training develops anaerobic and aerobic capacity through work periods of approximately 30 seconds to several minutes followed by recovery periods of one half to two times the length of the interval. This type of riding plays an important part in riding fast, but it is very different from speed, or sprint, training.

Speed training is used to develop quickness and explosive power and involves short, intense periods of 5 to 30 seconds, with heart rates reaching 95% to 100% of maximum during the longer sprints. Speed, power, and acceleration are the key elements, not heart rate. It is important that a long recovery period (at least 2 to 5 minutes) follow such sprints to allow for a total rebuilding of ATP in the muscle and to ensure a quality workout.

Your total speed includes reaction time and movement time. Reaction time (the time from the stimulus—such as an opponent's jump—until the beginning of your sprint) is a function of the nervous system. You can't change the speed of your nerve transmissions. Thus, any major improvement in reaction must be achieved by increasing your response to the stimulus and by repeating the appropriate responses, which will reduce the time it will take your central nervous system to process the information. Use jumping drills and group sprints to improve your reaction time.

Movement time (the interval from the beginning to the end of the movement) will often decrease (improve) with appropriate strength and sprint training. The key to your success in sprinting lies in the specificity of your training. Specificity applies to the rate of movement and the resistance employed, which means that your training should simulate the competition as closely as possible. If you want to be successful at sprinting, then you need to sprint train in several situations—in a group, up a hill, out of a corner, and at the end of several hours on the bicycle.

How much can you improve your sprinting ability? To be a pure sprinter, your body may need to have a high percentage (over 50%) of Type II (fast-twitch) fibers. But don't feel like you will never win a race if this isn't the case. Although you may never be as fast as Connie Pariskevin-Young or Djamolidine Abdujaparov, you can improve your reaction and movement times by practicing the drills presented in this chapter.

But first let's discuss the principle of power. Power = work ÷ time, or the rate of doing work. Work = force × distance. Power combines a cyclist's strength (force put into the pedals) and velocity (distance ÷ time). For example, suppose you cycle at a power output of 500 watts (watts are a unit of power) for 10 seconds. You have done a certain amount of work in that time. Because power is the rate of doing work, you produce twice the power if you do the same amount of work in 5 seconds. You can also produce twice the power by doubling the force you exert over the 10 seconds. In other words, power is not only a measure of how much force you can exert, but also of how quickly you can exert it. Later in the chapter you will find examples of how to increase your power by sprinting uphill, by sprinting in large gears, and by using high-speed repetitions in weight training.

Who Needs Speed Work?

Endurance training gives you base mileage that will get you to the finish line comfortably. Eventually, you will enter harder and faster races, and you will begin to struggle to finish well and stay with the group. You need to consider sprint or speed work if you

- lack the strength to sprint strongly at the end of a race or to attack during a race,
- need to improve your high-speed racing coordination,
- get dropped in the first few miles of a criterium because the pace feels too hard,
- need to peak for a key race or series of races,
- need to improve your ability to generate power while riding the hills, or
- feel it is difficult to hold a fast pace during a race.

Bernard Hinault once said, "If there is one area where experience counts, it's in the sprint. The best school is the mistakes you make as you begin your career. It's best to commit them when you're young.

You should try your luck even if you're not particularly gifted, in order to learn" (*Velo-News*, v. 7, 1988, p. 108).

Sprints should be part of your program at least once a week after you have a good endurance base, from early season until the cool weather. Many cyclists will not do any speed work until they have 1,000 to 1,200 miles in their legs. Generally, 95% to 97% of your training will be endurance and tempo training, and only 2% to 5% will be speed work.

Do not add a lot of speed work to your program until you have raced for about 1 year, have completed a few races of varying distances, and have a good base of endurance miles. Your body needs to be ready to take on the extra load of speed or sprint training.

Speed training may be part of a short distance ride (60 to 90 minutes) or may be part of a warm-up for an interval session.

Body Position

The position of your body on the bike, especially arm position, is important when working on your jump. Your arms counteract the strong forces being generated by your legs, hips, and back. Most sprinters prefer to sprint with their arms flexed. If you use this style, the angle of your elbows should remain constant during the jump and acceleration phases of the sprint. This allows your body to remain stable as your hips are brought up and forward with greater ease. Your wrists should be on the outside of the bars on the drops, not bent toward the inside. This allows you to bend the elbows to the outside, which will allow you to maintain your weight better over the pedals and to remain more stable if you get bumped by another rider in the sprint.

Your hips should be aligned vertically over your front foot as the forward crank approaches horizontal. This will allow you to use your body weight during the power phase (downstroke) of the pedal. Remember to keep your head up and in a comfortable position.

When you accelerate or sprint using a big gear, learn to use your arms in a manner coordinated with the rest of your body. Pull against the left part of the bar when the left foot is pushing down on the pedal. At the same time, apply enough counterforce with your right arm to keep from turning the front wheel. As the right leg begins its downward stroke the process is reversed.

Roger Young, U.S. Cycling Team track sprint coach, tells his athletes to remember these key points in a sprint that is initiated at a very slow speed. He says, "At the start, you should drive up and out of the saddle, hips forward and as square as possible, arms bent slightly, and act as if you are running on the pedals. Gradually, as you pick up speed, your shoulders should go forward and down as your elbows and hips bend. When you reach your top rpms, the hips and shoulders begin to come back, and you should make a smooth transition into the saddle."

Learn to keep your leg speed high; work on letting it reach 110 to 120-plus revolutions. In some sprints, it may help you reach top-end speed if you concentrate on pedaling faster instead of harder. Let the bike move slightly from side to side as you power the bicycle forward.

Sprint With Snap and Power

Davis Phinney once described sprinting as being comprised of snap and power, power being the ability to push big gears quickly, and snap being leg speed and the ability to pedal smoothly in high gear.

While training in Boulder, Colorado, Davis often finds short, steep rolling hills on which to practice his sprinting. To work on his power, he rides halfway up the hill, then shifts into a larger gear and sprints over the top. So it becomes a sprint that develops pure explosive power and strength. He never does this form of training alone because riding with one or two other cyclists makes for better competition and pushes him to ride harder.

Davis develops snap by sprinting down long hills. In the middle of the descent, the group will jump and then sit down and continue to sprint, trying to spin as fast as they can. It not only helps cyclists develop snap and speed but also trains them to develop a smooth pedaling motion.

Gearing practice should coincide with your fitness and time training in the competitive season. Remember, you are trying to achieve maximal effort, not just to mash big gears. Early in the season use smaller gears; then, when in peak form, use 53 × 15 to 53 × 13 gearing. Experiment with gears to find your best combination for fast acceleration and top-end speed. Juniors and some women, depending on their strength, may have to modify their gear selection.

Jumps

You can increase your reaction time on group rides by sprinting for city-limit or other specific road signs. The designated sprinter in the group decides when to initiate the sprint. The others respond and chase until the initial rider is caught or ends the effort. Take turns initiating the sprint, and vary the distance from 100 to 300 meters.

Or have someone act as a coach and follow your training group in a car or on a motorcycle. While the group is riding along at training pace, the coach will occasionally beep the horn and everyone will sprint until they hear the next beep. The coach can vary the distance and decide whether the sprint starts up or downhill.

Sprint Drills

These drills will force you to learn to sprint in various gears, uphill, downhill, into the wind, with the wind at your back, and at various positions in the group. Get off the saddle, charge down the road as you build speed and cadence, then sit down and increase your revolutions. Stay low on the bike and reasonably smooth—lots of erratic movement on the bike is unsafe and will slow you down.

• **Sprints in Progressively Bigger Gears.**   After a good warm-up, complete two sprints of 200 to 250 meters, one sprint of 300 to 350 meters, and one or two sprints of 200 to 250 meters. Rest for at least 5 to 10 minutes between sprints, or until your heart rate returns to 60% of maximum, while riding in an easy gear before you start another set. Use the first 50 to 100 meters to get up to speed, and then ride all-out until the finish. As the season progresses, gradually increase the longest sprint to 500 meters.

• **Declining Time Sprints.**   After a good warm-up, start with a sprint of 60 seconds, then 50 seconds, 40, 30, and 20. Allow your heart rate to return to below 60% before beginning the next sprint. Finish with two to four sprints of 30 seconds.

• **Race Sprints.**   While riding with several teammates (six at most) try to replicate sprints you have seen in race videos or from past race experiences. One rider should attack at a certain place or at a particular speed, and then everyone goes from there. The person who is selected to jump also decides how long the sprint should last. These sprints can be completed during the last few hours of longer road rides.

• **Ins and Outs.**   Connie Carpenter-Phinney likes to have younger or beginning cyclists practice sprinting while getting in and out of the saddle. You start by rising out of the saddle in a big gear for 10 pedal revolutions and then sitting back down, sprinting for another 10 revolutions. Repeat these sprints three times, jumping out of the saddle and then sitting back down. You will have sprinted 30 revolutions in the saddle and 30 revolutions out of the saddle, for a distance of about 400 yards. These sprints are best done with the wind at your back or on a slight downhill. This drill works on your ability to sprint and accelerate several times during a longer sprint. This often happens when riders keep jumping in the final kilometers of a race.

• **Motorcycle Sprints.**   This excellent sprint will teach you how to attack while riding in a group at high speeds. While riding behind a

The Element of Surprise

Recently, at a U.S. Cycling Federation training camp for beginning riders, Chris Carmichael, U.S. Cycling Team Director, gave the following recommendations to help cyclists surprise their opponents and cause them to lose their advantage in a road race or criterium. Chris stated, "This may sound simple, but in practice many cyclists do not take full advantage of this strategy. One of the most common racing mistakes is enabling your opponents to predict your attacks."

Here are his guidelines for attacking your opponents in a race: Attack your opponents from behind. Try dropping back a few yards and then taking a run at the riders just in front of you. By the time you pass them, you are traveling 2 to 3 miles faster and are at a decided advantage. Remember to attack your opponents in an area of the course, or time in the race, where they are least likely to expect an attack. You need to gamble a little in order to win races.

Chris gave the following example of how to use this tactic. In a flat, long road race, it may seem very predictable that the race come down to a field sprint or a small breakaway in the closing miles of the race. This race development benefits the strong sprinter. If you are not a strong sprinter, you might try a breakaway with about 10 miles to go in the hope of holding out until the end.

Carmichael also gave these guidelines for sprinting at the end of a race and how much work you should do in a breakaway: Study the last 500 yards of a race. Try to pick a landmark in that last 500 yards, knowing that from that landmark, if you were to take a straight shot for the finish, you could continue to accelerate all the way. If you're in a group and there is a strong crosswind, stay on the downwind side of the group to begin your jump.

While riding in a breakaway, remember that all the energy you expend should benefit you, so that you reach the finish area with strength to spare for the sprint. Ask yourself, "Am I the driving force in the break?" If the answer is yes, then chances are someone in the break is trying to level the playing field and get you to take the brunt of the work. The break should not live or die by your work. Try taking shorter pulls and maintaining the same pace as the rider who just finished pulling. It is possible to save considerable energy during a long breakaway if you reduce the length of your pulls in the pace line.

motorcycle at 28 to 33 miles per hour, practice jumping around the motorcycle, and try to pass or "slingshot" around the driver. This replicates trying to attack opponents while they are racing full-speed.

• **Hill Sprints.**   On a hill of about 5% to 9% grade, find a spot where it will take about 20 to 25 seconds to reach the top. From this spot, initiate each sprint with a jump of 7 to 10 pedal strokes and then return to the saddle and go all-out to the top; you may get out of the saddle again for the last 10 yards. Then turn around and pedal easily back down the hill. Do not begin another sprint until your heart rate drops below 60% of maximum. Keep the bicycle as straight as possible, and ride in as straight a line as possible to the top. Use a 42 × 17 gear for the first sprint, 42 × 16 for the second sprint, 42 × 15 for the third, and 42 × 14 for the fourth; if you feel really strong, go for a fifth sprint in a 42 × 13 gear.

Ergometer Speed Work

Davis Phinney, in an issue of *Winning Magazine*, gives this workout for developing leg speed, power, and quick recovery. You will have to adjust the gearing and sets according to your age and level of fitness.

Warm up for 10 to 15 minutes; include three or four accelerations of about 15 seconds at the end of the warm-up. Complete the following ride for 10 minutes with no rest. Ride 1 minute in 42 × 17 gear at a cadence of 90 revolutions per minute. Gradually increase the gearing (keeping the same cadence) over the next 9 minutes, allowing your heart rate to reach 90% to 95% of maximum as you try to reach a 53 × 17 gear. Follow this with 5 minutes of recovery in a moderate gear at a moderate cadence.

Then complete the following sprint five times: 45 seconds in a 53 × 17 gear at a cadence of 90 revolutions per minute; then raise the cadence to between 110 and 120 for about 15 seconds. Allow 1 minute between each sprint in a moderate gear. Finish the workout with three 30-stroke sprints (53 × 17 gear) at a 110 to 120 cadence. Warm down for about 10 minutes.

The Final Spin

Remember that any cyclist can become a good sprinter, regardless of size and muscular strength. You only have to recall the 1984 Olympics, when Alexi Grewal, a great climber, was able to beat Steve Bauer, one of the better road sprinters in the world, in the final sprint for the gold medal. By working hard on his sprint in the spring and summer of 1984, he became an Olympic champion.

There are many physiological reasons why speed work is necessary if you want to maximize your potential at any distance, from criteriums to long road races. During speed work you train your body to recruit the muscles necessary for fast riding. You also learn a sense of relaxation at race pace, which apparently comes as a result of training your muscles to function at an accelerated pace.

During speed work your muscles also begin to accumulate lactic acid. Eventually, so much lactic acid builds up that your muscles begin to lose their ability to contract. That is why your muscles begin to lock up after about 60 seconds of maximal sprinting. Training , especially speed training, can modify this physiological effect. One of the adaptations to the previous workouts is the ability of your muscles to buffer some or most of the lactic acid. You can sprint faster and for a longer time before lactic acid brings you to your knees.

Building power and speed into your cycling program is a good way to add variety to your workouts. And there is no reason to repeat the same speed work every week because there are many options to getting the same job done. It is possible to get your body to move faster, and speed training is the answer. Just give it a try!

© John Kelly

Training Modes

As competition for the top spots in every sport gets tougher, creative coaches are going to look for ways to develop an edge—cross-training is one way to give athletes that edge.

—*Chris Carmichael*

Perhaps one of the most important investments you can make to improve your cycling is the time you spend developing a stronger body and investigating supplemental equipment and techniques to improve your fitness and performance. Resistance training, cross-training, stretching, indoor training, and using a heart rate monitor are just some of the tools you can add to your training arsenal. Training with weights or machines, plyometrics, cross-country skiing, and stretching all provide multiconditioning effects and help reduce injuries.

Cyclists who have worked all spring and summer on their bicycles will find cross-training a good change of pace. Cross-training is a nice mental break and gives you something different to look forward to. For example, cyclists who cross-country ski look forward to snow-covered roads because they know that they will soon be gliding across them.

All cyclists can benefit from using a heart rate monitor during training and competition. Training with a monitor is like having a portable full-time coach attached to your body. A heart rate monitor and cyclocomputer serve as excellent motivators and take the guesswork out of evaluating your performance and adjusting your training program.

This chapter presents a menu of different modes of exercise that you can use year round for improved performance. These training modes and the various types of on-the-bike training presented in previous chapters can be knit together to form a yearly training program, which is the subject of chapter 7.

Stretching

If you are a serious cyclist, stretching regularly will help you avoid tight muscles and injuries. Hard riding is great exercise, but it does lead to a gradual loss of muscle elasticity and an overall decrease in joint flexibility. Fortunately, stretching enables your muscles and joints to adapt to the rigors of cycling.

Stretching improves flexibility and increases range of motion, so well-exercised muscles and joints will undergo less severe stress in competitive conditions. Proper stretching after a workout can also reduce or even eliminate your muscle stiffness after a ride. Stretching keeps the body fine-tuned and hastens recovery.

In his book *Road Racing*, Bernard Hinault, five-time winner of the Tour de France, speaks of the benefits of regular stretching in a cycling program. "Stretching just before competition, like a time trial, prepares the muscles for the effort by making them more supple and increasing their tone. The alternating pattern of contraction-relaxation is more completely guaranteed, enhancing your effectiveness if you must ride fast and gives you a more efficient style if you must ride for a long time" (p. 182).

Hinault further explains, "You will be able to raise your saddle and still be able to pedal with suppleness and retain good speed. You'll be able to do this because of an improved decontraction of the opposing muscles with each pedal revolution. The hamstrings, which instinctively attempt to hold back the descending leg, reap a great benefit from stretching. It is their imperfect decontraction that prevents you from raising your saddle enough." Raising your saddle will allow your leg muscles a greater range and will put less strain on your spinal column and lower back.

Bob Anderson, author of *Stretching* and a frequent lecturer at U.S. National Team training camps, says, "One of the best ways to stretch is with static stretching, in which you stretch each muscle group slowly and gently, until a mild amount of tightness (not pain) is felt in the muscle. Then maintain this position for about 30 seconds, or until the muscle begins to relax. As you hold the stretch, the feeling of tension should diminish. If it doesn't, just ease off slightly into a more comfortable stretch."

After holding the easy stretch, move a bit farther into the stretch until you feel mild tension again. This, the developmental stretch, should be held for another 10 to 30 seconds. The tension should again slightly diminish or stay the same. If tension increases or becomes painful, you are overstretching and should ease off to a more comfortable stretch. The developmental stretch reduces tension and will safely increase flexibility. Repeating this process a few times for each muscle group will yield the best results.

The rapid, jerky movements involved in ballistic (bouncing) stretches are ineffective and can lead to injury. If you bounce, the muscle responds by contracting to protect itself from overstretching. Thus, an internal tension develops in the muscle and prevents it from being fully stretched. Bouncing may also cause tiny tears in the muscle, leaving scar tissue behind, which can make the muscle less flexible than it was before.

I suggest you experiment with stretching for 5 to 10 minutes before and after you ride. The areas of your body that tend to tire first are the ones that you should pay particular attention to when you are preparing for a ride. Michael Alter's book, *Sport Stretch*, contains an excellent stretching routine for cycling (see Table 6.1).

Hold the degree of tension in the muscle that feels good to you. The key to stretching is to be relaxed while you concentrate on the muscles being stretched. Your breathing should be slow, deep, and rhythmical. Don't worry about how far you stretch. Relax into it and limberness will become just one of many by-products you receive from regular stretching.

Table 6.1   A Stretch Routine for Cycling

Achilles tendon stretch

1. Stand upright 4 or 5 steps from a wall.
2. Lean against the wall without losing the straight line of the head, neck, spine, pelvis, legs, and ankles.
3. Keep both heels down, flat, together, and parallel to the hips.
4. Exhale, bend your arms, move your chest toward the wall, and shift your weight forward.
5. Hold the stretch and relax.

Hip flexors stretch

1. Lie on a table near the edge, flat on your back.
2. Allow one of your legs to hang over the side.
3. Inhale, flex the opposite knee, grasp it with your hands, and bring it to your chest.
4. Inhale and compress your thigh to your chest.
5. Hold the stretch and relax.

Table 6.1

Adductors stretches

1. Sit upright on the floor with your legs flexed and heels touching each other.
2. Grasp your feet or ankles and pull them as close to your buttocks as possible.
3. Exhale, lean forward from the hips without bending your back, and attempt to lower your chest to the floor.
4. Hold the stretch and relax.

1. Assume a squat position with your feet about 12 inches apart and your toes turned slightly out.
2. Place your elbows on the inside portions of your upper legs.
3. Exhale, and slowly push your legs outward with your elbows. Remember to keep your feet flat on the floor to reduce strain on the knees.
4. Hold the stretch and relax.

Abdomen and hips stretch

1. Kneel upright on the floor with legs slightly apart and parallel and with toes pointing backward.
2. Place your palms on your upper hips and buttocks.
3. Exhale, slowly arch your back, contract your buttocks, and push your hips forward.
4. Exhale, continue to arch your back, drop your head backward, open your mouth, and gradually slide your hands onto your heels.
5. Hold the stretch and relax.

(continued)

Table 6.1 *(continued)*

Quadriceps stretches

1. Lie on your back at the edge of a table with your left side toward the edge.
2. Flex your right leg and slide it toward the buttocks to help anchor and stabilize your hips.
3. Grasp your leg under the right thigh with your right hand.
4. Exhale, slowly lower your left leg off the table, and grasp the ankle or foot with your left hand.
5. Inhale, and slowly pull your left heel toward your buttocks.
6. Hold the stretch and relax.

1. Kneel upright with knees together, buttocks on the floor, heels by the side of your thighs, and toes pointing backward.
2. Exhale as you continue leaning backward until you are flat on your back. Do not let your feet flare out to the sides.
3. Hold the stretch and relax.

Buttocks and hips stretch

1. Sit upright on the floor, resting your left leg in front of you with your knee flexed and your foot pointing to the right.
2. Cross your right leg over your left leg and place the foot flat on the floor.
3. Exhale, round your upper torso, and bend forward.
4. Hold the stretch and relax.

Table 6.1

Lateral neck stretch

1. Sit or stand upright with your left arm flexed behind your back.
2. Grasp the elbow from behind with the opposite hand.
3. Exhale, pull your elbow across the midline of your back, and lower your ear to the right shoulder. It is essential to keep your left shoulder stabilized.
4. Hold the stretch and relax.

Lower back stretch

1. Lie flat on your back with your arms by your hips, palms down.
2. Inhale, push down on the floor with your palms, raise your legs up in a squat position so the knees almost rest on your forehead, and bring your hands up to support your back.
3. Hold the stretch and relax.
   Use this stretch with care.

Posterior neck stretch

1. Lie flat on the floor with both knees flexed.
2. Interlock your hands on the back of your head near the crown.
3. Exhale, and pull your head off the floor and onto your chest. Keep your shoulder blades flat on the floor.
4. Hold the stretch and relax.

(continued)

Table 6.1 *(continued)*

Hamstrings stretch

1. Sit upright on the floor with both legs straight.
2. Flex your right knee and slide your heel toward your buttocks.
3. Lower the outer side of your right thigh and calf onto the floor.
4. Place your right heel against the inner side of your left thigh so that a 90-degree angle is formed between your extended left leg and flexed right leg.
5. Exhale, keeping your left leg straight, bend at the waist, and lower your extended upper torso onto your thigh.
6. Hold the stretch and relax.

Note. From *Sport Stretch* by M.J. Alter, 1990, Champaign, IL: Human Kinetics. Copyright 1990 by Michael J. Alter. Adapted by permission.

Stretching will get your blood circulating through your muscles and warm them up for the tasks ahead. Once you start riding, don't forget to pedal easily for a few minutes until your heart rate gets up to 120 before beginning any hard efforts.

It will take you about 10 minutes to do the stretching exercises shown in Table 6.1 before and after your ride—just 10 minutes to keep injuries and tightness to minimum. As you stretch, you will learn about how your body moves and feels. Stretching is a great form of physical education.

Resistance Training

Successful cycling requires a combination of muscular endurance, strength, and power. The particular discipline within cycling you are training for determines which of these attributes you should emphasize in training. A road race requires mostly muscular endurance, but you will also need power to climb steep hills and sprint at the end. A match sprint depends primarily on strength and power for an explosive sprint. Because of this, resistance training with free weights and/or machines has always been part of a good training program.

Resistance training has recently attracted interest among middle-distance and distance athletes in many sports: Is there compatibility between resistance training and aerobic conditioning during the same conditioning period? And will resistance training provide the necessary strength, power, suppleness, stamina, and potential?

Only in the last few years have researchers and coaches begun to investigate these issues. Several recently published studies and books have shown that strength training can increase leg strength and time-to-exhaustion during cycling without increasing maximal oxygen consumption. There is also evidence that increased strength will reduce endurance athletes' incidence of injury.

Robert Hickson and others from his laboratory at the University of Illinois at Chicago studied the impact of adding heavy-resistance training on leg strength in eight runners and cyclists who had already been training for several years. Strength training was performed 3 days a week for 10 weeks while the subjects continued their normal endurance training. After 10 weeks, leg strength was increased by an average of 30%, but maximal oxygen consumption did not increase (which would have indicated increased maximal aerobic capacity); however, time-to-exhaustion at maximal work rates increased by 13% in the running group and 11% in the cycling group.

The data do not demonstrate any negative performance effects from adding heavy-resistance training to ongoing endurance training. The authors concluded that certain types of endurance performance, particularly those requiring fast-twitch fiber recruitment (for example, the ability to chase down a break), can be improved by supplementing the training program with resistance training.

Recently, a group of researchers from the University of Maryland completed a study investigating the effects of resistance training on lactate threshold and endurance performance. Eighteen healthy males were randomly assigned either to resistance training for 12 weeks or to a control group. After 12 weeks, despite no changes in maximal oxygen consumption, there was a 33% increase in cycling time-to-exhaustion at 75% of peak oxygen consumption in the strength-trained group. The improved endurance performance was associated with a 12% increase in lactate threshold.

Steve Fleck, PhD, sports physiologist in charge of strength-training research in the division of sports medicine at the Olympic Training Center in Colorado Springs, says of this study, "A higher lactate threshold and endurance time-to-exhaustion means that an athlete can ride at a higher intensity before fatigue sets in and causes a reduction in cycling speed. Their findings indicate that resistance training improved endurance performance independently of changes in oxygen consumption. This improvement appears to be related to increases in lactate threshold and increased leg strength." Put simply, Fleck is saying that endurance training and resistance training are not mutually exclusive. Both may be needed for improved performance.

If resistance training can improve performance, then how much time should be devoted to it? Remember that any supplemental training, whether it is resistance training or some other activity, is only an aid to improve cycling, not a substitute for riding, and should not be overdone. During any week of training, cycling should be the major component. But as you will see later in this chapter, varying amounts of time and intensity of resistance training need to be part of your overall cycling program.

When you design a resistance program to fulfill your individual needs, keep these points in mind. First, track specialists need more power and strength than do longer distance cyclists. Second, you need to identify your individual weaknesses and strengths and put an emphasis on developing those muscle groups that need increased strength and power. Do maintenance work for those muscles that are already well-conditioned. Third, during the off-season, when higher volume training (more reps or sets) is done, resistance training should receive more emphasis than during other periods.

Resistance training offers the additional benefit of reducing injuries by helping to strengthen the muscles, tendons, and ligaments around the foot, ankle, knee, and hip joints. Thus, a strength program that uses moderate resistance and 12 to 15 repetitions per exercise and also emphasizes injury prevention may be appropriate for distance cyclists and not adversely affect their endurance performance.

Program Planning

When you design a strength-training program for yourself, have specific goals in mind. Consider the needs and energy demands of the different events; the prescribed exercises should increase the realization of your potential. Exercise prescription for resistance training demands considerable thought, planning, evaluation, and organization. The key motivating factor to your participation in a strength and conditioning program will be improved performance.

Your first emphasis should be on proper planning. As with road training, strength training should be developed within your yearly training program.

The various parts of the resistance-training program are matched against periods of the cycling season and shown in Table 6.2. (For more information about dividing the cycling season into specific periods, please see chapter 7.) The transitional phase of the resistance program begins with the end of the competitive season and is designed to help you reduce your time on the bicycle while adjusting your body to new stresses. These exercises are done with a minimum of equipment. Body resistance can be used for some, thus avoiding the common problem of using too much weight too soon. Actual workout time should be short— 15 to 20 repetitions of each exercise for one to three sets. The training can be done 2 or 3 days a week as you gradually taper your miles on the bike and let your body get adequate rest.

The foundation phase begins after the muscles have been properly prepared. You should now be using slightly heavier resistance while decreasing the number of repetitions. As the name implies, this phase is geared toward allowing the muscles to grow. Harvey Newton, strength training consultant to the U.S. Cycling Team, has commented on the concern many cyclists have that they may add too much muscle mass to their bodies. According to Newton, resistance training "does not mean that body weight will increase; in fact, body composition may change— body fat will decrease, while some muscle growth takes place—while body weight remains constant. By working the muscles more intensely and allowing some growth, the body will be properly prepared for the next phase."

The basic-strength phase is geared toward increasing strength of individual muscle groups and using these groups in a coordinated effort. Weight is increased as repetitions are decreased. The exercises may change during this phase in order to test your body's ability to move more effectively in a unified effort and to allow for variation in training. To increase your strength quickly is quite easy; the real benefit comes from converting strength gains into power.

Power is the ability to use force in an explosive fashion. Increased power will allow the sprinter to jump more quickly and the road cyclist to bridge gaps more quickly, and to do this repeatedly if necessary. Therefore, in the power phase, resistance is reduced, perhaps along with the number of strength-training sessions each week, to allow for more training on the bike. Exercises are all done in an explosive manner, using timing devices where appropriate.

As the power phase ends, you need to decide how much, if any, maintenance training you will do. This is the peaking phase. Because you will be racing on a regular basis, the amount, duration, and intensity of strength work should be reduced. Continuing to train those weak points not normally stressed on the bike is frequently a good idea. This can be done with simple exercises using your body weight. This additional work will allow you to maintain your new-found strength so that the next transitional phase is begun with a level of strength higher than in the previous year.

Table 6.2   Strength Training Program Phases

Road cycling season*	Resistance-training phase	Purpose	Sets
Transition period (Oct—4 weeks)	Transitional	To adjust to strength training	1 to 3
General preparation phase of the preparation period (Nov-Dec—4-6 weeks)	Foundation	To build muscle tissue	3 to 4
General preparation phase of the preparation period (Dec-Jan—4-6 weeks)	Basic strength	To gain strength	5 to 7
Specialization phase of the preparation period (Jan-Feb—4-6 weeks)	Power	To build explosive power	5 to 6
Competition period (March into the racing season)	Peaking	To maintain strength	1 to 3

*This season assumes the rider trains and rides in the Northern Hemisphere.

Cycling-Specific Exercises

Table 6.3 lists exercises you can do during the various phases of your resistance-training program. These are only meant as examples; other exercises that you are already doing may be added to the list. For example, to prepare your lower back musculature, you could begin the transitional phase with back extensions, isolating the muscles but not using any large resistance. During the foundation phase, stiff-legged deadlifts or good-morning exercises could be employed. Once your muscles have been properly prepared, power cleans and high pulls could be added during the basic-strength and power phases. For peaking, back extensions could again be employed. Use your imagination to design specific exercises, or consult other books on resistance training. It is beyond the scope of this book to outline every movement that could be of use. Rather, some basic exercises are listed in Table 6.4 along with figures showing key positions. Consulting a knowledgeable coach who is familiar with resistance training is always a good idea.

Reps	Exercises	Intensity	Days per week
15 to 20	General in nature: circuits, body weight as resistance, etc.	Minimum	2 to 3
8 to 12	4 to 6, specific muscle groups: quad/glutes, biceps, triceps, abdominals, back, deltoids, gastrocnemius	Moderate	3
1 to 6	3 to 5, combined muscle groups: concentrate on weak areas	Heavy (80% to 100% of your maximum capacity)	3
1 to 15	3 to 4, specific muscle groups for cycling: partial squats, lunges, rowing	Moderate	2 to 3
6 to 10	Work on 1 to 3 weak areas not directly strengthened while riding	Light	1 to 2

Note. From "Strength Training for Cycling" by H. Newton. In *Science of Cycling* (p. 24) by E.R. Burke (Ed.), 1986, Champaign, IL: Human Kinetics. Copyright 1986 by Edmund Burke. Adapted by permission.

General Guidelines for Resistance Training

You should begin and end each resistance-training session with some stretching and aerobic exercise to warm up and cool down. As an additional cool-down, you should also ride a bicycle, a wind-load simulator, or a stationary bicycle for 5 to 10 minutes to help loosen your muscles in a familiar fashion. You want to maintain your smooth pedaling style.

Always keep safety a top priority. Use spotters on certain exercises, such as squats, and use collars on all barbells and dumbbells. Wear proper shoes when lifting heavy weights—they should have firm soles and the heel should be designed to prevent instability or imbalance.

Plyometrics for Power

One problem for many cyclists is the inability to fully use their muscular strength in explosive-type actions, such as sprinting up a short hill or accelerating at the start of a sprint. What they need is a training

Table 6.3 Suggested Strength Training Exercises per Phase

	Transition	Foundation	Basic strength	Power	Peak
Day 1	Trunk curl Dips Leg extension/leg curl Pull-ups Back extension or General circuit	Squats Straight-arm pullover Trunk curl Calf raise Dips Back extension Pull-ups	Push press Power clean Squats Trunk curl Calf raise	Power clean Dips Heavy partial squats Trunk curl Bent-over rowing	Back extension Trunk curl Squats Dips Pull-ups
Day 2	Twist/side bend Leg press Lat pulldown Hanging leg raise Press or General circuit	Dumbbell press Hanging leg raise Good morning Leg press Trunk curl Bent-over rowing	Bench press High pulls Barbell twist (1 end weight) Partial squats	High pulls Push press Squats Trunk curl	Partial squats Dips Pull-ups Calf raise
Day 3	Trunk curl Lunges Calf raise (single leg) Back extension Upright rowing or General circuit	Squats Bent-arm pullover Trunk curl Stiff-legged deadlift Pull-ups Calf raise Dips	Power clean Speed squats Incline press Rowing	Power clean Pull-ups Heavy partial squats Trunk curl	

Note. From "Strength Training for Cycling" by H. Newton. In *Science of Cycling* (p. 27) by E.R. Burke (Ed.), 1986, Champaign IL: Human Kinetics. Copyright 1986 by Edmund Burke. Adapted by permission.

Table 6.4   Strength Training Exercises

Trunk curl

Your lower legs can be in a straight or crossed position above your body or on a bench. When the feet are not braced, only the abdominal muscles are used, not the thigh and hip muscles. Slowly contract your abdominal muscles, placing your chin on your chest and attempting to touch your elbows to your knees. The actual movement should be about 6 to 8 inches.

Dips

From a fully extended arm position lower your body by bending your elbows. After lowering your body as far as possible push back up to a locked-arm position.

If you are too weak to push back to the original position, perform only the first part of the exercise. Take about 6 seconds to lower your body, resisting the weight of your body and gravity all the way. Then use a bench or chair to get back up to Position A, and repeat. After several weeks, you will be able to perform the complete exercise. This technique can be used to modify pull-ups also.

Back extension

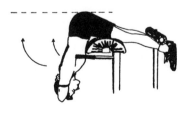

Although a padded apparatus is preferred, you may, with assistance, perform this exercise off the edge of a table or chair. From the position shown, slowly contract your lower back muscles until your trunk is parallel to the ground. There is no need to rise any higher. You can keep your back flat throughout the entire exercise or begin with your back rounded and finish with it flat. As you become stronger, you may hold additional weight behind your head during this exercise.

(continued)

Table 6.4   *(continued)*

Leg press

Various leg-press machines are available (slanted—as shown here—horizontal, or vertical). Regardless of the machine, bend your knees to the desired level and return them to a locked position.

Lunge

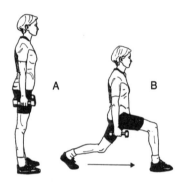

A   B

Stand with your feet shoulder-width apart, torso erect, arms straight down, head up, and eyes straight forward, as shown in Position A. With a firm grip on the dumbbells, step forward and sink down to Position B. Return to the original position, then repeat with the other leg. Very little weight is needed for this exercise to be effective. You can adjust the depth of your movement to mirror the knee flexion that matches pedaling.

Upright row

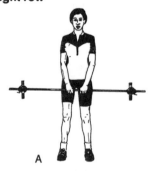

A   B

Assume Position A by gripping the bar with your hands shoulder-width (or slightly less than shoulder-width) apart. Using your trapezius, biceps, and middle deltoid muscles, raise the weight to the level of your sternum (Position B). Your elbows should rise to a point beside the top of your head.

Table 6.4

Squats

A

B

C

D

Squats are the base for any resistance-training program. They may be done throughout the training cycle; simply adjust the depth, intensity, and speed to match the phase of your program. Position A is the normal starting position. The bar is on the trapezius and shoulders. (Use a towel or pad as a cushion if you need to.) Keep your feet hip-width apart and your toes pointed slightly out or straight ahead. Throughout the movement, keep your back flat and make sure the bar remains over your feet. Control your descent, taking 1 to 3 seconds. Be sure not to bounce on recovery.

You can use full squats (Position D) during the foundation phase of your resistance-training program. As you increase the weight, you can adjust the level of your squat so that at your lowest point the tops of your thighs are parallel to the floor (Position C). The partial squat (descending only to Position B) can be used during any phase of your program, but it works best in the basic-strength phase. You may use a lot of weight as long as your trunk—your abdominal and lower back muscles—is strong enough to allow you to maintain a proper position.

During the power phase of your program, you may try speed squats, in which you descend normally but rise up as quickly as possible. Have someone time your ascent, starting a stopwatch as soon as he or she detects your upward movement and stopping it when your knees straighten out. Strive to improve your ascent times for given weights. Keeping each squat under 1 second at a weight that is 80% to 85% of the total weight you can squat will help recruit fast-twitch muscle fibers. For lighter weights, set faster goals. Keep a record of your repetitions, times, and weights.

(continued)

Table 6.4   *(continued)*

Straight-arm pullover

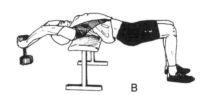

Use a light weight (15- to 20-pound barbell or dumbbell). Start in Position A, and inhale deeply while you lower the weight to Position B. Exhale as you return the weight to the original position. You can use this exercise to help you regain your breath after a round of squats. The amount of weight is not important. This is a breathing exercise.

Good morning

The motion of this exercise resembles the old-fashioned custom of gentlemen bowing to wish people good morning. Start with the bar on your shoulders (Position A), then flex your knees slightly while bending forward. Your lower back may be rounded (Position B) or flat. Return to your original position to complete one repetition. Use light to moderate weights only. This exercise can be stressful if too much weight is used.

Bent-over rowing

Keep your knees fully flexed and your back mostly flat. Draw the weight up to your chest or abdominal area using your arms, shoulders, and the latissimus muscles of your back. Do not allow the weight to drop as you return to the starting position. A variation of this exercise would be to lean your chest against an incline and use two dumbbells.

Table 6.4

Calf raise

For this exercise you may use a barbell across your shoulders, hold a dumbbell in one hand (for exercising one calf at a time), or have a partner help you with the "donkey raise" shown here. Put a board under your toes and stretch your calf muscles to the position shown and then raise your heels. Keep your knees straight. Do 15 to 30 repetitions.

Bent-arm pullover

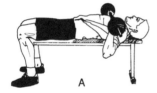
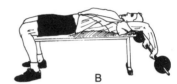

A   B

Place a weight on your chest (Position A), and inhale as you pass it over your face until it rests near the ground (Position B). Exhale as you return the weight to your chest. Use much less weight than in the straight-arm pullover.

Stiff-legged deadlift

A   B

Even though this is called a stiff-legged deadlift, keep your knees slightly bent. From Position A, round your back and lower the weight to Position B. Performing this exercise on the floor limits your range of motion. Using a bench will allow a maximum stretch of your back and hamstring muscles.

(continued)

Table 6.4   *(continued)*

Push press

This can also be called a "cheat press." Use your legs to start the bar's movement, but recruit your triceps and deltoids to finish the lockout phase. Hold the bar as shown in Position A, letting it rest on your frontal deltoids. Bend your knees a few inches (Position B). Then combine leg and arm thrust to get the bar over your head (Position C), rising up on your toes. Complete the lockout (Position D) with your feet flat on the floor. Do not allow yourself to bend backward. Return to the original position for the next repetition.

Heavy partial squats

Begin from the position shown, with the bar resting on pins in a power rack. Keep your back flat, and rise as quickly as possible. All cyclists should be able to work up to the 300- to 800-pound range.

Table 6.4

Power clean

A   B

C   D   E

This is an excellent exercise for the basic-strength and power phases of your program. Start with your feet flat, about hip-width apart, and your knees over your toes (Position A). Use your legs and hips to raise the bar to Position B. Keep your arms straight and back flat at this point. After the bar passes your knees, bend your ankles and knees and place the bar on your thighs above your knees (Position C). Jump up forcefully as you move the bar quickly up to Position D. Slightly dip your knees and affix the bar on your shoulders (Position E). This exercise uses the bigger muscles of your body and helps you develop a quick, explosive movement. It should take you 1 second to pull and place the bar on your shoulders.

High pulls

A   B

Be sure that your back is flat and your hips do not lift too quickly when you do this exercise. Use the same positions you did in the power clean; however, you can use heavier weights because the bar is only being pulled up to Position B, not being "cleaned" to the shoulders.

(continued)

Table 6.4   *(continued)*

Barbell twist

This exercise uses a rotational movement to work your muscles. Use your oblique muscles and the muscles of the abdominal wall to help rotate your body weight from Position A to Position B and back. Do not use your arm muscles. Be sure to keep your hips stable.

Note. From "Strength Training for Cycling" by H. Newton. In *Science of Cycling* (pp. 28-45) by E.R. Burke (Ed.), 1986, Champaign, IL: Human Kinetics. Copyright 1986 by Edmund Burke. Adapted by permission.

---

procedure that increases power—the ability to generate force quickly. In addition to the power phase of your resistance training program, a training modality known as *plyometrics* emphasizes the "explosive-reactive" power of training.

Plyometrics is often called *jump training*. Plyometric exercises are jumps that are designed to contract muscles in a specific way. Researchers have found that concentric muscle contractions, which shorten muscles, are more forceful when they are preceded by eccentric muscle contractions, which lengthen muscles. When you land from a jump during a plyometric exercise, your thigh muscles tense while lengthening (this is an eccentric contraction). This eccentric contraction puts those muscles in a stretched position prior to jumping again (i.e., a "prestretched" position). When you leap from this prestretched position, you are taking advantage of both the elastic and the contractile components of your muscle tissue as well as something called the *stretch reflex* to generate a more powerful concentric contraction.

To picture the elastic property of a muscle, think of a rubber band and how it responds to being stretched. When you increase the stretch on the band, both the tension in the band and the velocity of shortening when you let it go increase. Similarly, when you stretch the elastic component of a muscle, you develop tension due to the muscle's elastic resistance to the stretch. When this tension is released, it aids the resulting muscle contraction.

When muscles lengthen quickly, the stretch reflex (also known as the *myotactic reflex*) is invoked and causes the muscle to contract. Inducing the stretch reflex in conjunction with the voluntary muscle contraction results in a more vigorous concentric contraction. Both the elastic component and the stretch reflex contribute to the total force generated in concentric contraction.

In a plyometric exercise like stadium hops (shown in Table 6.5), the rapid stretching (loading) of the muscles activates their stretch receptors and sends a very strong stimulus by way of the spinal cord to the muscles, causing them to contract powerfully. In sports, plyometrics can be used to improve the leg muscles' force and speed of contraction.

An excellent book offering elementary drills is *Jumping Into Plyometrics* by Dr. Donald Chu. A few drills taken from Dr. Chu's text that are specific to cycling are listed in Table 6.5. Plyometrics should be initiated in the later part of the transition phase and can be continued into the power phase of your resistance-training program.

Like other exercises, plyometrics can lead to poor results if not used properly. Indeed, symptoms of tendinitis and synovitis, particularly of the knee, can result from too much plyometric training. The frequency and duration of your plyometric training session should be determined by your level of fitness and experience. Stronger athletes can train more often and include more jumps into their routines, but even the most experienced individual should perform no more than two sessions a week, with a maximum of 60 to 80 jumps per session. You should have a sound conditioning base and have incorporated stretching into your program before engaging in plyometrics.

Indoor Cycling

The biggest problems with cycling in the winter are early sunsets and foul weather. For most of us, who must juggle training with real-world schedules, indoor cycling on a wind or magnetic trainer is the only real choice. Many great cyclists, such as Greg LeMond and Eve Stephenson, incorporate indoor cycling into their off-season training by using either these trainers or rollers. They enjoy working out at home because it gives them time to concentrate on specific exercises to improve their cycling performance.

Before you complain about indoor cycling as a boring alternative to "real" cycling, you should acknowledge some specific benefits. The controlled environment of a trainer allows you to isolate and concentrate on specific areas of cycling fitness and technique.

Rollers

Rollers consist of three round cylinders mounted on bearings and fixed to a frame. A belt connects one of the rear cylinders to the front cylinder to keep the front wheel spinning at the same speed. Rollers

Table 6.5   **Plyometric Drills for Cyclists**

Split squat with cycle

Equipment: None.

Start: Standing upright, spread the feet far apart, front to back, and bend the front leg 90 degrees at the hip and 90 degrees at the knee.

Action: Jumping up, switch leg positions—the front leg kicks to the back position and the back leg bends back and comes through to the front. While bringing the back leg through, try to flex the knee so that it comes close to the buttock. Land in the split-squat position and jump again immediately.

Alternating push-off

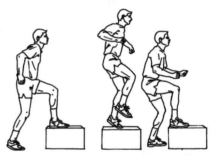

Equipment: A box 6 to 12 inches high.

Start: Stand on the ground and place one foot on the box, heel close to the closest edge.

Action: Push off of the foot on the box to gain as much height as possible by extending through the entire leg and foot; land with feet reversed (the box foot lands a split second before the ground foot). Use a double-arm swing for height and balance.

Squat-depth jump

Equipment: A box 12 to 42 inches high.

Start: Stand on a box in a quarter- to half-squat, toes close to the edge.

Action: Step off the box and land in a 90-degree squat position; explode up out of the squat and land solidly in a squat. For added difficulty, land on a second box of equal height after doing the jump.

Table 6.5

Single-leg push-off

Equipment: A box 6 to 12 inches high.

Start: Stand on the ground and place one foot on the box, heel close to the closest edge.

Action: Push off of the foot on top of the box to gain as much height as possible by extending through the entire leg and foot. Land with the same foot on top of the box and push off again. Use a double-arm swing for height and balance.

Stadium hops

Equipment: Bleachers or stadium steps.

Start: Stand in a quarter-squat at the bottom of the stairs, with hands on hips or back of neck and feet shoulder-width apart.

Action: Jump to the first step and continue up for 10 or more jumps. Make landings light and quick; movements should be continuous up the stairs without pauses. Generally, the athlete should be able to take two steps at a time.

Note. From *Jumping Into Plyometrics* (pp. 29, 40, 43, and 50) by D.A. Chu, 1992, Champaign, IL: Human Kinetics. Copyright 1992 by Donald A. Chu. Adapted by permission.

sharpen your bike-handling ability because you must rely on skillful steering and balance. They teach you to work on smooth, fast spinning but offer little resistance unless you add a fan or magnetic unit. It takes weeks to be able to ride on rollers and feel relaxed enough to lift your hands off the handlebars. Once you get past the first learning stages, the bike-handling skills you obtain will make you a more confident and successful cyclist.

Magnetic and Wind Trainers

Magnetic, or mag, trainers have powerful magnets and a nonconductive disk that produces resistance and dissipates energy as heat. Performance mag trainers have six resistance settings (low to high) and are controlled by a bar-mounted lever. Wind, or turbo, trainers have two fans with slotted blades that churn the air.

A wind trainer's greatest advantage is that it closely mimics the resistance you experience on the road—it increases resistance exponentially. If you were to increase your speed on the wind trainer from 15 to 30 miles per hour, you would need to increase your power output by a factor of about 8. The disadvantages of wind trainers are the noise generated by the fans and the lack of resistance adjustment.

With mag trainers, the resistance increases in direct proportion to speed, which is less realistic, but they do provide enough resistance to elevate your heart rate. Several magnetic training units incorporate a small, precisely weighted flywheel that creates a slight coasting sensation and helps you pedal through the dead spots in your stroke for a more realistic road-feel. An advantage of mag trainers over wind trainers is that they are much quieter to use.

Improving Your Riding Technique

Surprisingly, working on an indoor trainer can afford you rapid improvements in riding technique. The isolated environment of indoor training allows you to concentrate on specific skills without distraction. Spinning, the ability to maintain a high cadence with a continuous application of power, can be improved simply by listening to the trainer's noise. If you hear a steady "whoosh" on the downstroke, you are not pedaling properly. Concentrate on pedaling in circles. You will find that this helps you begin the power stroke earlier at the top and pulls your foot across the bottom of the stroke. After a while, you will develop a longer and smoother delivery of power to the pedals.

Another exercise on a trainer that has dramatic results is one-legged cycling. Most cyclists are not symmetrical in the application of power to the pedals. Most favor one leg over the other and exert more force on the pedal with this leg. The result is asymmetrical pedaling, which leads to loss of power.

To alleviate this problem, try this exercise: Place one foot on a 16- to 18-inch box and, with the other leg, force yourself to pedal smooth circles for 5 to 10 minutes. You will find that this technique improves your ability to apply power over a longer portion of the crank circle because you do not have the inertial support of the other leg. After several weeks of alternating work with both legs, slip the trainer into a very low gear and, using both legs, attempt to pedal with a smooth application of power. This is what professional cyclists refer to as pedaling with suppleness.

Indoor-Cycling Workouts

As with any workout, remember to spend a few minutes warming up and cooling down after each session on the bicycle. Cycling indoors is quite different from cycling outdoors. Within 5 minutes you'll be over-heated if you don't have a cooling system. It is easy to forget how the wind keeps us cool. So use a fan or ride in the coolest part of your house. Or you might want to try riding in an unheated garage, where it is cooler than a house but where you do not have to fight the cold winds of winter. Remember to fill your water bottle before you start your workout.

Cycling to music is a personal choice. Make a couple of training tapes of your favorite songs (preferably songs with a strong beat) and put on your headphones. Use a cyclocomputer to monitor your progress.

Chris Carmichael, National Coaching Director for the U.S. Cycling Federation, recommends that you not spend more than 2 hours at a time on the trainer. He has seen many inexperienced riders spend a great deal of time on stationary trainers, peak too soon in the season, and then fade by midseason.

If you want to emerge in February or March in the best early-season shape of your life, here is the indoor-cycling program for you. Each workout is designed to provide variety, build the cycling muscles, and train your body's different energy systems.

• For general conditioning, find a resistance-and-gear combination that elevates your heart rate into your training zone. After you warm up, raise your cadence to 85 to 100 revolutions per minute, maintaining your heart rate at no more than 85% of your maximum.

• For climbing strength and to become accustomed to pushing larger gears, put the bike into a big gear, or use a trainer and increase to the resistance that forces you to drop your cadence about 15 revolutions per minute. Maintain this cadence for a few minutes and repeat several times during a training session.

• For speed work and to work on your anaerobic capacity, intervals on a trainer are just the answer. You can structure on the trainer many interval programs similar to those you use on the road. The key is to remember to not overwork.

Table 6.6 lists several technique-specific workouts that can be performed on trainers. Variations of these workouts can also be performed on indoor stair-climbers and rowers.

Table 6.6 Technique-Specific Workouts Using a Bicycle Trainer

1. Start with a 10-minute hard effort followed by 2 minutes of easy spinning for recovery. The next interval should be 8 minutes hard, 2 minutes easy. Each hard interval decreases by 2 minutes but increases slightly in intensity. The easy 2 minutes remains the same. The workout ends when you reach 2 minutes hard and 2 minutes easy.

2. Ride progressively harder gears. Start in a relatively low gear and ride for 1 to 2 minutes (keeping the same cadence); then shift to the next higher gear, and to the next, etc. When you're finished with the highest gear you plan to ride, ride back "down the ladder." Usually, riding up four or five gears is sufficient for a good workout.

3. There are dozens of variations on #2 (for example, hard gear, easy gear, back to hard, up two gears, down one). You can also vary the cadence, increasing it to 110 or 120 revolutions per minute, but always keep it above 80.

4. To develop speed, throw in some intervals: 10 to 12 all-out 15-second pedaling sprints, alternating with 45 seconds of easy pedaling.

5. To develop power, try between 3 and 6 repetitions of 3 minutes at 90 revolutions per minute in a big gear, with 3 minutes of low-gear spinning between efforts.

6. Here's a good workout when you want to do an endurance ride at a specific heart rate zone. For example, if you want to work out at between 75% and 80% of your maximum for a good aerobic workout, follow this plan:

   • Warm up for about 5 minutes, starting with low to moderate gears and gradually raise your rpm or gearing until your heart rate is 75% of your maximum.

   • For the next 30 minutes, keep your heart rate within the 75% to 80% target zone. That's the range you calculated before getting on the bike. The challenge of this workout is to keep your heart rate there. If it rises above or falls below this zone, increase or decrease your effort.

   • Cool down for 5 or 10 minutes until your heart rate has returned to below 110 to 120 beats.

   • A final tip: Ride your trainer only every other day. Otherwise, you're likely to get stale. On days you don't ride, get your aerobic workout by rowing or stepping. You can also row or lift weights the same day you ride.

Cross-Training

In many parts of the world, late November through March is considered downtime for many outdoor activities. Cyclists may turn to weight training and wind trainers as their sole forms of conditioning. But with all the new and wonderful winter sporting gear available at reasonable prices, there is no longer any reason to stay indoors. The outdoors and backcountry in winter are beautiful, and cyclists are increasingly discovering the thrills and benefits of training outside. New ultralight skis and snowshoes make the mountains and woods more accessible. Instead of plodding along with heavy gear, you can do what you wanted to do all along—make outdoor exercise a four-season sport.

Skinny Skis, Big Legs

Greg LeMond, Tony Rominger, and Bunki Bankiatis-Davis are just a few of the cyclists who have found that cross-country skiing provides an excellent complement to a year-round cycling program. For cyclists, cross-country skiing is an opportunity to work not only the lower body but also the upper body and torso, which get rather minimal use during cycling. In addition to building upper body and leg power, cross-country skiing is a great way for cyclists to maintain a high level of aerobic conditioning.

Another advantage to cross-country skiing is psychological: Most of us get stale doing the same activity day in and day out. Skiing can be a break in the routine: a chance to do something different, at a different pace, and with different people. For cyclists, skiing in the quiet of the forest is a welcome change from working out indoors or dodging cars on snow-packed roads.

Virtually all ski racers use the skating technique rather than the traditional diagonal stride. Skate skiing requires you to push off the inside edges of your skis. Your skis are no longer confined to tracks; you use the better part of a wide path; and once you learn the technique, you can travel at a rapid clip and get in a great workout. You can experience the power and endurance required to get up a hill and then the excitement of descending and carrying all that speed around the turns. Technique and style are important to success in both cycling and skiing.

Dan Simoneau, cross-country ski manager at Fisher skis and an accomplished cyclist, says, "Besides being a great cardiovascular conditioner, the technique used in skate skiing works the power muscles of cycling: the quadriceps, the gluteals, and the back. The power a cyclist gains from skate skiing carries over into time trials, steep climbs, and sprinting."

If you have tried skiing but have never learned to ski fluidly—pushing off, gliding, and using your poles as more than crutches—you're basically walking on your skis. This is fine if you like it, but it doesn't provide much more exercise or cardiovascular benefit than walking. Take lessons and you'll be amazed at the difference. It takes time to become proficient on skis.

Don't plan to use skiing as a complete replacement for conditioning. You still need to be on the bike and in the weight room. Once you are comfortable on skis, and if there's reliable snow cover, you can take a short break from cycling and ski every day. If you can only ski on groomed trails on the weekends, then add one or two sessions a week on roller skis.

The National Cycling Team spends several weeks on skis at Snow Mountain Ranch in Colorado. Chris Carmichael, the athlete development coach, gives these guidelines for training in winter: He suggests skiing about 2 days a week—a day of endurance training and a day of anaerobic-threshold training, where your heart rate stays at anaerobic-threshold level or slightly higher for 30 to 90 minutes. The rest of the time, ride either indoors or on the road.

Nathan Sheafor, 1992 Olympian and several-time national champion, skis about 3 days a week, goes on road rides twice a week, and mountain bikes twice a week. He uses the road rides for steady endurance work and the mountain bike for climbing. He gets in four or more rides a week for aerobic maintenance, and he finds that skiing, though hard work, is a refreshing change. Skate skiing gives his mind a rest, works his cardiovascular system hard, and allows him to approach spring with increased energy.

With road races sparse in the winter and the inevitable snow- and ice-covered roads always a hassle, this might be the time to put on a pair of skis, get a lesson, and discover the world of skate skiing. A winter on skis won't necessarily help you win the National Championships, but Nordic skiing has one real cross-training benefit: Instead of losing your fitness in the winter months, you're more likely to increase it.

Snowshoeing 101

If you don't have the time to learn the technique to master cross-country skiing, then I have the activity for you. It will develop strength, power, and aerobic capacity. If you can walk, you can snowshoe.

Snowshoeing doesn't require special skills, expensive lessons, or groomed trails. Today's snowshoes, used for racing or as cross-training tools, are made of lightweight metals and synthetic webbing and are about 8 inches wide, 2 feet long, and less than 2 pounds total. Now you only need warm clothes and the desire to get in some great exercise.

The combination of physical exertion and fun has Skip Hamilton recommending snowshoeing to many cyclists. The accomplished mountain biker and personal coach to top riders on the mountain-bike circuit is a veteran snowshoer. "For cross-training in winter," says Hamilton, "snowshoeing is an excellent training option. You use many of the same muscles as in cycling; it's a great aerobic workout and does not subject one to the injuries of running."

Compared to running on roads, running in snowshoes involves lower knee carriage, shorter strides, and harder arm pumping. The lower body range of motion is similar to that used in cycling.

If you have never snowshoed, find a trail with packed snow, or loose snow that is only a few inches deep. The first lesson is to keep your strides compact, and in a few outings you will have developed a natural rhythm and will be able to cover terrain that is not accessible on skis. Frozen and snow-covered lakes become huge flat highways for speed work and intervals. Ski areas and hills become playgrounds and offer lung-searing vertical climbs and downhills.

Some snowshoers use poles when the snow is deep or the terrain uneven. Poles can be a hindrance to running, but for steep ascents, poles may provide that extra thrust. The claw on the bottom of the shoe provides traction for climbing, so you can attack the steepest hills with only your cardiovascular system as your limiting factor. Your quadriceps will feel like you are riding up a steep hill during a power workout.

Snowshoeing downhill is really fun. The snow gives you a smooth surface to run on, and if you fall, so what—just get up and keep going. Says Hamilton, "Snowshoe running is low impact, easy to do, and addictive."

Snowshoe racers train with intervals, hill work, and distance runs— the same as training for road races. "Interval workouts completed on uphill slopes simulate tough power workouts," says Andre Bozell, winner of the Vail Mountain Man and coach at the Carpenter-Phinney training camps.

You can rent snowshoes from outdoor shops and Nordic centers, where they should be able to help you select a suitable pair. Day rentals generally cost from $10 to $15 plus deposit. If you choose to buy them, snowshoes are moderately expensive: from $160 for the training models to over $200 for racing shoes. One pair should last the average snowshoer several seasons.

Imagine yourself surrounded by snowfields and snow-covered hills. You are about to attempt a grueling workout. But with your feet strapped to snowshoes, this won't be an ordinary winter workout. You're partaking in the hottest winter cross-training sport— snowshoeing.

In-Line Skating

Skating offers another excellent outdoor, off-season activity for cyclists who do not have access to snow. Until recently, "blading" was only for kids or for recreation when you visited Venice, California. But now droves of athletes—including runners, cross-country skiers, and cyclists—cross-train on blades because the motion works both the upper and the lower body. Using the quadriceps and gluteal muscles, in-line skating provides the extra lower body workout that cyclists need in the off-season. And in addition to giving your cycling muscles a good workout, in-line skating allows you to train away from the bicycle for a psychological recharge.

In-line skating is every bit as good for developing your quads, glutes, and hamstrings as cross-country skiing and snowshoeing. Now the message is out, and more cyclists are taking up in-line skating. But before you join them, there are several things to consider to ensure an effective and safe workout.

Three main components determine the performance of in-line skates: boots, bearings, and wheels. The fit of the boot is critical. Buy skates that are fairly snug. Your toes should just touch the tip when you're standing up. Most in-line skates come in unisex sizes and run wider than what most women are used to. Get fitted properly, and consider adding insoles to accommodate narrow heels or flat feet.

Beginners and individuals who want more resistance in their training should consider using wheels with lower precision bearings, "lower rebound" polyurethane wheels with hubless construction, and wheels of a smaller diameter. By purchasing skates from a quality dealer you can tailor the wheel/hub combinations to your specific requirements. I recently switched to Rollerblade Max-trainer wheels for greater resistance and aerobic benefits. For racing, you'll want high-precision bearings and quality Kryptonic wheels.

Know that sooner or later you will fall—and on a hard surface. Most beginners put out their hands to break their falls, and as a result some may fracture their wrists. I recommend buying wrist guards and putting them on before you put on your skates. Knee and elbow pads, to help prevent abrasions, and a helmet may also be prudent.

Avoid traffic at first. Begin by skating on bike paths or in empty parking lots. Practice stopping; stopping and turning will be difficult at first. Don't try any hills until you can safely stop and securely turn back and forth across the road. After gaining experience, skate on hills that have safe run-outs, good-quality pavement, and little traffic. Pebbles and cracks in the road can cause dire problems when they meet the small wheels of your skates.

So how good an exercise is in-line skating? Dr. Carl Foster, coordinator of sports science for the U.S. Speed Skating Team, recently completed a study for Rollerblades. In the laboratory, 11 subjects performed incremental running and cycling tests, during which oxygen uptake, heart rate, and lactic acid in the blood were measured at 10-minute intervals. Subjects were then studied during an incremental in-line skating workout. They skated 1 mile four times at progressively faster speeds. Again, oxygen uptake, heart rate, and lactic acid were measured during each trial.

The study found that in-line skating at a steady, comfortable rate for 30 minutes produced a mean heart rate of 148 beats per minute and a caloric expenditure of 285 calories, or 9.5 calories per minute. For interval skating, the caloric expenditure was 450 calories in 30 minutes, or 15 calories per minute. Running and cycling burned 350 and 360 calories, respectively, at the same heart rates. The times to burn 300 calories through running, cycling, easy and continuous in-line skating, and interval in-line skating are 25, 24, 32, and 22 minutes, respectively.

In addition, skating places less impact than running does on the musculoskeletal system and may reduce the risk of injury to hip, knee, and foot joints. In-line skating also develops the hip and knee extensor (thigh) muscles better than running does. Though in-line skating may not be the perfect imitation of cycling (nothing is), it can be a great training tool if used properly.

Cardiovascular Training

Control of your training is critical to peak performance. Through the systematic use of heart rate monitors, many athletes have scientifically monitored their training to progress more rapidly or to a higher level. Rebecca Twigg, Claudio Chiappucci, Miguel Indurain, and Tony Rominger are just a few of the athletes who have experienced the benefits of training and competing with heart rate monitors. In this portion of the chapter you will be given key information on how to use heart rate monitoring to help you ride and train at your optimal heart rate.

The cyclocomputer has also become a necessary accessory for the competitive cyclist and the multisport athlete. Along with heart rate, measurements such as current speed, cadence, elapsed time, and trip distance allow you to quantitatively measure and track your performance. A heart rate monitor and cyclocomputer are performance-monitoring tools for the serious cyclist and triathlete.

Your Heart Rate

All of the control and monitoring you could ever want is contained in an instrument built into your body: your heart. The heart is an amazingly sophisticated organ that reflects every change in your physical and mental state. The heart adjusts heart rate and contraction force automatically to respond to the demands put on it during exercise. So your heart can tell you how hard your body is working with remarkable accuracy. The heart is your built-in monitor, telling you when to pick up the pace or slow down.

You need to be aware of three different heart rates: your resting, maximum, and exercising heart rates. Resting and exercising heart rates are good indicators of your fitness and capacity for exercise. Maximum heart rate is probably not a good fitness indicator since it varies quite a bit with age.

Your resting heart rate can be obtained just after you awaken in the morning. The better condition you are in, the lower your resting heart rate will be. Some athletes sleep with their monitors on and are able to record their heart rates during sleep. True resting heart rate is obtained about 1 hour before your normal wake-up time. Some mornings your resting heart rate may be higher, and this may be a sign of overtraining, lack of rest, or emotional stress.

Maximum heart rate is the highest number of beats your heart can attain when you are exercising at maximum effort. The standard method of estimating your maximum heart rate is to subtract your age from 220 for males or from 226 for females. However, for trained cyclists there may be a more accurate method.

I have determined that the average heart rate during a 5-kilometer time trial is approximately 95% of a person's maximum heart rate. Use your heart rate monitor during an all-out effort of 5 kilometers and determine your average heart rate at the midpoint of the ride. This is your exercising heart rate. A heart rate monitor with a memory function and a cyclocomputer will come in handy. Manually plot your heart rate against your time and speed on a graph. You'll see that your heart rate levels off in the midportion of the ride. This corresponding heart rate is your average heart rate. Multiply that number by 105% to arrive at your maximum heart rate.

Another method is to simply record your heart rate several times when you are putting out a maximum effort. Sally Edwards, in her book *The Heart Rate Monitor Book*, suggests finding a long hill or series of hills and, after warming up, hitting the bottom of the hill relatively fast. Work the hill extremely hard until your heart rate reading no longer rises and you approach exhaustion. This number is your maximum heart rate.

Cardiovascular Monitoring During Training

Medical authorities use the term *target heart rate* to prescribe the amount of cardiovascular exercise that is sufficient to achieve fitness without exceeding safe limits. This target zone is the level of activity that produces a heart rate of 70% to 85% of maximum heart rate. In other words, your own heart rate can be used to gauge how much exercise your body needs for optimum fitness.

A heart rate monitor and cyclocomputer have a place in all aspects of your training and competition. First let's look at how they will help you gauge and adjust your cycling workouts.

- *Resting Heart Rate*: Strap your heart rate monitor on at night, and the next morning you'll have a good baseline to go by. Use this number to monitor your body for signs of overtraining or incomplete recovery. Any major deviation from the norm may indicate that you need extra rest.

- *Easy Days*: Many cyclists are more likely to exercise too hard than to undertrain. They believe the more and harder they train, the faster and longer they will ride in competition. This is true to a point. But you *can* overtrain, which will ultimately lead to diminished performances rather than to success. On days when you know you should be taking it easy after a previous hard interval or distance workout, use your heart rate monitor and cyclocomputer to hold yourself back. Many cyclists like to work at a heart rate of 25% lower than their lactate-threshold heart rate.

- *Hard Days*: A heart rate monitor can also prevent you from training too hard on your hard days. On long climbs, if your heart is working too hard, the heart rate monitor will beep, telling you to slow down and return to your ideal heart rate range. This only works if your monitor has a high and low alarm system. You can also track your speed and cadence to monitor your training effort.

- *Intervals*: You can get the most from interval training by using your heart rate monitor to help you recover properly between intervals. After riding for several minutes you may feel it is time to start the next interval, but your heart may not have recovered enough. A heart rate monitor tells you exactly when your heart rate has slowed to the proper level of recovery so you can begin your next interval. If you do intervals without adequate recovery in between, you will notice a drop in your speed and cadence and you will benefit less from the workout.

- *Comeback From Injury*: If you have been off the bike because of injury or illness, the monitor can help you gradually work your way back to fitness. A heart rate monitor and cyclocomputer help keep highly motivated cyclists from overdoing too soon.

- *Postexercise Recovery*: One of the best indicators of fitness is the ability to recover and return to normal heart rates following exercise. Routinely record your heart rate at 1, 2, and 5 minutes after exercise. As the weeks pass, you will see a more rapid return to your resting heart rate. Then, if you notice an unusual rate of recovery—such as your heart rate staying elevated longer than normal—you might conclude that your training effort was more intense than you had planned, and you can adjust your next workout accordingly.

• *Cycling Cadence*: In most situations, you will want to pedal around 90 or more revolutions per minute. As a general rule, higher revolutions per minute emphasize leg speed and lower revolutions emphasize leg power. Ideally, you want a blend of leg speed and leg power; 90 to 100 revolutions per minute is the best compromise. During sprinting your cadence may climb as high as 120, and during climbing it may drop as low as 75. Use your cyclocomputer to monitor your cadence in various training situations of sprinting, climbing, and time trialing.

• *Cycling Efficiency*: Find a hill about 1 mile long and mark the beginning and the end. Ride the hill in your normal riding position and gearing. Time yourself and record your cadence and heart rate during the whole effort. Ride the section again and again using different techniques: Use a bigger gear, pedal at a higher or lower cadence, climb in and out of the saddle. Through this process you will determine the most efficient technique for climbing (the fastest method at the same energy expenditure). The same procedure can be used for time-trial training.

Cardiovascular Monitoring During Competition

A heart rate monitor and a cyclocomputer are also valuable tools to use during competition. During a race, the monitor can be used to judge when you should push and when you shouldn't.

• *Racing*: During time trials, breakaways, or hill climbs, use a heart rate monitor to determine if you are going into anaerobic debt or a cyclocomputer to monitor when your cadence is too low. For example, by not pushing too hard you may be able to save yourself from "blowing up" on a climb, which will enable you to catch the group on the descent. Remember, though, that during a race you will be able to push yourself a little harder due to the release of adrenaline and "race psych" factors that in practice can affect your sustainable heart rate.

• *Before the Race*: Before important races, wear your monitor from the time you get up until the race is over. Just wearing a monitor will probably remind you to relax, and it will give you feedback about how uptight you're getting. You have limited energy, so it's best to use it for racing, not for worrying about the race before it happens.

• *Time Trials*: In the past, a cyclist measured the intensity of competition by the time or speed it took to cover a familiar course—for example, 25 miles in 64 minutes, or about 2 minutes and 34 seconds per mile. But on a given day many environmental and physiological variables can affect the speed of a particular time trial. Temperature, wind, humidity, altitude, and terrain vary from course to course and affect intensity. A heart rate monitor allows you to measure intensity by monitoring heart rate along with speed, distance, time, and cadence. By riding at your lactate threshold you will finish the event with maximum effort and not "blow up" by riding too fast.

• *Race Feedback*: Use your monitor to collect data when you are racing to help you improve your training sessions. If you get dropped in breakaways, you can design your interval training to incorporate longer intervals at higher heart rate intensities. If you get beat in the sprint, check your cadence and speed and see if you can turn over the big gears for a short burst of energy output.

Fast Decisions

There have been many claims by manufacturers that their cycling equipment or how the equipment positions you on the bike will make you go faster during competition. Regardless of such claims, you need to examine the efficiency of your cycling using various equipment options. A cyclocomputer and heart rate monitor can help you. Here are some ideas:

Equipment: Use your cyclocomputer to evaluate new handlebars, wheels, or tires. Keeping the same speed, ride a known loop with different pieces of equipment and review your heart rates. This method will give you an idea of which pieces of equipment are faster for the same energy output.

Position: You can spend a lot of time working to achieve a more aerodynamic position on the bike. You need feedback as to how subtle changes will improve speed without increasing energy cost. A heart rate monitor will help you find a good all-around aerodynamic position that is both efficient and comfortable. Although some positions may be more aerodynamic, they may restrict your breathing or increase your energy cost because they require more use of your back to support your position. Ride a familiar course and check out various positions against speed, cadence, and heart rate. The more aerodynamic positions will allow you to ride faster laps at a constant heart rate.

You should test a position change only after you have had sufficient practice in the new position; testing too soon will probably net a slower performance. If after several weeks you see a significant increase in speed without a rise in heart rate, you know you are on track to a faster position.

The Final Spin

Until a few years ago, training to be a cyclist was relatively simple. To improve, you hopped on your bike and headed for the road. To develop speed, you rode hard. To build endurance, you rode farther. During the off-season, you took about 8 weeks off to help your body recover. Simple stuff.

Well, times have changed. Off-season training and conditioning is very important to overall conditioning and injury prevention. After a short break at the end of the season, think about integrating some cross-training into your cycling skill work to increase your strength, endurance, and speed. Many top riders say their cycling performance has improved dramatically with a winter training schedule that combines resistance training with other activities, such as cross-country skiing or in-line skating.

In addition to supplemental training, the times have brought heart rate monitors, cyclocomputers, and, consequently, high-tech biofeedback training to all cyclists. These tools have allowed cyclists to develop sophisticated training programs, the likes of which were unheard of just 10 years ago. We have seen the benefits of being able to accurately monitor training, time, speed, distance, and cadence during training and racing. A monitor takes much of the guesswork out of training intensity and serves as an excellent motivator: It's like having your own personal coach. Monitor your performance during your next workout or race and receive the encouraging personal feedback that you are indeed improving physiologically.

Heart rate monitors, resistance-training equipment, and in-line skates are tools you might expect only elite cyclists to use. But now this equipment is within reach of almost everyone. When you have the chance to use these tools, you'll probably wonder how you ever did any serious exercise without them. The answer is simple: You probably didn't.

7

© Graham Watson

Your Yearly Training Program

One thing you learn in racing is that they don't wait for you.

—*Roger Penske*

As a cyclist, you know how hard it is to design a training program. In addition to evaluating your physiological capabilities, you must also consider other training principles, such as tapering (gradually reducing training mileage and intensity), peaking (attaining your maximum potential before major competitions), and recovery (resting between sessions and seasons). How do you incorporate all these elements into a comprehensive, useful training program? The answer lies in periodization.

Periodization is the long-term planning and scheduling of training. Each period prepares the cyclist for the next, more advanced training period, until the cyclist peaks at the most important competition of the year. Chris Carmichael has used periodization for several years with his athletes. This planning led to Lance Armstrong's peaking to win the World Championship road race. By systematically varying the volume, intensity, and recovery of various "periods," you can maximize your performance while reducing the risk of overtraining and injury. This chapter will show you how.

A Yearly Plan

To create a yearly training schedule, first look at your yearly competition calendar. Try to determine some specific training periods and phases, like general preparation, specialization, competition, and transition. Establish the peak point in your competition season (for example, the regional championships, National Championships, or World Championships). You will want to peak physically, mentally, and tactically during this period. Figure 7.1 is an example of a model similar to the one used by the U.S. Cycling Team's senior men. It shows training and competition miles logged at each stage of the season. Their yearly cycle begins with general preparation in November, and they peak at the World Championships in August.

Many cyclists refer to the annual training cycle as the *macrocycle*. A macrocycle is a complete training cycle, from the start of training to a peak at a major competition and then through the concluding transitional or recovery period. The macrocycle may have to be modified for individuals who live in areas where the competitive seasons do not match up with the schedules illustrated in this chapter. Also, you may have to adjust the mileage or the time you wish to peak to fit your competition or fitness goals.

Periodizing the Training Cycle

The advantage of a yearly training schedule is that if you have solid information about your strengths and goals, your time to train will be well planned. A yearly training schedule enables you to work in certain

Senior men—road

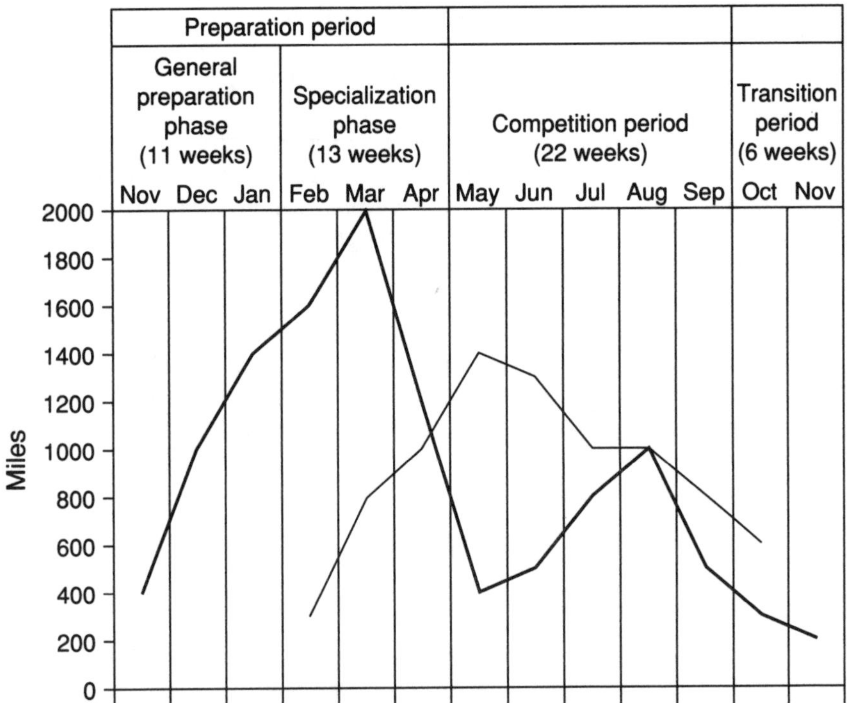

	General preparation phase (11 weeks)			Specialization phase (13 weeks)			Competition period (22 weeks)					Transition period (6 weeks)	
Preparation period													
	Nov	Dec	Jan	Feb	Mar	Apr	May	Jun	Jul	Aug	Sep	Oct	Nov
Training	400	1000	1400	1600	2000	1200	400	500	800	1000	500	300	200
Racing				300	800	1000	1400	1300	1000	1000	800	600	

——— Training miles

——— Racing miles

Figure 7.1 A yearly racing and training mileage schedule for senior men road racers.

time frames of specific training. To reach your best training and competition results, you will have to divide the annual training cycle into various periods.

The annual training cycle for cycling is conventionally divided into three main periods of training: preparation, competition, and transition (or active rest). Some cyclists refer to these intermediate or medium-length cycles as *mesocycles*. Within each period you try to control the training volume, intensity, frequency, and skill work to direct yourself toward a peak performance.

Some periods are further divided into phases. You can divide each period into as many phases as necessary as long as these parts all lead to your main competition goal. Road cycling in the United States can mean competing from March to October. That means that your general preparation phase will have to begin four or five months prior to your competition period. The transition period usually starts when the competition period is over, usually around the beginning of October. Readers from other countries will have to adjust the months to fit their seasons of training and competition.

Table 7.1 is the yearly schedule for senior men who are competing on the elite international level or are close to turning professional. Their training starts out rather slowly in November, and more racing miles are added to the program as they get closer to competition and to the predetermined peaking points of the National Championships and World Championships.

Figure 7.2 and Table 7.2 show the example of a yearly schedule for senior women who are competing at the elite national and international levels. These women will also peak in the late summer months. If you have been racing for only a few years or want to compete at only the national level, then you can cut the training and racing miles and hours

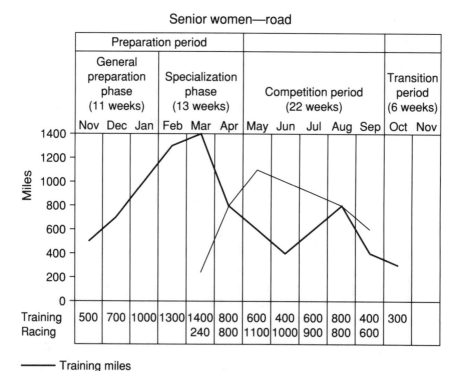

Senior women—road

	Preparation period			
	General preparation phase (11 weeks)	Specialization phase (13 weeks)	Competition period (22 weeks)	Transition period (6 weeks)
	Nov Dec Jan	Feb Mar Apr	May Jun Jul Aug Sep	Oct Nov
Training	500 700 1000	1300 1400 800	600 400 600 800 400	300
Racing		240 800	1100 1000 900 800 600	

——— Training miles

——— Racing miles

Figure 7.2 A yearly racing and training mileage schedule for senior women road racers.

Table 7.1 A Yearly Training and Racing Schedule (Senior Men—Road)

Month	General preparation phase (11 weeks)			Specialization phase (13 weeks)			Competition period (22 weeks)					Transition period (6 weeks)		Total
	Nov 16	Dec	Jan	Feb	Mar	Apr	May	June	July	Aug	Sept	Oct	Nov 15	
Training miles	400	1000	1400	1600	2000	1200	400	500	800	1000	500	300	200	11300
Race miles				300	800	1000	1400	1300	1000	1000	800	600		8200
Training and race miles	400	1000	1400	1900	2800	2200	1800	1800	1800	2000	1300	900	200	19500
Body exercise hours	48	96	86	43	20									293

General preparation: November 16–January 31
Body exercise: mostly aerobic training, running, swimming, skiing, hiking, cyclo-cross, resistance training, road training, indoor cycling. Build mental and physical performance.
Specialization: February 1–April 30
Training and races only for training. Work on endurance, power, speed, speed endurance, sprints, technique, and tactics.
Competition: May 1–September 30
Races: national and international, World Championships, and Olympics.
Transition: October–November 15
Move from racing to regeneration. Rehabilitate the body for the general preparation phase.

Table 7.2   A Yearly Training and Racing Schedule (Senior Women—Road)

| | Preparation period | | | | | | Competition period (22 weeks) | | | | | Transition period (6 weeks) | | Total |
| | General preparation phase (11 weeks) | | | Specialization phase (13 weeks) | | | | | | | | | | |
Month	Nov 16	Dec	Jan	Feb	Mar	Apr	May	June	July	Aug	Sept	Oct	Nov 15	Total
Training miles	500	700	1000	1300	1400	800	600	400	600	800	400	300		8800
Race miles					240	800	1100	1000	900	800	600			5440
Training and race miles	500	700	1000	1300	1640	1600	1700	1400	1500	1600	1000	300		14240
Body exercise hours	70	96	86	43	20									315

General preparation: November 16–January 31
Body exercise: mostly aerobic training, running, swimming, skiing, hiking, cyclo-cross, resistance training, road training, indoor cycling. Build mental and physical performance.

Specialization: February 1–April 30
Training and races only for training. Work on endurance, power, speed, speed endurance, sprints, technique, and tactics.

Competition: May 1–September 30
Races: national and international, World Championships.

Transition: October–November 15
Move from racing to regeneration. Rehabilitate the body for the general preparation phase.

of general body conditioning by about 25% to 35% across the season to fit your program.

Figure 7.3 and Table 7.3 show the yearly schedule for national-class junior men (ages 16 to 18) who have a later seasonal peak due to the World Championships being held in late September. Again, juniors who are just beginning to race or who want to race only on the regional level should cut the suggested mileage and hours of training by 25% to 35%.

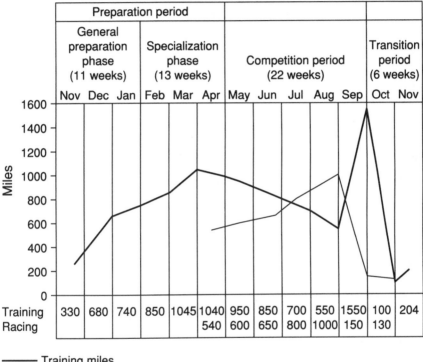

Junior men age 16-18—road

	Preparation period			
General preparation phase (11 weeks)	Specialization phase (13 weeks)	Competition period (22 weeks)	Transition period (6 weeks)

	Nov	Dec	Jan	Feb	Mar	Apr	May	Jun	Jul	Aug	Sep	Oct	Nov
Training	330	680	740	850	1045	1040	950	850	700	550	1550	100	204
Racing						540	600	650	800	1000	150	130	

———— Training miles

———— Racing miles

Figure 7.3 A yearly racing and training mileage schedule for junior men road racers.

Figure 7.4 and Table 7.4 show a yearly schedule that may be used by a serious college student or working individual who is peaking for a major competition in August. This schedule is for the senior male cyclist who wants to race seriously on the regional level but is not committed to international racing. As you can see, the mileage has been reduced due to other time constraints, but it is still very serious mileage.

Table 7.3 A Yearly Training and Racing Schedule (Junior Men—Road)

Month	Preparation period						Competition period (22 weeks)					Transition period (6 weeks)		Total
	General preparation phase (11 weeks)			Specialization phase (13 weeks)										
	Nov 16	Dec	Jan	Feb	Mar	Apr	May	June	July	Aug	Sept	Oct	Nov 15	
Training miles	330	680	740	850	1045	1040	950	850	700	550	1550	100	204	9589
Race miles						540	600	650	800	1000	150	130		3870
Training and race miles	330	680	740	850	1045	1580	1550	1500	1500	1550	1700	230	204	13459
Body exercise hours	26	50	51	50	61									238

General preparation: November 16–January 31
Body exercise: mostly aerobic training, running, swimming, skiing, hiking, cyclo-cross, resistance training, road training, indoor cycling. Build mental and physical performance.
Specialization: February 1–April 30
Training and races only for training. Work on endurance, power, speed, speed endurance, sprints, technique, and tactics.
Competition: May 1–September 30
Races: national and international, World Championships.
Transition: October–November 15
Move from racing to regeneration. Rehabilitate the body for the general preparation phase.

Table 7.4 A Yearly Training and Racing Schedule (Working Individual/College Student—Road)

Month	Preparation period						Competition period (18 weeks)				Transition period (10 weeks)			Total
	General preparation phase (15 weeks)				Specialization phase (9 weeks)									
	Nov 16	Dec	Jan	Feb	Mar	Apr	May	June	July	Aug	Sept	Oct	Nov 15	
Training miles	200	450	650	750	850	700	600	500	500	500	350	180	120	6350
Race miles				100	200	300	400	500	500	400	200	100		2700
Training and race miles	200	450	650	850	1050	1000	1000	1000	1000	900	550	280	120	9050
Body exercise hours	50	100	80	30	20									280

General preparation: November 16–February 28
Body exercise: mostly aerobic training, running, swimming, skiing, hiking, cyclo-cross, resistance training, road training, indoor cycling. Build mental and physical performance.

Specialization: March 1–April 30
Training and races only for training. Work on endurance, power, speed, speed endurance, sprints, technique, and tactics.

Competition: May 1–August 31
Races: National Championships.

Transition: September 1–November 15
Move from racing to regeneration. Rehabilitate the body for the general preparation phase.

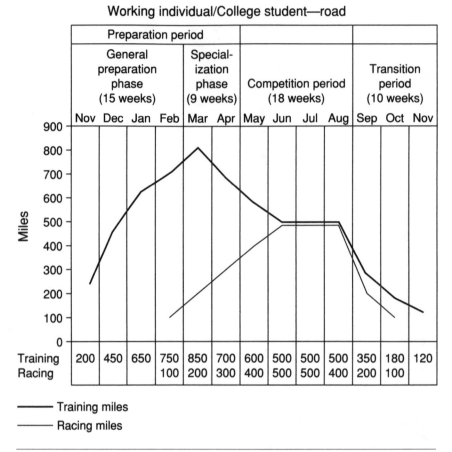

Working individual/College student—road

| | Preparation period | | | |
| General preparation phase (15 weeks) | Special-ization phase (9 weeks) | Competition period (18 weeks) | Transition period (10 weeks) |

	Nov	Dec	Jan	Feb	Mar	Apr	May	Jun	Jul	Aug	Sep	Oct	Nov
Training	200	450	650	750	850	700	600	500	500	500	350	180	120
Racing				100	200	300	400	500	500	400	200	100	

——— Training miles

——— Racing miles

Figure 7.4 A yearly racing and training mileage schedule for road racers who are working or are in college.

From these schedules you can see that the proper planning of conditioning, training, and racing is crucial to peaking during a specific time of the year. Again, you may have to adapt the periods and phases to your particular climate and competitive season. Also, if you are new to the sport, you may even have to reduce the schedule in Figure 7.4 and Table 7.4 by 25% to 30% your first year. You can also easily see how a yearly schedule employs the concept of periodization, or training according to prescribed periods. The purpose of periodization is to divide the annual cycle into three distinct periods, which allows for the development and improvement of the physical, technical, and psychological aspects of cycling. Let's examine each period so that you can better plan your season.

The Preparation Period

The preparation period of the yearly program is the longest, lasting up to 6 months. Because of its length and the different tasks that need to be accomplished, this period is divided into two phases. The first phase consists of general conditioning through weight training; off-road (mountain bike) riding, which is also known as cyclo-cross training; and cross-country skiing. The second phase is marked by specialized training on the bicycle. You work on endurance, speed, and power and begin racing.

The General Preparation Phase. During this phase of the preparation period, you want to begin with activities of relatively low intensity and long duration. Train 5 to 6 days a week for 3 to 4 hours each day. Toward the end of this phase, training intensity will increase and more miles will be put on the bicycle.

You want to engage in activities that will build your overall body conditioning. To build general endurance, for example, go on long, hilly hikes or cross-country ski for several hours. Your intensity during these efforts should be 60% to 80% of your maximum heart rate. Keep the intensity below anaerobic threshold for the majority of these workouts.

Cross-country skiing, snowshoeing, running, hiking, and in-line skating are useful for developing endurance. Your resistance training should now switch from the transition phase to the foundation and basic-strength phases (see chapter 6), and you will begin using slightly heavier weights while decreasing the number of repetitions.

Around December, you will also need to start putting in miles on the bicycle. During December on-the-bike training becomes increasingly important, and supplemental training starts to taper off in January. Consider riding your road bike (indoors and outdoors) and mountain bike during this phase. The following is an example of a typical week—of course, there really is no such thing as a typical week at this time of year due to weather and daylight considerations. Cycling may have to be done indoors and broken up into several sessions to relieve boredom.

Monday: *Morning*: One hour of easy endurance training
Afternoon: Resistance training

Tuesday: Easy endurance training for 2 hours, one jump, and one 3-minute effort at anaerobic-threshold pace

Wednesday: Resistance training and 60 to 90 minutes of endurance training

Thursday: An easy day of very little effort (30 minutes max) or a day of total rest

Friday: *Morning*: 1 to 3 hours of endurance training

Saturday: Endurance training off the bicycle for 2 to 4 hours with a few short efforts of 1 to 5 minutes at anaerobic threshold pace

Sunday: A long bicycle ride for 2 to 3 hours with one or two jumps

The Specialization Phase.   At this point racing starts to enter the program. General exercises come to an end. Resistance training enters the power phase, and once racing begins you will continue into the peaking phase of resistance training (see chapter 6). Some cyclists may consider continuing with one to three sets of 6 to 10 resistance exercises once a week to maintain the strength they developed in the off-season.

The physiological requirements for this phase increase in intensity. You begin doing intervals, power work, sprints, and anaerobic-threshold training. Heart rates climb to between 85% and 95% of your maximum. Allow yourself adequate rest between hard training or racing sessions. You can now add short stage races of 3 to 4 days to your program. As the season comes closer, your mental preparation has to become increasingly competition-related.

Your racing program during this phase must stay within the goals of the preparation period: to develop endurance and to increase speed and power. Participation in races should be considered only when they do not interfere with these goals. In other words, you do not want to compete in races that are too difficult. Races during this phase can be ridden as "training races." Training races are ridden not necessarily to win but to get in miles on the bike and to occasionally test yourself in breakaways and sprints.

Training intensity should increase steadily along with duration. March will be your biggest month in terms of training and racing miles. In the specialization phase, a week's work may go like this:

Monday: An easy, flat ride of 2 to 3 hours; heart rate at 60% to 65% of maximum

Tuesday: A good warm-up and 2 hours of long intervals (use small gearing); heart rate up to 95% of maximum

Wednesday: 2 to 3 hours of jumps, sprints, and anaerobic-threshold riding: five or six sprints of 400 to 500 yards, 20 to 30 minutes of riding at anaerobic-threshold pace, and two jumps of 150 to 200 yards

Thursday: 2 hours of mixed long intervals and one long climb of 20 to 40 minutes; heart rate at 70% to 95% of maximum

Friday: A day of rest or an easy ride of 1 hour; heart rate at 60% to 65% of maximum

Saturday: A club or team ride of 3 to 4 hours (heart rate up to 80% of maximum) or a local road race

Sunday: A club or team ride of 2 to 3 hours (heart rate at 60% to 95% of maximum), one hill effort, and six to eight sprints; or a local road or criterium race

The Competition Period

The specialization phase leads directly into the competition period. You should be in top form as your competitive season begins, and later in this period your physical, mental, and tactical training must come to a peak. Your main concern now, besides producing results, is to maintain your racing performance as long as the competition period lasts. Because a season can last from May until the end of September, this may be difficult to accomplish. For this reason, you should schedule small rest or recovery phases into the competition period.

Top performance and optimal fitness are variable, and it is difficult to maintain optimal fitness for 5 months. Top performance may escalate and decline; if you observe your race results dropping, you may have to adjust your training program immediately. First determine whether the decline is due to mental or physical factors. If the problem is mental, reevaluate your goals as outlined later in the chapter. If the problem is physical, you may have to take some time off the bicycle. One or 2 days is usually enough; then gradually add intensity back into your program. You may consider entering a shorter race or one in which you have less competition to allow yourself to perform well again. If your performance is down due to illness, make sure to recover adequately before your next hard training session or race.

If you need to prepare for a major event, such as the National Championships, plan a short break of about 2 weeks without a competition in the training schedule. The 2-week period should start with 3 to 4 days of easy riding followed by 9 to 10 days of specialized work in preparation for the event. For example, if the race will have a lot of climbing, you need to spend a few training sessions working on your climbing technique and power. High-intensity and race-simulated intervals, sprints, motor pacing, and other exercises should be part of your program. At 2 days to go before the race, you should include only light training of low duration with two or three jumps each day and then prepare mentally and nutritionally for the competition.

Every cyclist needs competition in order to properly prepare for a major peak point in the season. Planned competitions cannot be replaced with hard training and are necessary to reach top physical performance. The amount of competition needed to reach top fitness, however, varies from cyclist to cyclist. If you train and compete with other cyclists, you may not be able to race as often as the strongest cyclist on the team. You have to compete in the right amount of races of the right caliber to ensure *your* success. Occasionally entering lower caliber races and having a

Does Altitude Training Improve Performance?

Although there seems to be debate among sports scientists concerning the value of altitude training as preparation for sea-level competition, there is no doubt about its value among some of cycling's most famous coaches and athletes. Charley Walsh and George Hubner, the successful coaches of the Australian and German cycling teams, have been taking their athletes "to altitude" in both Mexico and the United States several times each year to enhance their athletes' performance. Tony Rominger spent 3 weeks in the thin air of Vail, Colorado, in preparation for the 1993 Tour de France, where he finished second overall and won the King of the Mountains jersey.

Most athletes see coming to altitude as a way of stimulating the body to produce more red blood cells, which, upon returning to the oxygen-rich environment of sea level, enables them to transport more oxygen to the working muscles.

Many cyclists used to think they had to move to towns such as Boulder, Colorado, to take advantage of the physiological effects of altitude. But published scientific research and practical evidence from world-class coaches seem to show that several 3-week stays at moderate altitudes may also have physiological benefits. These 3-week stays at altitude seem to be beneficial for endurance athletes, because research demonstrates that 3 weeks is long enough to raise red blood cell concentrations but short enough so that overall fitness does not deteriorate, which has happened with stays lasting a few months.

Owen Anderson, PhD, in a recent issue of *Running Research News*, pointed out that athletes may want to adjust their training programs at altitude during these 3-week stays to provide short-interval, high-intensity exercise combined with distance training to achieve the most out of their stays. He based his recommendations on the research conducted on seven elite Norwegian cross-country skiers who lived and trained at a moderate altitude of 6,200 feet for 3 weeks. Training durations ranged from 2 to 4 hours a day, and on several days the training program included many high-intensity efforts. Before and after the 3 weeks of training at altitude, the athletes were asked to run on a treadmill at sea level for 6 minutes at a 10-kilometer race pace. Blood lactates were measured at 1 and 3 minutes after the run. Hemoglobin, $\dot{V}O_2$max, and hematocrit (the ratio of red blood cells to total blood volume) were also measured before and after the 3 weeks at altitude. The control segment of the study was to train the same subjects a year later at sea level at their previous altitude intensity.

After 3 weeks at altitude, the group's average for hemoglobin increased from 15 to 15.8 grams per 100 milliliters of blood, and hematocrit increased from 46.3% to 48.6%, but $\dot{V}O_2$max did not change. The athletes' blood values returned to prealtitude values after about 2 weeks at sea level.

Although $\dot{V}O_2$max did not change, there was a significant change in the athletes' lactate profiles: a decrease in blood lactate at the 10-kilometer pace after returning from altitude. Prior to altitude, the group's lactate profiles rose to about 4.8 mmol/l during a 6-minute run; after 3 weeks at altitude and upon returning to sea level, the lactate profiles only rose to 4.0 mmol/l. Interestingly, the athletes who improved their lactate profiles the most were those with the biggest gains in hemoglobin and hematocrit.

F.W. Dick, of the British Athletic Federation, shared similar information at the 1991 European Athletics Coaches Association Endurance Congress in his lecture on when to use altitude training relative to target competitions. He gives the following recommendations to athletes wishing to use altitude training for improved performance.

First, you should stay at an altitude of about 6,200 feet for about 3 weeks twice a year. The first stay should fall at the end of winter training and at the commencement of preseason training. In our yearly training schedule, this would be during the month of January. The second ascent to altitude should be in the final preparation period prior to a major championship.

This second stay should be scheduled so that the competition is about 15 to 24 days after returning from altitude, because many athletes feel quite fatigued after 3 weeks of hard training at altitude and need time to recover. F.W. Dick reported that it takes many athletes about 8 to 11 days to feel like they have reacclimated to sea level and that peak performance will be within 15 to 24 days. Tony Rominger planned his return from Vail so that the Tour de France fell on the 20th through 40th days after returning to sea level.

(continued)

Altitude Training   *(continued)*

If you plan to experiment with this method of altitude training, you should realize that the range of days that are best for performance varies among athletes. You should practice this procedure several times before using it for a major competition. Experiment with the amount of days needed for you to reach top form once you return to sea level.

For the past 10 years the Australian track and German time-trial teams have been dominant at the World Championships. Both coaches feel that their teams' short exposures to altitude have improved their athletes' abilities to perform their best at this competition. They return to sea level with fortified blood and with leg muscles that have a large capacity for oxygen utilization. As Rominger's coach and doctor, Michele Ferrari stated before the Tour de France, "I will tell other cyclists about the advantages of altitude, but if Tony does well in the Tour, I will not need to." I believe he was right.

greater chance of success may be extremely good for you, especially if you find it hard to finish well for a period of time. See the upcoming information on planning your weekly and daily training sessions for an example of a weekly program during the competition season.

When successful athletes are in top form for the big events, we say they have peaked, or are at their peak for an event. Occasionally an athlete goes through the whole season in top form—Eddy Merckx and Bernard Hinault did for several cycling seasons—but such an optimal level of performance is rare. Whether optimum peaking rarely occurs because the season is too long for most athletes to perform at their peak or because so few know how to stay at their peak is an ongoing argument.

Peaking for a race does not just happen. Months, even years, of preparation are required for events such as the World Championships. Peaking at the right time requires setting goals for yourself, and it requires the discipline to establish the priorities needed to achieve those goals.

Self-discipline is enhanced and priorities are more easily established if you have goals to work toward. One goal may be to set a personal record on a course you have raced before, another to win in your age category at a particular race. Goals should be established early in the season. Choose goals based on your past performances, your body's and your bike's physical and mechanical capabilities, and input from other athletes and coaches. Goals are not absolute and may be adjusted as your training progresses.

This peaking concept need not be restricted to one season but can be approached on a much broader scale. For example, you may peak for a few regional events during the upcoming season, add longer events to your schedule the next year, and have as your goal for the third year to place well in your age group at the National Championships.

Peaking is often difficult to plan for because of the crowded race schedule and the variety of events offered. It's one thing to peak at a specific event such as the district championships; it's another thing to peak for a series of races spread out over 2 weeks. Now throw the National Championships into your program, and you begin to appreciate the difficulty of scheduling for peaks. Add to this the pressure of sponsors, press, and coaches—you may begin to wonder if peaking is even possible during the season. Many times you will have to decide which events you must train through in order to prepare for your next major race.

Most cyclists, coaches, and sport scientists say that you can only peak two or three times a year. You need to allow a minimum of 6 weeks between events to perform well. For example, you may peak for an event in late spring, again for a race in midsummer, and a final time for the National Championships in the fall. Between the events you will need to recover and rebuild, and you will enter races for the purposes of training and fine-tuning your performance.

Prior to a major event you should cut down on distance work and add speed and last-minute technique training to your program. All hard training should end a few days before the event and be replaced with easy or moderate rides, with a few short bursts of speed when you feel good.

In order to peak effectively to attain your goals, use the following guidelines throughout the season to ensure success:

1. Emphasize consistency in your training program. Have a program that plans for the whole season.
2. Realize that a sound, successful training program is your best source of self-confidence.
3. Rest sufficiently after all races to restore your energy levels.
4. Don't train hard when you are sick.
5. Identify your nutritional needs and nourish yourself properly. (See chapter 8 for information on proper nutrition.)
6. Do not consider any one aspect of your training more important then another. Off-season *and* in-season training are integral to your total program.
7. Avoid injury. Don't do anything foolish in training or racing that could lead to a serious crash or overuse injury.

8. When possible, train in an environment that promotes a concentrated effort.
9. Maintain a strong commitment to being fit and healthy.

What I've outlined here is a systematic approach to planning your season and peaking for important events. Remember that though the annals of cycling are filled with stories of outstanding athletes who succeeded at big events, other stories tell of the individuals who lined up at the start as leading contenders . . . and failed. It should have been their time, but they were not prepared because in many cases they had not properly peaked for the competition. The secret to success in any sporting event is being prepared for optimum performance at the right time.

The Transition Period

The transition period is the end of the competition season and serves as your transition time to the beginning of the preparation period. After a season of competing and peaking for major events, you need a period of reduced training to emotionally and physically recover from the bike.

However, according to Jiri Mainus, national team operations manager of the U.S. Cycling Team, total time off the bike is not good: "Cyclists should gradually reduce their cycling mileage. It is important to keep in touch with the bicycle. Off-season training usually consists of low-volume, low-intensity workouts." Mainus also emphasizes the importance of psychological recovery: "It is important to replace the stress of training with things you enjoy." Many coaches encourage athletes to participate in other recreational activities.

In this period of active rest your goal is to maintain a specific performance level and a training condition of medium to high fitness. It is important to continue to exercise during this period because passive rest will make it difficult for you to start training in the general preparation phase.

The transition period should not be longer than 8 weeks. Cross-training in other activities should be part of your program, and if you choose to race in cyclo-cross or mountain bike races during this period, the psychological pressure of performing should be as low as possible. You should also begin your resistance-training program now.

Planning Your Weekly and Daily Training Sessions

Weekly training sessions are often referred to as *microcycles*, though microcycles can be as short as 3 days. The daily training program or session is a single workout, such as an afternoon workout on sprinting tactics. You may have up to two training sessions per day.

Your Weekly Training Plan

This is where you focus in on your daily training variations of intensity, mileage, and exercise selection. Here is an example of a weekly training plan during the month of July in the competition period:

Monday: A recovery ride of 1 to 2 hours at low intensity

Tuesday: 2 hours of training with a few jumps and short intervals, a local night race, motorpacing, or lactate criss-cross training

Wednesday: *Morning*: Endurance riding for 3 to 4 hours on mixed terrain at varying tempos
Afternoon: Weight training: six to eight exercises for lower back, shoulders, arms, and abdominals

Thursday: 2 to 3 hours with jumps and short sprints

Friday: An easy ride for 1 hour

Saturday: *Morning*: An easy ride for 30 minutes
Afternoon: Criterium

Sunday: A 75-mile road race or long group ride

Your Daily Training Plan

A typical daily training session includes a warm-up, the body of the training session, and a cool-down. You need to organize your daily training session for the optimal value of the workout. You may deviate from your daily training session due to weather conditions or if you have not recovered from the previous day's efforts. Here is an example of a training session designed for the middle of July, about 4 days before a local race:

Tuesday, July 6th
- A warm-up of about 10 to 15 miles
- Two 200-meter sprints
- Three 2-minute intervals
- 20 minutes of lactate criss-cross training
- A cool-down of 10 to 15 miles

Designing a Training Diary

Every cyclist is an individual and responds differently to training, so every training method cannot satisfy the training needs of every cyclist. What is good for Greg LeMond may not be good for Lance Armstrong, or for you. Rather, every cyclist must develop his own training methods and yearly training schedule. The guidelines in this book will give you direction, and then you must monitor how your body responds to the various training methods. The only way to do this is to keep a detailed training diary.

The basis of your training diary is your daily record (see Figure 7.5). On this record you enter the details of your physical condition: your waking and exercising heart rates, your sleeping patterns, morning body weight, how you feel during training and racing, and how you perform in races. Training diaries are available through bookstores or catalogs, or you may want to design your own using a standard notebook.

Here are some important points to record in your diary:

- As specifically as possible, describe the training session: Did you work on long, slow distances? What type of intervals did you do? Record who you rode with, on what routes, and what the weather and wind conditions were.
- Record the time you went to bed the previous night and the number of hours you slept. Record any naps you took during the day. Research has shown that athletes who are overtraining start going to bed later at night, sleep less, and wake up tired in the morning. So your sleep patterns are a vital indication of whether or not you are overtraining.
- Record your body weight in the morning after you have emptied your bladder. If you have lost several pounds since the day before, you are dehydrated and need to drink plenty of fluids before your next training session. A continual fall in body weight over a few weeks is an ominous sign and indicates progressive overtraining.
- Record your heart rate upon waking. Count your pulse for 15 seconds, multiply by 4, and record this number. A sudden rise of more than five or six beats per minute in the early morning may mean that you have not recovered from the previous day's training or that you are getting ill. You should not train hard that day. A persistent elevation of 5 or 6 beats in your morning pulse rate indicates a more serious form of overtraining. It may be wise to take a few days off until your waking pulse returns to normal.
- Each morning record how you feel. Use a scale from *A* to *F*: *A* for "feeling great" and "cannot wait for the day's training session," and *F* for "feeling terrible" and "don't want to even see a bike."
- Besides recording your feelings, you can train and track your mental toughness by focusing on motivation. Most riders neglect this form of mental training because they fail to verbalize their goals. Don't make this mistake. Recording your long-term, short-term, and daily goals and their achievement should be an integral part of your training diary. Meeting your daily goals is a tremendous confidence builder.

Day: _____   Date: _____

Last night's bedtime: _____   Hours slept: _____

Body weight: _____   Waking heart rate: _____

Feeling rating: _____

Long-term goal: _____

Short-term goal: _____

Today's goal: _____

Training/race session notes:

_____

_____

_____

_____

_____

_____

_____

_____

_____

_____

_____

_____

_____

Figure 7.5   A sheet from a cyclist's diary.

- Create a comments section. Record any minor ailments such as colds, influenza, muscle soreness, or injuries. Record your general state of well-being: Are you enthusiastic, positive, or lethargic? Write about how motivated you were for the practice or competition, and, if you were psyched up, record the thoughts and feelings that helped you. Record training or race results. Record the conditions of the race if it is a race day—size of field, gears used on climbs, sprints, tactics, mistakes, who was in the break, and your final placing. And keep records of any medical tests or physiological tests completed that day.

For an example of a completed diary entry, see Figure 7.6.

In cycling, as in any sport, you can't know where you are going if you don't know where you have been. A training diary is a map and record of where you've been and a guide to where you want to go. In addition to your diary, you occasionally may want to summarize your data. Figure 7.7 is an example of a blank page from one rider's weekly summary of physiological and psychological variables.

Day: *Monday*   Date: *May 6, 2001*

Last night's bedtime: *10 pm*   Hours slept: *8 1/2*

Body Weight: *157*   Waking heart rate: *49*

Feeling rating: *B+*

Long-term goal: *Break 1 hr. in the 40 K Natl. Championships Time Trial*

Short-term goal: *Win Geneva 10 mile trial on Memorial Day*

Today's goal: *Work on Sprint Technique*

Training/race session notes:

Weather was cool – 60's – a little windy.

Easy ride 20 miles with 2 jumps of 200 yards.

Felt good after the hard race yesterday.

Knee problem seems to be going away.

Figure 7.6   A sample entry from a cyclist's diary.

Summary Data

Week	Waking pulse rate (beats/min)	Sleep (hours)	Cycling time (hours)	Cycling distance (km)	Effort rating (points)	Body weight
1						
2						
3						
4						
5						
6						
7						
8						
9						
10						
11						
12						
13						
14						
15						
16						
17						
18						
19						
20						
21						
22						
23						
24						
25						
26						

(continued)

Figure 7.7 Summary data sheet.

Summary Data *(continued)*

Week	Waking pulse rate (beats/min)	Sleep (hours)	Cycling time (hours)	Cycling distance (km)	Effort rating (points)	Body weight
27						
28						
29						
30						
31						
32						
33						
34						
35						
36						
37						
38						
39						
40						
41						
42						
43						
44						
45						
46						
47						
48						
49						
50						
51						
52						

Figure 7.7 *(continued)*

Counting the Miles to Race Day

Data from your daily training log can be summarized on a yearly mileage graph (see Figure 7.8). This summary data can then be compared to your yearly racing and training mileage schedule that was drawn up at the beginning of the season. This will give you a quick estimate of how you are living up to your yearly plan and if you are reaching your mileage goals for racing and training. Your yearly mileage graph can also help you compare your present mileage achievements to a previous year's. Every year as you become stronger and fitter you will see an increase in your mileage and intensity. This information, along with the summary information on physiological and psychological factors (Figure 7.8) will help you evaluate your program and make necessary short-term adjustments. For example, if you see a continued rise in your waking pulse rate, this may be a sign that you are fatigued and on the verge of becoming overtrained. You may need to adjust your mileage and intensity downward for the next few days (or week) to allow for recovery.

Results of your yearly races can be recorded on a summary chart (see Figure 7.9). You can use information you recorded first in your training diary. Then you will have a running commentary on your races, placings, and how you fared against the rest of the starters. Under the comments column you can record the terrain of the course, gearing used at various points in the race, details of the finish area, and any other particulars important to this race. Then next year you can use this information to train for and select equipment for this particular event.

The Final Spin

Planning at the yearly, monthly, weekly, and daily levels will provide you with clear goals and objectives for the season. By keeping both the plan and your daily training diary you will be able to review your training plan to determine what may have been a deciding influence in the success or failure of your season.

A well-planned yearly training program, supplemental resistance training, stretching, and a training diary are a cyclist's best friends for

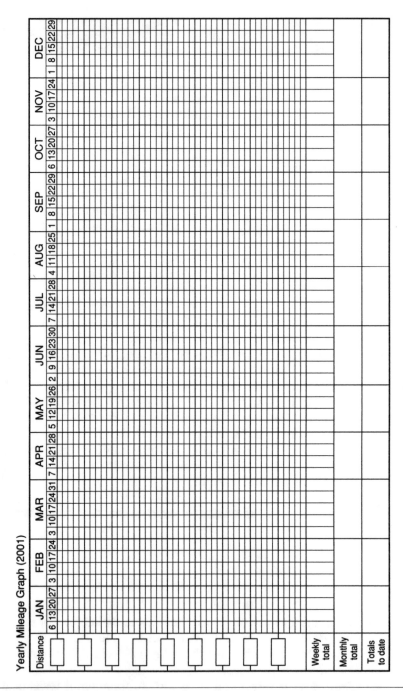

Figure 7.8 Complete a yearly mileage graph to compare your actual miles ridden to the goals you set. Set distance goals along the left-hand side of the chart, and color in a bar each week to reflect your mileage.

Races of the Year

Date	Event	Distance, time, pace	Place, starters	Comments

Figure 7.9 Use a races-of-the-year chart to track your performance in competition.

continued success. A well-thought-out plan and a complete training diary are continued sources of motivation and provide essential clues as to which training methods have been successful or not so successful. Many great cyclists, such as Miguel Indurain, Lance Armstrong, and Inga Thompson, attribute a large measure of their success to developing a sound yearly training program and keeping detailed logs.

Steve Johnson, a national-class master road cyclist and exercise physiologist from the University of Utah, emphasizes the importance of planning and keeping detailed records. "Training is all about setting performance goals and, most importantly, reaching them. Periodization provides a cyclist with a methodical, organized approach to scheduling the training year so preseason goals can become medal-winning realities," says Johnson.

© Graham Watson

Fueling Your Body

When I first started racing, a bottle would last me 150 kilometers. But now, for a 300-kilometer race in moderate weather, I need 10 to 12 bottles including nutritional drinks. Normally, a rider should lose hardly any weight during a stage, and that means drinking a lot.

—*Bernard Hinault*

As a cyclist, you may be tempted to purchase a high-tech bicycle to improve your performance, but you may only need to look at your diet to elevate your performance to new heights. No amount of money spent on equipment, training, and coaching will help ensure a winning performance if you do not have the proper fuel in your tank.

Nutrition and fluid replacement play a significant role in successful training and competition. You have trained hard, purchased the proper equipment and have honed your cycling skills. Now I will show you how proper nutrition may be all you need to perform at your maximum in training and competition. This chapter will provide you with information on optimal nutrition, which is an essential component in achieving top physical performance in cycling.

Total Nutrition for Improved Performance

The main nutritional need of cyclists is an increased energy. The more intensive your cycling, and the longer it lasts, the larger your total energy expenditure.

From published reports on cyclists in the Tour de France and personal observations, it can be estimated that racing cyclists require 3,000 to 7,000 calories daily. Sedentary, normal-weight women typically consume between 1,400 and 2,000 calories per day; their male counterparts between 2,500 and 2,800. This wide range highlights the need for individual assessment. In daily practice, you may estimate your energy needs by monitoring your weight and satisfying your appetite. Inadequate energy intake will lead to decreased physical performance, weight loss, and chronic fatigue.

Fluid Facts

You may not think of water as a nutrient, but it is the most critical one in your diet. You can only live about 3 to 4 days without water. About 60% to 70% of an adult's body weight is water.

You lose water from the body in many ways. Through breathing, urinating, and sweating, you lose up to 12 cups of water each day. And if you exercise in hot weather, you could easily double or triple that amount.

Without sufficient water intake, fatigue will set in, and your performance will be affected. Even small variations in your fluid levels will begin to affect your performance. Losing only 2% to 3% of the body's fluid through sweat (about 3 to 4 pounds in a 150-pound individual) will decrease cycling performance by 3% to 7%. Figure 8.1 shows the effects of dehydration on cycling performance.

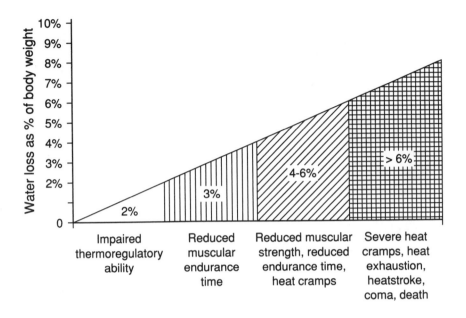

Figure 8.1 The effects of various levels of dehydration on endurance performance.

Note. From *Serious Training for Serious Athletes* (p. 135) by R. Sleamaker, 1989, Champaign, IL: Human Kinetics. Copyright 1989 by Robert Hayes Sleamaker. Reprinted by permission.

It is best to drink about 1 to 2 cups of fluid before exercise and then drink often during exercise. It is also important to include some form of carbohydrate with the fluid to help supply energy to your muscles.

Carbohydrate: The Main Source of Energy

Carbohydrate, the primary fuel for muscle contraction, is the nutrient most important for cycling. The energy released from carbohydrates can be released within exercising muscles up to three times faster than energy from fat. There are two major types of carbohydrates: complex (found in spaghetti, potatoes, breads, and rice) and simple (naturally occurring simple sugars). Carbohydrate stores in the body (glycogen) are limited. When depleted, cyclists can't train or race hard and may experience fatigue.

To accomplish glycogen repletion on a daily basis, you must consume a significant amount of carbohydrates, from 60% to 70% of your total caloric intake. This amounts to between 500 and 600 grams of carbohydrate (2,000 to 2,400 calories per day). Such a diet means eating very large quantities of carbohydrate foods (see Table 8.1). Eat carbohydrate-rich breakfasts, such as cereals and pancakes, instead of eggs. For lunch

Table 8.1 Foods Containing High Sources of Carbohydrate		
Food	**Energy (calories)**	**Carbohydrate (g)***
Banana, medium	105	27
Apple, medium	81	21
Baked potato, large	240	55
Rice, 1 cup	205	45
Raisins, 1/4 cup	120	30
Whole wheat bread, 4 slices	224	44
Sports bar, 1 bar	225	40
Pancakes, 3 4-in.	260	51
Peas, 1/2 cup	60	10
Carrot, 1 medium	40	10
Green beans, 1/2 cup	30	7
Spaghetti, 1 cup	200	40
Bagel, 1	160	30
Fig cookie, 1	50	11
Cream of wheat, 1 serving	100	22
Instant oatmeal, maple, 1 serving	160	30
English muffin, 1	130	25
Honey, 1 tablespoon	60	15
Pizza, cheese, 2 slices	340	42
Stuffing, 1 cup	220	40

*1 gram of carbohydrate = 4 calories. Some of these foods contain fats and proteins.

and dinner, have large portions of rice, pasta, potatoes, vegetables, and fruits. Your plate should be two thirds covered by carbohydrates. The remaining calories in the diet should be obtained from fat (20% to 30%) and protein (10% to 15%).

Not only does the amount of carbohydrate in your diet affect your performance, but your daily carbohydrate stores will dictate your day-to-day energy level. Figure 8.2 shows what can happen to your muscles' glycogen stores if you do not eat a diet high in carbohydrate on a daily basis. A high-carbohydrate (high-CHO) diet allows you to recover faster from your workouts (see Figure 8.2). Getting inadequate carbo-

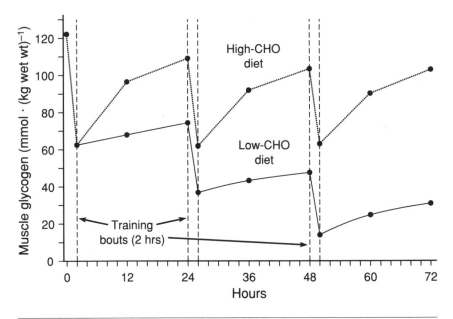

Figure 8.2 A high carbohydrate (high-CHO) diet speeds recovery from training.

Note. From "Nutrition for Endurance Sport: Carbohydrate and Fluid Balance" by D.L. Costill and J.M. Miller, 1980, *International Journal of Sports Medicine*, **1**, p. 2. Reprinted by permission of Georg Thieme Verlag.

hydrate stores can lead to chronic fatigue. Without adequate carbohydrate stores, you'll feel like you are always riding in low gear.

Protein Needs

High-protein intake is usually associated with weight lifting and bodybuilding, but recent evidence suggests that endurance athletes may also need additional protein. The extra protein is probably necessary to repair damaged muscle tissue and as an auxiliary fuel source during long-term exercise. Such exercise would increase your protein demands from the .8 grams per kilogram of body weight as suggested by the Recommended Dietary Allowance (RDA) for protein to between 1 and 1.5 grams per kilogram. For a 120-pound cyclist this would be 60 to 85 grams of protein per day.

Most cyclists will not have to make major changes in their diets to meet this requirement. For example, a cyclist who consumes 3,500 calories a day in a diet that is about 12% protein will easily be meeting this requirement. Aim for 1.5 grams per kilogram of body weight. If you eat 10% to 15% of your diet in protein, your protein intake will be adequate to meet the increased needs of hard training and racing.

A rule of thumb to get adequate protein in your diet is to include 2 cups of low-fat milk or yogurt plus 4 to 6 ounces of protein-rich foods per day. Foods high in protein are meat, poultry, fish, eggs, dried peas, beans, and lentils.

Some individuals may need to modify this diet. A female cyclist eating a low-calorie diet of mostly vegetables and salads may be at risk for protein deficiency, which would manifest itself in anemia, fatigue, and possibly amenorrhea. She should consume more protein-rich foods like dairy products, fish, poultry, and lean meats. Be sure to include products such as yogurt, lean meats, and low-fat milk, which are considered complete proteins when you are on a high-carbohydrate diet.

Fat Facts

The recommended diet for healthy and active individuals has 20% to 30% fat. There is no need to supplement your diet with fat. Research on Tour de France cyclists confirms this statement. On average, the diets of these cyclists contained 23% fat, 62% carbohydrate, and 15% protein. Although cycling stimulates adaptive changes that increase the body's ability to mobilize and utilize fat as an energy source, you do not need to increase fat intake above the prescribed percentages. Adequate carbohydrate and fat intake can be obtained from a diet containing grains, vegetables, fruit, dairy products, and lean meats.

All fats—saturated (found in butter, beef fat, coconut and palm oil, and hydrogenated vegetable oil), monounsaturated (found in olive and canola oil), and polyunsaturated (found in most vegetable oils such as corn and safflower oil)—have 9 calories per gram, compared to the 4 calories per gram of carbohydrate and protein. By having fat in the diet, cyclists who expend a lot of calories each day can get the calories they need with less food. It can be difficult for a cyclist who needs 4,000 to 6,000 calories a day to eat this large amount of calories on a diet of less than 20% to 25% fat.

In getting your 20% to 30% fat allotment, you should try to consume similar amounts of saturated, monounsaturated, and polyunsaturated fats. Fats help provide energy, help store and use fat-soluble vitamins (A, D, E, and K), and are vital to moving nutrients into and out of cells. Fat is needed in your diet, but it needs to be kept in the recommended range of total calories.

Vitamins and Minerals

Although a lot of research on vitamins and minerals has focused on their use as enzymes to speed up metabolic reactions in the body, there is now evidence that they protect your body from the damage of hard cycling.

Little did you know that increased exercise may have a negative effect on your body. Yes, after all these years of telling about the benefits of exercise—reduced body fat, increased cardiorespiratory fitness, increased strength, and less stress—scientists are now discovering a link between exercise and the formation of free radicals. They sound like a group of terrorists loose in your body, and they are.

We inhale a lot of free radicals from the air that we breathe. Yes, oxygen is critical for life and for the production of energy for strength training, running, cycling, or swimming. But, ironically, some of the chemical reactions oxygen triggers within your body create toxic compounds called free radicals—highly reactive, unstable entities that have the potential to cause severe damage to a cell's structure. They attack the walls of the cells of your muscles, mitochondria, heart, and blood vessels. They damage the structure of the cell and reduce the cell's ability to function and regulate itself.

Free-radical damage has been linked not only to reduced exercise ability but also to problems specifically associated with aging, such as declining immune systems, atherosclerosis, and Parkinson's disease. They may also be directly linked to cancer and heart disease, which together account for 80% of all deaths in the United States.

Fortunately, our bodies are equipped to fight the ravages of free radicals with substances called *antioxidants*, which halt or inactivate these dangerous molecular by-products and help repair the cellular damage. Antioxidants keep the damage from getting out of control. Traffic lights are to cars what antioxidants are to cells: They both prevent destruction and mayhem, but the more activity there is between oxygen and the cells of your body (traffic), the more antioxidants (traffic lights) you need.

The body creates antioxidants in the form of enzymes such as superoxide dismutase (SOD). But they are also found in vitamins C and E and in beta carotene, a precursor of vitamin A. Selenium, zinc, the peptide glutathione, and bioflavonoids are other minerals and nutrients that have been found to be synergistic in the fight against free radicals. Also, scientific research has shown that some herbs may be linked to combating free radicals. Siberian ginseng, tumeric, rosemary, ginkgo, and milk thistle are some of the more popular antioxidant herbs.

Exercise and Free Radicals

As a cyclist, you may be at a greater risk than more sedentary individuals for higher levels of free-radical production in your body. Here is why:

While you exercise you take in many more times the oxygen than you would at rest, which leads to an increased number of mitochondria in the muscle cells. Mitochondria are the structures involved in your muscles' aerobic metabolism. The resulting mitochondrial activity is thought to increase oxidation and free-radical production.

Exercise increases the release of the hormones epinephrine and norepinephrine, which helps charge up your nervous system, release fats from your body's stores, and supply glycogen to the muscles. The oxidation of these hormones has been shown to be related to free-radical formation.

Just as exercising leads to greater oxygen intake, exercising in smoggy conditions can lead to the increased intake of ozone and nitrogen oxide. When the oxygen combines with the ozone or nitrogen oxide, even more free radicals are produced.

Combating Free Radicals With Vitamins

Free radicals are at least partially to blame for muscle damage, soreness, and reduced endurance. Free radicals damage muscle cells during hard exercise, which leads to inflammation and acute muscle soreness. Several studies have shown that optimal levels of antioxidants may reduce muscle injury and improve endurance.

Research at the University of California showed that when athletes ran to exhaustion on the treadmill, two important enzymes normally found in the muscle cells appeared in high concentrations in the athletes' blood.

In a second trial the runners received supplements of 1,000 milligrams (mg) of vitamin C, 10 mg of beta carotene, and 800 international units (IU) of vitamin E for 8 weeks. When the tests were repeated, the athletes had much lower concentrations of the enzymes in their blood. This suggests that the athletes had less muscle-cell damage when they took the antioxidants. They also had significantly higher levels of glutathione preoxidase in their blood, an antioxidant that helps prevent damage to muscle-cell membranes.

Vitamin C has many important functions, including enhancing iron absorption, producing collagen, assisting in wound healing, and stimulating the immune system. As an important water-soluble antioxidant, vitamin C specializes in scavenging oxidants and free radicals in the watery fluids of cells and blood. The U.S. RDA for vitamin C is 60 mg a day, but many researchers are recommending anywhere from 250 to 1,000 mg per day to prevent cell damage, serve as an antioxidant, prevent heart disease, and help prevent cancer.

Beta carotene and vitamin A are related. Beta carotene is a precursor to vitamin A and also serves as an antioxidant in itself. Although vitamin A is not a very active antioxidant, it helps your body resist infection, neutralizes the effect of free radicals, and has been shown to reduce the incidence of cancer. The U.S. RDA for vitamin A is 5,000 IU per day.

Many people now believe that you need about 10,000 to 20,000 IU of vitamin A to help fight infections and battle free radicals.

Beta carotene is a plant pigment your body converts to vitamin A if the need exists. When you eat a carrot or an orange, part of the beta carotene is converted to vitamin A. The remaining beta carotene acts as an antioxidant, dousing free radicals and preventing oxidative damage. There is no RDA for beta carotene, but most scientists recommend a minimum intake of 5 to 10 mg per day.

Many in the medical community claim that vitamin E is the master antioxidant. Vitamin E has been shown to mend some of the signs of aging and other changes that occur as the result of oxidative damage. Older individuals have greater levels of markers called *lipid peroxides*, which are signs of oxidative damage. Yet when elderly people in one research study took vitamin E supplements in amounts 20 to 40 times the U.S. RDA, the levels of these markers went down, which suggests the slowing down of cell aging.

What about the effects of vitamin E on athletes, who experience oxidative damage to muscle cells during exercise? In one study, athletes who received vitamin E supplements of as little as 400 IU per day showed decreased levels of malondialdehyde (MDA, a marker for muscle-cell oxidation) after running. Twenty-five female runners were measured for MDA before and after a 30-minute treadmill run. The postrun levels of MDA increased over 30% in the group that did not take vitamin E supplements.

The U.S. RDA for vitamin E is 30 IU, but studies have used much higher levels, up to 800 IU for 3 years, without finding toxic effects. A minimum intake of 200 IU is recommended for people who exercise intensely or are routinely exposed to air pollutants during exercise.

Exercise may also have an effect on your immune system. There is probably a link between hard exercise, immunity, and antioxidants. When you exercise vigorously and often, fighting free radicals may strain your immune system, leaving you susceptible to colds, flu, and infection. After hard exercise your immune system needs a boost, and antioxidants are essential for optimal functioning of your immune system.

Additional Free-Radical Fighters

It is fast becoming an established reality that when you exercise hard, when you are exposed to stress or poor air quality, or when you are ingesting certain medications or processed foods, you may not be obtaining enough key antioxidant nutrients. Recently, numerous studies have reported that the RDA of antioxidants may not be sufficient to provide a strong defense against free radicals and infections. You might want to use glutathione and N-acetyl cysteine, selenium, zinc, or bioflavonoids for supplemental protection against free radicals.

Glutathione and N-Acetyl Cysteine.   The peptide glutathione converts oxidized vitamin C back into a form that can once again serve as an antioxidant. Research on animals has shown that intense exercise can reduce muscle glutathione by 40% and liver glutathione (from which muscles increase their supply) by 80%. After exercise, liver and muscle glutathione levels continue to fall, indicating continued use of this antioxidant in fighting free radicals. If glutathione levels drop too low, severe muscle damage may take place.

Glutathione can be taken preformed, but some of it will be destroyed in the digestive tract. Glutathione is produced in the body from L-cysteine and other amino acids. Research has shown that increasing your intake of N-acetyl cysteine will help your body supercompensate its levels of glutathione. N-acetyl cysteine is preferred over L-cysteine because it is more stable and less toxic.

To ensure that your intake of cysteine to produce glutathione is adequate, eat quality protein or take a supplement containing N-acetyl cysteine. Currently there are no RDAs for glutathione *or* N-acetyl cysteine, but intakes of 50 mg or more of *each* antioxidant should be ingested. Read the label on any antioxidant supplement you purchase to ensure that these forms of peptide and amino acid are on the label. And be sure to take three times the amount of vitamin C as N-acetyl cysteine to avoid the possibility of it precipitating in the kidneys as cysteine and possibly causing kidney stones.

Selenium.   Selenium is a potent antioxidant that works synergistically with antioxidant nutrients such as glutathione preoxidase, vitamin E, zinc, and vitamin C to combat cellular damage caused by free radicals. We receive selenium from plants, and plants from the soil, but many areas have too little selenium in the soil. If the soil that produces your food is too low in selenium, chances are you will not receive enough from your diet alone.

The RDA for selenium is 50 mg, but Colgan Institute, a leading center dedicated to sports nutritional research, and other exercise-research institutes have shown that 200 to 400 mg of selenium per day may help fight against free-radical damage of heart tissue and decrease incidence of cancer.

Dr. Michael Colgan also recommends the Seleno-L-Methionine form of selenium for better absorption into your body. Seleno-L-Methionine is one of the most potent and nutritionally safe forms of selenium. Be sure to keep your daily intake of selenium under 800 mg per day; selenium can become very toxic above this dosage.

Zinc. Zinc stimulates superoxide dismutase (SOD), the main antioxidant enzyme manufactured by your body. This enzyme is crucial to cell life. Most of the clinical research on SOD has centered on the inflammation resulting from excess free radicals, such as in arthritis, bursitis, and gout. SOD supplements do not work; they are often missing cofactors or are mostly destroyed in the digestive tract. Eating a balanced diet and taking zinc and other supplements will ensure production of SOD. You should be taking a minimum of 15 mg of zinc per day.

Bioflavonoids. The bioflavonoids are a family of related compounds that includes rutin, flavones, flavonols, and the flavonones. The bioflavonoids are not vitamins or minerals, although at one time they were called vitamin P or substance P. They are found in the inner peel of citrus fruits, the white core of peppers, buckwheat, and leafy vegetables.

Bioflavonoids are essential for the proper absorption and use of vitamin C. They assist vitamin C in keeping collagen, the intercellular cement, in healthy condition. Bioflavonoids also act as antioxidants to keep vitamin C and adrenaline from being oxidized by copper-containing enzymes. Limited evidence shows bioflavonoids might prevent the bruising and damage to artery walls caused by free radicals.

There is no RDA for bioflavonoids. Ensure a daily intake of good food sources of bioflavonoids, and take a supplement that contains bioflavonoids to aid in vitamin C uptake.

Your Personal Antioxidant Program

So what should a smart athlete do? First, eat lots of fresh fruits, vegetables, and whole grains. Citrus fruits provide vitamin C. Two to three servings per day of dark-green and orange vegetables, like spinach and carrots, will increase your beta carotene intake. Whole grains are good sources of selenium and zinc. Vitamin E can be found in wheat germ, nuts, and sweet potatoes.

A balanced diet is important to the complete profile of antioxidant support to fight free radicals and infection. But getting a balanced diet in today's society may be as difficult as riding a 40-kilometer time trial in less than an hour. We often do not like the foods that are high in antioxidants, often eat processed or overcooked foods, and often cannot eat enough food to reach the necessary antioxidant levels. According to the National Cancer Institute, less than a tenth of the population of the United States eats five or more daily servings of food sources of antioxidants—the minimum recommended by most health and nutritional organizations. And the RDA for antioxidants may not be adequate for persons who exercise regularly.

Many experts now recommend that you enhance your antioxidant and immune systems with supplements of vitamins, minerals, and herbs. Your best bet is a multivitamin and mineral supplement that includes antioxidant-helping herbs. The decision to supplement is one only you can make. However, given the harmful effects of free radicals and a lowering of your immunity during hard training and competition, your best offense may be an adequate diet and a solid multivitamin-and-mineral defense. There is now enough research available to make it clear that antioxidant vitamins and minerals are very important nutrients for health—and that many athletes are probably not getting enough.

Iron-Poor Blood

It had been a long, hard road back in the first half of the 1989 season for Greg LeMond, and the results had not been promising. To not do well after putting in many miles of hard work and training was frustrating. As late in the season as the Tour of Italy, he still felt that he was running on empty and decided it was time to have a physical examination and blood test. He was diagnosed as having a low iron count and anemia. Once this physical problem was resolved, the season turned around for him, and he went on to win the Tour de France and the World Championships.

Hard-training athletes must maintain a proper level of iron in order to compete in top form. Iron helps the hemoglobin molecule carry oxygen to your exercising muscles. Iron also plays a key role in energy production in the working muscles. If the body's iron stores are not adequate, an individual can develop anemia, a condition that can be identified by low hemoglobin and/or serum (blood) ferritin. The normal value for males is 14 to 18 grams per 100 milliliters of blood and for women 12 to 16.

Cyclists reduce their iron stores in several ways. Iron stores are reduced during periods of heavy sweating. Cyclists who sweat 2 to 3 liters per day may double their loss of iron. This increased drain of iron, if it continued for months, could lead to exhaustion.

Cyclists who are vegetarian can have reduced iron stores because their diet is poor in iron. Heme-iron, the iron-rich red pigment in the blood hemoglobin, is found only in meat, not in vegetables. Cyclists who are vegetarians should be conscious of their iron consumption and make an extra effort to eat plenty of whole grains, nuts, dried fruits, and other iron-rich foods.

Female cyclists also need to be concerned with iron loss. The average cyclist, male or female, normally loses .9 milligrams of iron every day in urine, sweat, and in their stool. Women lose an additional 15 to 45 milligrams each time they menstruate and may not eat enough iron-rich foods to compensate for that loss. For this group, RDA is 18 milligrams.

Amenorrheic (nonmenstruating) cyclists have reduced blood losses and reduced iron needs, and their requirements are similar to those for men—10 milligrams.

To reduce your risk of becoming iron deficient or anemic, incorporate the following practices into your diet:

1. Eat foods rich in vitamin C at every meal. Vitamin C helps the body absorb iron. For example, a glass of orange juice with an iron-enriched breakfast cereal enhances vitamin C absorption by 250%. The enhancing effect is proportional to the amount of vitamin C ingested. You may also consider taking a vitamin supplement.

2. Make lean meat a part of your diet three times a week. Other good sources of iron are beans, spinach, broccoli, prunes, and dried apricots. But remember, fruits and vegetables do not contain the essential heme-iron your body needs.

3. Eat enriched or fortified breads, cereals, and pasta whenever you can.

4. When it's feasible, cook your meals in a cast-iron pan or skillet; this will help increase the iron content of the foods.

5. If you eat primarily fish or chicken, eat them with vegetable proteins such as lentils, chili beans, or split peas. The heme-iron from animal protein enhances the absorption of vegetable protein.

6. Avoid drinking tea and coffee at meals. They reduce iron absorption by as much as 40%.

You may wonder how vitamin B-12 affects iron absorption and prevents anemia. Actually, vitamin B-12 is known to cure only one form of anemia—pernicious anemia—which occurs when you cannot adequately absorb vitamin B-12 in the intestine. Vitamin B-12 is important for the proper development of red blood cells, and deficiency of this vitamin can lead to improper oxygen transport in the circulatory system. People who eat meat are assured an adequate intake of vitamin B-12. Strict vegetarians will have to supplement their diets with vitamin B-12 because they will not receive any in their meals.

With an iron-rich diet, iron supplementation may not be needed. But if your diet is deficient in iron, consider taking a multivitamin. A multivitamin supplement will provide not only iron but also the vitamin C to advance iron absorption. If you are experiencing recurrent iron deficiency, your physician can prescribe an iron supplement. A common supplement is 325 milligrams of ferrous sulfate two or three times a week. Be careful not to take megadoses of iron because it can cause intestinal distress and may result in conditions such as cirrhosis of the liver, diabetes, and possible damage to the heart.

If you find yourself suffering the symptoms of chronic fatigue that Greg LeMond had, don't waste time. Review your entries in your training diary, because lack of sleep, lots of travel, or overtraining may also produce the same symptoms. Then call your physician and have a blood test. Early diagnosis, proper diet, and supplementation can be keys to restoring peak performance.

Carbo Loading

Glucose is a simple form of sugar and is the basic form of carbohydrate used in your body. Almost all ingested carbohydrates are converted to glucose before they are used in your body. Blood glucose serves as the metabolic fuel for your skeletal muscle. Some glucose supplied to your muscles is converted to glycogen and is stored intramuscularly. Glycogen is a polymer of glucose—that is, a number of glucose molecules chemically linked together. Glycogen is the stored form of glucose and serves as a metabolic fuel for cycling.

The amount of glycogen stored in your muscle will determine how long and at what level you will perform in training and racing. As you can see in Figure 8.3, the glycogen level is low on a high-fat, low-

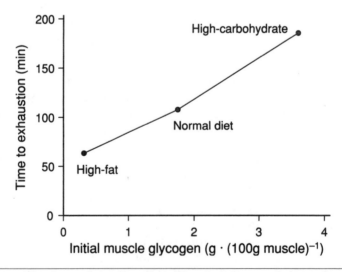

Figure 8.3   This figure shows the effects of various diets on time to exhaustion in endurance athletes. The time to exhaustion is related to the amount of glycogen stores the athlete has. A high-carbohydrate diet is the most effective means of building glycogen stores.

Note. From "Diet, Muscle Glycogen and Physical Performance" by J. Bergstrom, L. Hermansen, E. Hultman, et al., 1967, *Acta Physiologica Scandinavica*, **71**, p. 140. Reprinted by permission of *Acta Physiologica Scandinavica*.

carbohydrate diet. Cycling on low levels of glycogen will lead to early fatigue. If you eat a low-carbohydrate diet (40% or less) your cycling abilities will be greatly reduced, and you will fatigue more quickly than if you ate a high-carbohydrate diet (60%-70%).

Glycogen supercompensation, or carbohydrate loading, is the term used to describe the technique whereby muscle-glycogen levels are over-loaded in an effort to enhance cycling performance. You may want to practice this technique several times during the season to ensure that your muscles are filled with carbohydrate. The classic approach to carbohydrate loading has been to exercise hard and eat a low-carbohy-drate diet for 3 or 4 days. This depletion phase is followed by 3 or 4 days of high-carbohydrate meals while tapering training intensity for an upcoming event. Several studies showed that a cyclist could enter the event with increased carbohydrate stores.

However, this regimen has its problems. It increases your chances of injury and your workout quality suffers during the depletion phase. And many athletes have complained of not peaking physiologically and psychologically for competition after following this program.

Recently, a modified regimen has become popular with athletes who want to supercompensate before major competitions. Athletes follow a diet of 50% carbohydrate for 3 days followed by a diet of at least 70% carbohydrate for another 3 days before competition (see Table 8.2). During this 6-day period, cycling exercise is decreased from 90 minutes on Day 1, to 40 to 60 minutes on Days 2 and 3, and to 20 to 30 minutes on Days 4 and 5, with complete rest or a short ride the day before competition. This method has been shown to be just as successful in loading the muscles with glycogen but with fewer side effects than the classic method.

Table 8.2 Modified Carbohydrate (CHO) Loading Regimen		
Day	**Exercise time**	**Percent dietary CHO**
1	90 minutes	50
2	40-60 minutes	50
3	40-60 minutes	50
4	20-45 minutes	70
5	20-45 minutes	70
6	Rest to 30 minutes	70
7	Race	

Glycogen supercompensation results in a 1- to 4-kilogram weight gain because each gram of glycogen is stored with 3 to 5 grams of water, and some athletes complain of feeling heavy or bloated during this loading program. For this reason, you may want to practice this regimen in training or before a minor competition before trying it prior to a major competition.

Such overcompensation does lead to increased performance in events over 60 to 90 minutes but is of no value in shorter races, such as track events or short criteriums. Glycogen loading should not be used on a routine or weekly basis but reserved for a few major competitions each year.

It is not easy to eat a diet of over 70% carbohydrate. The volume of food eaten in a high-carbohydrate diet is enormous, and several companies have come up with liquid products to help athletes increase their carbohydrate intake. In addition to the foods listed in Table 8.1, Table 8.3 identifies liquid carbohydrate products that can supplement your meals. One advantage to liquid carbohydrates is that they do not provide the bulk of solid carbohydrates.

Table 8.3 Liquid Sources of High Carbohydrates*			
Product	Energy (calories)	Carbohydrate	
		(g)	(%)
GatorLode (Quaker Oats)	187	47	20
Exceed, High Carbohydrate (Weider)	235	59	25
Ultra Fuel (Twinn Labs)	200	50	21
Carboplex (Unipro)	220	55	23
Muscle Pep (Sports Pep)	260	45	70
Carbo Energizer (Weider)	237	59	25

*All drinks are given in 8-ounce serving size for comparison.

Competition and Nutrition

A pre-event meal prevents hunger during cycling. Food eaten at least 3 to 6 hours before an event can raise blood glucose and liver glycogen, particularly after an overnight fast. This may supply a small competitive edge for an upcoming road race. The liver, which helps maintain blood glucose during exercise, relies on frequently scheduled meals to fill its stores of glycogen.

A pre-event meal should be low in fat and fiber and contain from 70 to 150 grams (280 to 600 calories) of carbohydrate. Choose high-starch foods like English muffins, pancakes, waffles, bagels, and pasta because these foods are easily digested and will help maintain your blood glucose levels. Drink low-fat milk, juice, or an energy drink with your meal.

The closer to competition the meal is consumed, the smaller it should be. For example, a meal containing 2 or 3 calories per pound of body weight is suggested during the last 1 or 2 hours before competition, whereas a meal of 7 to 8 calories per pound is all right 3 or 4 hours before the event. This should help prevent an upset stomach before a race.

Balanced liquid meals may be an excellent alternative for cyclists who have difficulty eating solid food right before events. These products leave the stomach quickly and provide quality nutrients.

Eating on the Line

Cyclists often consume simple carbohydrates such as energy drinks, honey, and sports bars on the line before the start of their event. Does this late intake of carbohydrates have an effect upon race performance? It seems that athletes differ in their responses to eating 30 to 45 minutes prior to exercise. Some athletes experience hypoglycemia (low blood glucose) because of high insulin levels induced by the pre-exercise sugar. Other athletes are not as sensitive to these pre-exercise snacks and do not experience fatigue during cycling. The best time to experiment with pre-exercise eating is in training.

Consuming sugar before short events such as the kilometer, match sprints, or a pursuit will not improve performance because the body already has enough energy stored in the muscles in the form of glycogen and ATP. However, you may benefit from such snacks before a long road race because they will provide you with additional glucose during the first hour of the race. If you are concerned about a possible insulin reaction and hypoglycemia, you should not eat sugar until a few minutes before the event. The rise of specific hormones prior to racing, such as epinephrine and growth hormone, will inhibit insulin responses.

Carbohydrate and Fluid Intake During Training and Racing

Consuming fluids during cycling is vital to your optimal performance. Dehydration of as little as 2% of your body weight can impair your endurance.

You can prepare for cycling in warm weather by drinking 15 to 20 ounces during the last 15 minutes before training or racing. If you are participating in events lasting over 60 minutes, continued fluids and carbohydrates are essential to improved performance.

Consuming carbohydrates during prolonged cycling enhances performance by providing glucose for the muscles to use when their glycogen stores begin to drop. When you consume carbohydrates during the ride, your blood glucose levels are maintained and used to supply energy to the working muscles. Your body will utilize carbohydrates at a higher rate and your endurance will improve.

Research has shown that trained cyclists need to ingest carbohydrate at the rate of 1 gram per minute (60 grams per hour, or about 240 calories) to maintain normal blood glucose levels during prolonged rides. As shown in Table 8.4, you can accomplish this by drinking beverages containing various combinations of fluid and carbohydrate. From this table you can formulate your own ideas for mixing weaker or stronger concentrations. The amount of carbohydrate athletes feel they can tolerate in their drinks does vary. The best time to discover your preference is in training, when you can experiment with different concentrations of carbohydrate.

Table 8.4   Volume of Carbohydrate (CHO) Drink to Provide Indicated Amount of CHO

Concentration of carbohydrate in drink (%)	Rate of CHO supplementation grams/hour (milliliters/hour)			Comment
	(40 g/hr)	(60 g/hr)	(80 g/hr)	
2	2000	3000	4000	Volume too large
4	1000	1500	2000	Volume too large
6	667	1000	1333	Volume too large
8	500	750	1000	Fluid & CHO supl.
10	400	600	800	Fluid & CHO supl.
15	267	400	533	CHO Supplement
20	200	300	400	CHO supplement
25	160	240	320	CHO supplement

Note. From "Carbohydrate Feeding During Prolonged Cycling to Improve Performance" by Andrew Coggan, 1990, *Cycling Science*, **2**(1), p. 10. Copyright 1990 by Cycling Science Publications. Adapted by permission.

Caffeine and Performance

Caffeine has been shown to enhance cycling performance by increasing the fat available for muscle energy, thus preserving glycogen and postponing the onset of fatigue. So caffeine has a glycogen-sparing effect in that it enables more fat and less glycogen to be used as fuel. Caffeine may also influence performance by reducing perceived effort or acting as a stimulant on the central nervous system. On the down side, caffeine, especially if you do not normally consume it, may cause dehydration, stomach distress, irregular heartbeats, and other discomforts.

There is no agreed-upon dose to take before competition. Research shows that individuals differ greatly in their responses to caffeine. You might experiment with two or three cups of coffee before competition; this amount seems to work for most athletes. However, if you are a habitual consumer of coffee, cola, tea, cocoa, or chocolate, then the extra caffeine before competition may not help. Because caffeine is present naturally in so many foods, drinks, and medications, you probably do get some caffeine every day.

Here is some age-old advice: If you use caffeine, moderate amounts of it are advisable. If you do not use caffeine, don't start using it to boost your performance.

Fluid Choices

As indicated in Table 8.4, beverages containing 6% or less carbohydrate probably cannot be ingested in large enough volumes to provide adequate carbohydrates and should be viewed only as fluid-replacement drinks. Drinks of greater than 10% carbohydrate can easily provide 1 gram of carbohydrate per minute, but they supply very little fluid. They are best used only as carbohydrate-supplement drinks. Drinks of between 8% and 10% carbohydrate in volumes of 600 to 1,000 milliliters per hour provide both adequate carbohydrate and fluid.

I would suggest the following regimen to help maintain an optimum flow of fluid and carbohydrate from the stomach and intestine into the bloodstream. Drink about 400 milliliters (about 14 ounces) of an energy drink of 10% or less carbohydrate just before a long race or training ride and then ingest about 100 milliliters (3 to 4 ounces) every 10 minutes during the race.

This pattern of filling your stomach before a race and then taking in more fluid at regular intervals will keep your stomach full enough to maximize gastric emptying. As a result, you'll optimize water absorption during hot weather, and the carbohydrate in the drink will be carried into the intestine along with the fluid. Remember, drink only a few minutes before the start of the race to ensure that the fluid will end up in the bloodstream, not in the bladder.

This volume of fluid in the stomach during cycling may take some getting used to. You should practice this regimen in training. If you "train" the stomach and intestine to tolerate a particular energy drink by using the drink during your practice rides, you will be less likely to have stomach problems during a race.

Some athletes do not have as many stomach problems when they consume drinks that have maltodextrins or glucose polymers as their primary carbohydrates. Glucose, maltodextrin, and sucrose all stimulate fluid absorption in the small intestine. It may be best to avoid a fructose-based drink. Fructose, which is absorbed more slowly in the intestine than other carbohydrates, does not stimulate as much fluid absorption. In fact, diarrhea and gastrointestinal distress are common side effects in athletes who consume large volumes of fructose drinks during exercise. Table 8.5 compares the sources of carbohydrates, percentages of carbohydrates, calories, and sodium in commercially available energy drinks.

Table 8.5	Commercial Sports/Energy Drinks			
Product	Carbohydrate source	Carbohydrate (%)	Calories per 8 ounces	Sodium (mg)
Gatorade	Sucrose, glucose	6	50	110
Exceed	Glucose polymer, fructose	7.2	70	50
Cytomax	Fructose, polylactate, maltodextrin	8	83	100
Powerade	High-fructose corn syrup, glucose polymers	8	70	70
Hydra-Charge	Maltodextrin, fructose	8.0	80	50
All Sport	High-fructose corn syrup	8.5	80	55
HydraFuel	Glucose, glucose polymer	7	66	25
Max	Maltodextrin	10	96	13
10-K	High-fructose corn syrup, fructose	6.3	60	55
Break Through	Maltodextin, fructose	8	80	56

Food Intake During the Ride

As you have seen, drinking small amounts of carbohydrate and fluid through the ride can ward off hunger, provide needed calories, help maintain blood glucose, and meet your fluid needs. If you prefer something to eat during the ride, a nutritious, convenient energy bar may be the answer. Top road cyclists often consume large quantities of energy bars during road races. Some cyclists have suggested that on cooler days or when they cannot tolerate a lot of fluid in their stomachs, energy bars supply their carbohydrate. Be careful, though, in selecting energy bars: The majority of the calories should come from carbohydrate, not from fat and protein. PowerBars, FinHalsa, and other sports bars are excellent products for active cyclists.

Taste: An Important Factor

Don't underestimate the importance of taste. If a drink tastes good, you will drink more of it. Research by Gatorade has shown that the optimal beverage or bar must strike a balance between physiological effectiveness and palatability. What seems pleasant-tasting when you are at rest may not be right several hours into the race on a hot day. So try out various nutritional products and volumes during training.

When possible, drink cool fluids. A cool fluid tastes better and is more refreshing; it helps lower body temperature and may empty from the stomach quicker.

Electrolyte Addition

Athletes often wonder how important electrolytes—such as sodium, potassium, phosphorus, magnesium, and calcium—are in energy drinks. Well, there is good reason to think that a small amount of sodium in an energy drink is beneficial.

An electrolyte imbalance called *hyponatremia*—low blood sodium, also called "water intoxication"—has been reported in endurance athletes. Hyponatremia may occur during endurance events for a couple of reasons. First, sodium is lost in sweat, and after several hours this amount may be significant. Second, consuming only water and/or carbohydrate drinks dilutes the amount of sodium in the bloodstream. Although water intoxication is rare, the potential for it still exists. Water intoxication causes headaches, cramping, loss of strength, and nausea. Drinking sports drinks that contain sodium can help reduce the risk of hyponatremia and its symptoms.

Ingesting sodium during exercise can help maintain blood plasma volume, the fluid portion of the blood volume. Beverages containing sodium help maintain water in the bloodstream and plasma volume.

Meals on Wheels

Most sports bars are high-carbohydrate, with moderate amounts of fat and protein. They also supply vitamins, minerals, and fiber. Along with energy drinks, these bars should have a definite place in your pantry.

Check the bar's label to ensure that it is high-carbohydrate, low-fat, and low-protein. Select bars that are over 80% carbohydrate, less than 10% fat, and not much more than 10% protein. Remember, there are 4 calories per gram of carbohydrate, 4 calories per gram of protein, and 9 calories per gram of fat. A 225-calorie bar that contains 11 grams of fat and 5 grams of protein is 44% fat calories, 9% protein calories, and only 47% carbohydrate calories.

While riding—or even cross-country skiing in the off-season—over long distances, it may be wise to consume some solid food. Energy bars not only will supply carbohydrates but will also give you a sense of having something solid in your stomach.

Some athletes do not like drinking excessive fluids during exercise. Nutritionists have suggested that exercise-induced nausea can be accentuated by having liquids sloshing around in the stomach for a long time. Eating solid food will help settle the stomach when large volumes of fluid are being digested.

Remember these points about eating energy bars before, during, or after training or competition:

- Drink several ounces of fluid with the energy bar, especially during exercise when you need the fluid in addition to the energy from the bar.
- Stay away from high-fat, high-protein bars. Your primary fuel during exercise is carbohydrate, and that should be first on the label.
- Eat before you are hungry. If you wait until you are hungry, your blood glucose and muscle glycogen stores may be too low for peak performance.
- During cold weather, you may need to keep your energy bars close to your body to prevent their freezing.
- Just as you do with energy drinks, you need to experiment with energy bars in training before using them in competition. Trying something new on race day can increase your risk of abdominal distress.

Energy bars—along with sports drinks, bananas, and other fruits—are important tools in the nutritional arsenal of any cyclist. Try several of the brands and flavors available at your local sports or nutrition outlet. Whichever one works best for you is the one to use in training and competition—taste and palatability are your biggest concerns. Keep the carbohydrate content high, the fat content low, and, most importantly, your energy level high.

Fred Brouns, PhD, from the Department of Human Biology at the University of Limburg, the Netherlands, who has worked with many professional cycling teams, recommends that you look for the following on the label of a sports drink: sodium, 400 to 1,100 milligrams per liter (mg/L); chloride, 500 to 1,500 mg/L; magnesium, 10 to 100 mg/L; and potassium, 120 to 225 mg/L. Many sports drinks report electrolytes in milligrams per 8-ounce serving. To convert that amount to milligrams per liter, simply multiply that amount by 4.

Recovering Nutritionally

The race is over. You pack up your bike and drink 10 to 12 ounces of water. After collecting your prize, you jump into your car and drive the 3 hours home before you sit down to dinner. This is your first food after a hard road race.

Then you're tired the whole next day, and even after a good warm-up, you still feel sluggish while riding a 42 × 21 during your afternoon workout. For many years we thought that you just went too hard in the race and may not have had enough training miles in your legs to recover. We know better now.

Your muscles and liver have not completely refilled themselves with glycogen. Research has shown that training rides or races that last over 60 minutes can put severe demands upon your body's glycogen stores. If the ride was long and hard enough, your muscles may even "bonk" during the event.

After a hard race or training session, fluids and carbohydrates are crucial to your recovery. No matter how much you drank during the event, you will not have been able to keep up with dehydration. For every pound you are down from your preride weight, you will need to drink 1 pint. If you became very dehydrated during the ride, you may need 12 to 24 hours to completely replace sweat losses.

Keep your alcohol intake to a minimum after exercise because it will only further dehydrate you. Beer and wine are poor sports drinks because they act as diuretics and are low-carbohydrate. So make sure you consume primarily water, energy drinks, or juices.

You need to consume between 100 and 200 grams of carbohydrate within the first hour after the ride, and then an additional 100 grams every 2 to 4 hours thereafter. Your initial intake can be a highly concentrated energy drink (20% to 25% carbohydrate), supplying not only carbohydrates but fluids too (see Table 8.3). Recent work by John Ivy, PhD, has shown that adding a little milk-protein powder to this recovery beverage will speed up glycogen resynthesis. The protein has an effect on the increased release of insulin, which means a greater uptake of carbohydrate by the muscles. It takes at least 20 hours to completely resynthesize the muscle glycogen lost in training or competition.

The Final Spin

Everything you do influences your performance, but your food choices can have the most effect because of their long-term and short-term benefits. A proper diet will help your training and performance.

The ideal training and competition diet should include the following percentages of calories: 60% to 70% from carbohydrate, 20% to 30% from fat, and 10% to 15% from protein.

There are four stages in cycling where nutrition can impact performance:

1. Nutrition During Training. You will spend most of your time training; therefore, training is the most critical stage. A diet high in carbohydrates is important, because it is not uncommon to train from 4 to 6 hours a day and burn 2,500 to 5,000 calories. The best way to replenish these calories is with a high-carbohydrate diet. By consuming high-carbohydrate foods and/or drinks in the first 30 minutes following a workout, you can minimize the depletion of your energy stores.

2. Pre-Event Nutrition. Your main dietary concern before an event is to ensure sufficient energy and fluids. Two or 3 days before competition, a high-carbohydrate diet with plenty of fluids should be emphasized.

3. Nutrition During Competition. You will need to ingest adequate amounts of fluids and carbohydrate during rides lasting 60 minutes or longer. Proper nutrition during exercise will help maintain glucose in the bloodstream, which will then supply the muscles with glucose for energy.

4. Nutrition After Competition. Long-duration and/or high-intensity cycling will deplete the muscles' energy supplies. So carbohydrates play an important role after competition to make sure energy stores are maintained.

Optimal nutrition is essential to achieving top physical performance in cycling.

9

© Graham Watson

The Biomechanics of Cycling

Cycling is a marriage between the cyclist, who is somewhat adaptable, and the bicycle, which is somewhat adjustable.

—Andy Pruitt, EdD

Understanding the basic biomechanical factors involved in driving the bicycle forward will help you pedal more efficiently—get more push for your effort. The problem of applying biomechanics to cycling is that the enormously complex web of physical and mechanical variables is completely interrelated. You have physical factors that deal with the muscles you use to pedal and how you position yourself on the bike. And you have mechanical factors of the bike that you can adjust. But the whole system taken together—for example, position on the bike, frame geometry, crank length, cadence, power output, muscle-fiber type, and speed—is so interdependent that if one variable is changed, it affects several others, making the study of one variable in isolation impossible.

Most of the important determinations of crank length, frame size, pedal cadence, and so on have been empirically developed by cyclists, coaches, manufacturers, and scientists. These individuals have done quite a good job of filling our needs for improved performance and injury prevention. The challenge in the future will be to integrate our ever-increasing knowledge of cycling mechanics with rapidly improving computer and instrumentation technology to improve cycling performance.

Let's begin our exploration of the biomechanics of cycling with an examination of the physical factors in pedaling, in converting muscle power to pedal power. We will examine the pedaling motion as it relates to ankle position and to your position on the bike. Then we'll look at the mechanical side of things, examining how the makeup of the bicycle affects rider position and pedaling motion. Finally we'll draw some conclusions about optimal pedaling cadence per minute.

Pedal Motion—The Science Behind the Effort

The pattern of force applied throughout the complete pedal cycle begins at top dead center. Force output has been shown to change continually during one complete revolution. Figure 9.1 shows changes in the various forces as the crank rotates through the 360 degrees of a revolution. This figure represents one complete leg cycle at 20 points (about 18 degrees apart) in the crank revolution.

The crank (dotted line) and the pedal (short bold line) are shown in correct relationship to each other. The angle of the pedal with respect to the vertical line is called the *ankling angle*. The size of the force being applied to the pedal, referred to as *resultant force*, is shown by the size of the bold arrow. This arrow's orientation to the pedal shows the angle at which the force is applied. The scale in the lower right-hand corner of 600 newtons equals about 135 pounds of force on the pedal.

Not surprisingly, most cyclists attain peak force at about 90 degrees, or with the pedal at about 3 o'clock. However, significant downward

TDC

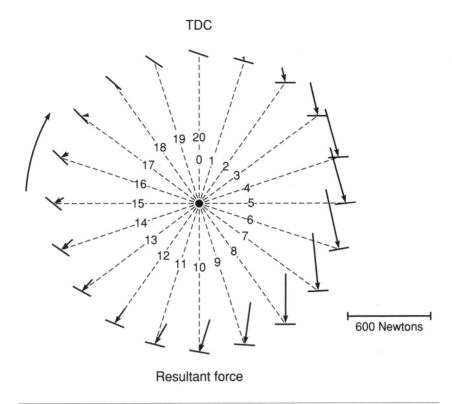

Resultant force

Figure 9.1 The force applied to the pedal during one complete pedal cycle.

Note. From "The Biomechanics of Cycling: Studies of the Pedaling Mechanics of Elite Pursuit Riders" by P.R. Cavanagh and D.J. Sanderson. In *Science of Cycling* (p. 105) by E.R. Burke (Ed.), 1986, Champaign, IL: Human Kinetics. Copyright 1986 by Edmund Burke. Adapted by permission.

force is still being applied at the bottom of the pedal stroke (180 degrees); cyclists refer to this as trying to stretch the crank arm. Downward force decreases but is not totally eliminated during the upstroke, acting in opposition to the other leg.

Biomechanists use the different forces a cyclist applies to the bicycle pedals to characterize pedaling technique. These forces are typically measured with pedals that have built-in piezoelectric measuring devices and are described in component terms. Biomechanists refer to the force that is perpendicular to the pedal as the *normal-force component* and the force along the surface of the pedal as the *tangential-force component*. The *effective component* acts perpendicular to the bicycle crank arm and is responsible for powering the bicycle forward. The *ineffective component* acts parallel to the crank arm and thus only acts to lengthen or compress the crank arm.

Early research by Peter Cavanagh at Penn State University has shown that to be most effective it is necessary to apply force perpendicular to the crank. The product of the effective force and the crank-arm length is called *torque*.

This research has shown several interesting observations, which can be seen in Figure 9.1. The cyclist upon which this figure is based was seated and riding a simulated pursuit at about 100 revolutions per minute with close to maximum power output during a steady-state ride of 4 minutes. Notice that the force on the pedals is rarely vertical (a direct push downward to the ground). In the first 130 degrees of the pedal cycle (positions 0 to 7) the force is downward and forward. For much of the remainder of the pedal cycle it is downward and backward. At position 4, the force is close to a 90-degree angle with the crank arm and is very close to being 100% effective. This is the position that corresponds to where the most force is being applied to propel the bicycle forward.

From this point forward, the angle of the crank and pedal decreases and the effectiveness of the force put into the pedal decreases. By the time the pedal reaches the bottom of the stroke a fairly large force exists, but you can see from its orientation that it is not very effective.

During the recovery phase of the pedal cycle (180 to 360 degrees) a force is still pushing down on the pedals. The weight of your foot and leg on the pedal is a negative force during recovery that tends to produce a countertorque, opposing the forward movement of the bicycle. Notice that, under the conditions of the study, during the recovery phase hardly any pulling-up force was applied to the pedals. Pulling-up forces would be shown on the diagram as an arrow underneath the pedal and would point upward.

Remember, though, that your legs are moving in a synchronous motion, but 180 degrees opposite each other. When the right leg is pushing down in the propulsion phase, the left leg will be in the recovery phase. The small downward force from the leg in recovery is easily overcome by the other (propulsive) leg. During sprinting, climbing, and starting on the track, the recovery forces would probably indicate that the rider actually pulls up on the pedals.

From Figure 9.1 we see that propulsion occurs whenever the effective component of the applied force to the crank arm is positive and in the direction of pedaling. In Figure 9.1 it is obvious that the resultant force is still effective beyond bottom dead center. Your goal should be to make the propulsive phase of the pedal cycle as long as possible.

In this example, the fact that the cyclist was able to remain seated while pedaling indicates that his maximum steady-state resultant force was less than his body weight. If he had produced forces greater than his body weight, he would have lifted himself off the saddle unless he used his arm and back muscles to hold himself down.

Leg Movement Patterns

By using high-speed film, it is now possible to film pedal action while a cyclist is pedaling. The developed film can then be digitized (converted to numbers), and when these numbers are entered into a computer, the rate of leg movement and joint angles of the foot, ankle, knee, and hip can be calculated. Researchers have been able to give us clearer answers to where maximum knee flexion occurs in the pedal stroke, how straight the knee is at the bottom of the pedal stroke, and how the cyclist "ankles" during the pedal cycle.

Figure 9.2 represents the composite drawing of the mean data collected by Dr. Peter Cavanagh on six National Team pursuit cyclists as

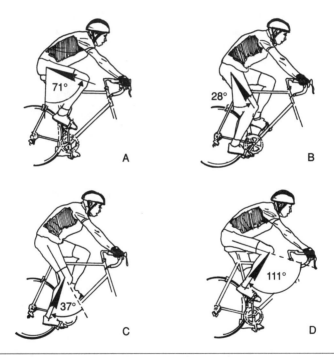

Figure 9.2 The body position and crank at the times of (a) maximum hip flexion, (b) minimum hip flexion, (c) maximum knee extension, and (d) maximum knee flexion. These values are the means from six different elite riders who had individually adjusted the cycle to their own requirements. The small dark-shaded sectors represent the range of values for the particular position found among subjects.

Note. From "The Biomechanics of Cycling: Studies of the Pedaling Mechanics of Elite Pursuit Riders" by P.R. Cavanagh and D.J. Sanderson. In *Science of Cycling* (p. 93) by E.R. Burke (Ed.), 1986, Champaign, IL: Human Kinetics. Copyright 1986 by Edmund Burke. Reprinted by permission.

they rode their own bikes at 100 revolutions per minute in a 53 × 13 gear combination.

Looking at one complete revolution of the crank cycle, we can see the range of motion of the major leg joints and segments. The thigh moves through about a 43-degree range of motion. It moves from about 71 degrees of vertical just after top dead center (TDC; Figure 9.2a) to within 28 degrees at bottom dead center (BDC; Figure 9.2b). Through this range of motion, the upper body stays relatively motionless at about 35 degrees of horizontal. This means that the hip joint never moves into full extension (full extension would be if the thigh moved behind a line drawn through the center of the trunk). These observations have implications for designing your strength-training program.

The knee's range of motion is about 75 degrees (Figure 9.2, c–d). Near the bottom of the pedal stroke the knee is flexed at about 37 degrees, and at just before TDC, the maximum knee flexion is 111 degrees.

The shaded areas in all four diagrams show the variations in range of motion among all the cyclists in the study. It is quite small, about 10 degrees. This points out that the adjustments made by the cyclists to their bicycles have fairly standardized their body positions once they begin riding.

Although the leg's range of motion is fairly constrained by the rider's position and the geometry of the bike's frame, there are significant changes in technique when the rider changes positions. When a cyclist climbs or sprints out of the saddle, for example, her joint patterns will be different. Even when she is seated and climbing or pedaling hard, as in time-trialing, the pattern can change due to body and bike movement.

Muscle Activity Patterns

Robert Gregor, PhD, and others from the University of California have identified the major cycling muscles of the leg using a technique called *electromyography* (EMG). Electromyography is based on the fact that contracting muscles generate electrical impulses. The unique advantages of EMG are that it reveals both the intensity and the duration of a muscle's action and discloses the precise time sequences of muscular movement. Their EMG shows that many major lower extremity muscles produce hip extension (propulsion) (see Figure 9.3).

Figure 9.4 shows that the gluteus maximus (GM) and biceps femoris (BF) play a major role in hip extension from 0 degrees (at TDC) to 180 degrees (at BDC). The rectus femoris (RF), vastus medialis (VM), and vastus lateralis (VL)—the principle extensors of the knee—are active at the same time as the hamstrings, from 0 degrees to 75 degrees, and

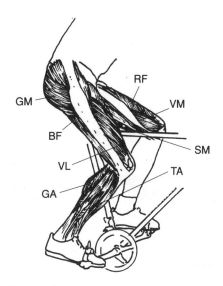

Figure 9.3   Some of the major lower extremity muscles used in cycling include the gluteus maximus (GM), biceps femoris (BF), vastus lateralis (VL), gastrocnemius (GA), tibialis anterior (TA), semimembranosus (SM), vastus medialis (VM), and rectus femoris (RF).

Note. From "Effects of Saddle Height and Pedaling Cadence on Power Output and Efficiency" by R.J. Gregor and S.G. Rugg. In *Science of Cycling* (p. 74) by E.R. Burke (Ed.), 1986, Champaign, IL: Human Kinetics. Copyright 1986 by Edmund Burke. Reprinted by permission.

during the last 90 degrees of the recovery, helping to flex the hip. Their primary use, however, is during the propulsion phase of the pedal stroke.

There is no doubt that knee extension and flexion are important in the production of force during cycling. The semimembranosus, biceps femoris, and gastrocnemius play a role in knee flexion. Many weight-training programs tend to ignore the knee flexors while working the knee extensors. The cyclist must plan a strength-training program (see chapter 6) that works both knee flexors and knee extensors.

Ankling

Many traditional cyclists will tell you to drop your ankle as you pedal through top dead center (for example, from 30 degrees before TDC to 30 degrees after TDC) and to drop your toe across the bottom of the pedal stroke. From the information we've received from measures of pedal force (Figure 9.1) and from high-speed filming, we know that the pedal varies from almost horizontal in position 3 to slightly heel-

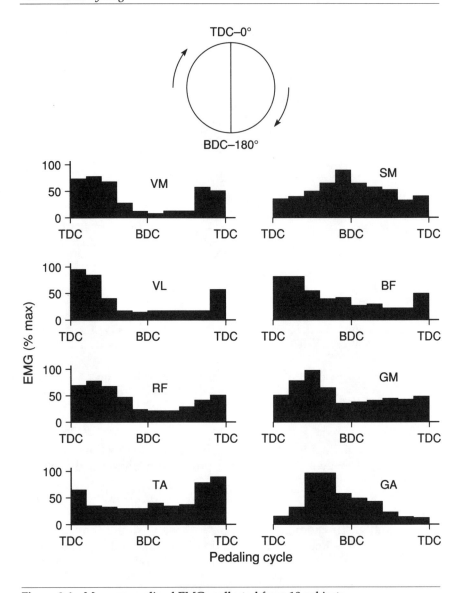

Figure 9.4   Mean normalized EMGs collected from 10 subjects.

Note. From "Effects of Saddle Height and Pedaling Cadence on Power Output and Efficiency" by R.J. Gregor and S.G. Rugg. In *Science of Cycling* (p. 74) by E.R. Burke (Ed.), 1986, Champaign, IL: Human Kinetics. Copyright 1986 by Edmund Burke. Reprinted by permission.

down in position 6, to a maximum toes-down position in position 16. The maximum toes-down position occurs at about 75 degrees before TDC.

The total ankling pattern that Peter Cavanagh and David Sanderson have measured is shown for one complete crank revolution in Figure 9.5. The dark solid line is the mean, or average, pattern from seven elite pursuit riders; the two other lines represent values for a single rider. Notice that this rider is off of the mean pattern for most of the revolution. In general, he keeps his heel a little higher than average. This is particularly noticeable on his left foot during the recovery phase (180 to

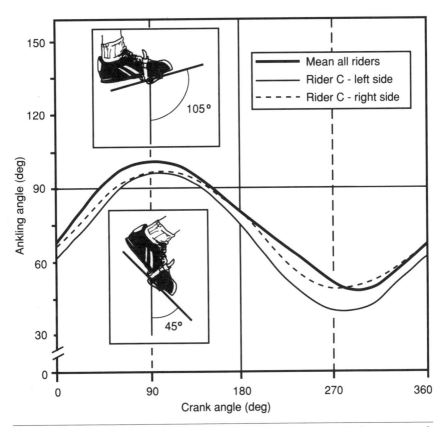

Figure 9.5 The mean ankling pattern as a function of crank angle for a group of pursuit riders during 100-rpm pedaling with a 400-watt power output. Zero degrees is the first top dead center (TDC), and 360 degrees is the end of one crank revolution. The inset diagrams show the conventions used for measuring the angle of ankling. Also shown on the diagram is the ankling pattern for a particular rider (Rider C of the study). See text for a discussion.

Note. From "The Biomechanics of Cycling: Studies of the Pedaling Mechanics of Elite Pursuit Riders" by P.R. Cavanagh and D.J. Sanderson. In *Science of Cycling* (p. 95) by E.R. Burke (Ed.), 1986, Champaign, IL: Human Kinetics . Copyright 1986 by Edmund Burke. Reprinted by permission.

360 degrees). There is also an approximate 10-degree difference in the range of motion of his left and right feet.

The ankling pattern used by the 7 cyclists (Figure 9.6b)—and by other nonelite cyclists they have studied—departs considerably from what has been accepted in the popular literature. The pattern suggested in some lay articles (Figure 9.6a) is likely both anatomically and mechanically impossible if the rider remains in the saddle. Your ankling pattern should look like that in Figure 9.6b, in which you can increase your effective force on the pedal by pushing through at the top of your stroke and pulling back at the bottom.

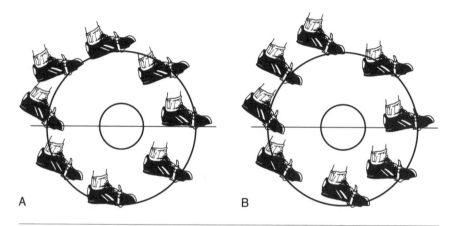

A   B

Figure 9.6   Pattern A is the ankling pattern that is recommended in popular bicycling literature. Pattern B is the ankling pattern that Peter Cavanagh and David Sanderson have discovered highly successful elite pursuit riders using.

Note. From "The Biomechanics of Cycling: Studies of the Pedaling Mechanics of Elite Pursuit Riders" by P.R. Cavanagh and D.J. Sanderson, 1986. In *Science of Cycling* (p. 95) by E.R. Burke (Ed.), 1986, Champaign, IL: Human Kinetics. Copyright 1986 by Edmund Burke. Reprinted by permission.

Foot Position

Your foot should be positioned so that the ball of the foot is directly over the pedal axle. To avoid knee pain later on, your cleats should be adjusted so that your foot rests on the pedal naturally. Experienced cyclists have their cleats set with a rotational adjustment device (RAD) at their local bicycle shops. Most cyclists today use clipless pedals that allow the foot to "float" a few degrees inward or outward on the pedal as it moves through the pedal cycle. Research has shown that these new pedal systems put less strain on the knee and allow a more natural pedaling motion.

Is There a Need for Floating Pedals?

Bicycle pedal and shoe design has changed significantly since Bernard Hinault won the Tour of Italy and the Tour de France in 1985 using Look pedals, which he helped design and which helped him avoid falling on several occasions. Since then, clipless pedals have become the most popular among competitive, road, and mountain bike cyclists. In 1993, history was made again when Sean Kelly finally turned in his toe straps and clips for clipless pedals.

But with the introduction of clipless pedals in the mid-1980s the medical community saw a rise in the incidence of overuse injuries to the knee, such as tendinitis, chondromalacia, and illiotibial band friction syndrome. The increase in injuries was attributed to clipless pedals that locked the foot more firmly in place and to the stiffer-soled shoes that were used with them.

Andy Pruitt, EdD, ATC, director of Western Orthopedic Sports Medicine and Rehabilitation in Denver, says, "In the old days, cycling shoes had soft leather uppers and the cleat wore in quickly, allowing one to have quite a bit of pivot around the ball of the foot. Most injuries occur in trying to make the knee adapt to a fixed pedal position, which puts chronic stress on the knee joint. The 'static' or 'fixed' clipless-pedal systems hold the foot and knee in a rigid position. The foot wants to move during the pedal stroke."

Because of the increased incidence of knee problems, in 1987 Jean Beyl, the inventor of Look pedals, created the Time pedal-and-shoe system and introduced the first "floating" pedal design. His floating system was the first attempt to make the pedal adapt to the cyclist. Now every major pedal manufacturer produces floating systems that allow as much as 37 degrees of lateral pivot in road pedals. Speedplay has recently introduced a mountain bike pedal with 54 degrees of lateral pivot.

Andy Pruitt says that any cyclist's knees are safer in a pivoting pedal. Andy adds, "The ultimate cycling position for maximum performance is secondary to cycling injury- and pain-free. The floating-pedal systems are ideal because there is no loss of power and they allow for some knee and foot movement. The natural rotation of the large bone of the lower leg [tibia] is to rotate in as you push down on the pedals. If your foot is fixed, your knee and

(continued)

Floating Pedals *(continued)*

supporting tendons and ligaments must absorb this rotation, which leads to chronic knee problems. Remember, chronic injuries in cycling occur over time. If your foot is improperly fixed to the pedal, and you pedal at about 95 revolutions per minute, you will complete 5,700 revolutions per hour, per leg. If you are riding about 10 hours per week, you will pedal approximately 57,000 pedal strokes per week. Do this for several weeks and it is easy to see why knee injuries may occur."

Recently, in research at UCLA's biomechanics department, cyclists rode both "fixed" and "float" pedals on an instrumented-force pedal system, which shows the force placed on the pedals while cycling. Data from this investigation suggest that the torsional force applied at the shoe/pedal interface is attenuated with the use of the floating-pedal design. Cyclists who had existing knee pain exhibited more internal and external rotation of the foot while cycling. Although this is preliminary research, it confirms the need for floating systems.

If you are experiencing knee pain, first evaluate your cleat position with the use of the Fit Kit's rotational adjustment device and consider using a floating-pedal system if you do not already. If you own a fixed-pedal system and don't want to invest in floating pedals, you may want to experiment with the Bio-Cleat, which are Look-compatible, bolt-on cleats that offer 5 degrees of pivot on either side of neutral.

After you change shoes or pedals, be sure to recheck saddle height and fore/aft position. The only disadvantage is that some floating motions take getting used to, and some cyclists say they experience hamstring soreness in the first few days of use, but this will eventually go away.

If your knee pain is severe or continues after your adjustments, I suggest that you make an appointment to see a medical specialist who is familiar with cycling mechanics and injuries; you may have a leg-length discrepancy, excessive foot pronation, or other anatomical problems.

The floating-pedal systems allow your tibia (the large bone of the lower leg) to move in and rotate as you push down on the pedal. In a fixed-pedal system, your knee and its ligaments must absorb much of this rotation, which can cause knee problems.

Sitting Pretty

If you are interested in optimum performance, proper body position on the bike is paramount. A properly fitted bicycle will help you feel comfortable and be more efficient on the bicycle. An efficient position is one that enables you to produce more power without working any muscles needlessly.

The importance of a proper fit between you and your bicycle can be seen in your increased economy of oxygen consumption. A study conducted by Mark Hodges at the Olympic Training Center measured the oxygen consumption of elite juniors before and after being positioned properly on bicycles. After a proper fitting the group was able to reduce their average oxygen consumption by 8% to 14% at a given workload.

The Right Frame

The most important angle on a bicycle is that formed by the seat tube with the ground. As you will see later in this chapter, a good fit requires your knee to be over the pedal spindle when the crank arms are horizontal. The angle of the seat tube with the ground is usually designed to accomplish this. The typical range for all bicycles is 70 to 75 degrees, although some triathletes' seat tubes are at 90 degrees to the ground. The most common angles are from 72 to 74 degrees, which will allow an average-sized cyclist to position the knee over the pedal spindle with only minor adjustments in fore and aft movement of the saddle.

Consequently, the seat-tube angle is related to the length of the femur (thighbone). The longer the femur, the smaller the angle, the farther back the cyclist tends to sit on the bicycle. If you have a short femur, the seat-tube angle has to be larger to position your knee far enough forward. In general, the smaller the bicycle, the larger the seat-tube angle. Professional cyclists who ride long road races with many climbs increasingly opt to ride bicycles with a 72-degree seat-tube angle.

Frame Size

Your seat tube length, which is determined by your leg length, will allow for proper positioning of the saddle in relation to the pedals. John Howard, during his School of Champions clinics, recommends allowing between 1 and 2 inches of space between the rider's crotch and the top tube when the rider is standing barefoot over the bicycle. An acceptable frame will have 4 to 5 inches of seat post showing when the seat is properly adjusted.

The latest trend is to choose the smallest frame size that will allow proper biomechanical relationships. A smaller frame will be stiffer, lighter, and will handle better due to its lower center of gravity.

Top-Tube Length

The top-tube length is determined by the relationship of your upper body to your lower body. Mark Hodges, past director of coaching for the U.S. Cycling Team, recommends the following formula for determining top-tube length. First divide your height in inches by your pants inseam in inches. If your answer is greater than 2.2, you have a long torso in comparison to your legs. Values less than 2.0 mean your torso length is disproportionately short. If you are average, your value will fall between the two. If you are at either extreme, selecting a frame with proper top-tube length is crucial.

According to Hodges, if you have short legs and a long torso, you will need a frame with a closer relationship between the seat-tube length and the top-tube length (commonly measured from the center of the seat tube to the center of the head tube). A "long" frame, for someone with a long torso, might have a 58-centimeter seat tube and a 59-centimeter top tube; a "short" frame, for someone with a short torso, might have a 54 × 52 combination.

Average frames normally have top tubes that are 2 or 3 centimeters shorter than their seat tubes. Selecting a frame with the inappropriate ratio for your body type may adversely affect breathing, steering, and weight distribution and eventually strain the muscles that support the torso. Do not believe anyone who says you can compensate for an incorrect tube length by adjusting the stem extension or the position of the saddle on the rail. That approach just screws up many other adjustments on the bike.

Women generally have proportionally shorter torsos and longer legs than men, which often makes it difficult for some women to ride frames built for men. As the awareness of women's needs grows, we see more and more bikes being designed for women.

Saddle Height

Changes in saddle height affect the muscle activity of your legs. Research conducted by Michael Desipres in France studied muscle-activity patterns using electromyography (EMG). Three male cyclists were asked to ride their own bicycles at three different intensities and two saddle heights. EMG measurements of eight leg muscles were sampled at 95% and 105% of inseam length (measured from the ground to the crotch). Desipres concluded that as saddle height increased, the leg muscles turned on earlier in the pedal cycle and stayed on longer. The magnitude of muscle action did not appear larger; the EMG activity was just recorded for a longer period of time.

Saddle height does seem to make a difference, and cyclists and coaches all seem to have their own methods for achieving the optimum. But if you look at a few of the most popular methods, you will see that the saddle heights they produce end up fairly similar.

The John Howard Method

John Howard, past Olympian and Iron Man champion, recommends having a 30-degree bend in your knee when you're seated on the saddle, with the ball of your foot on the pedal and the pedal in the 6 o'clock position. The 30-degree bend is measured with a goineometer. You can buy one at a medical supply store or make one of your own using a ruler and protractor. The goineometer is lined up with the femur and tibia, with the axis being the midpoint of the femur (see Figure 9.7). Your foot must be in its natural pedaling position to properly take the measurements.

Rocking of the hips is a sign of too high a saddle position. Excessive upper body movement and frequent saddle standing are signs that it is too low.

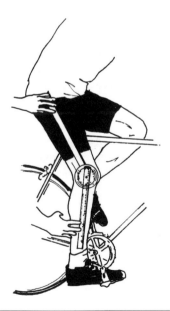

Figure 9.7 John Howard recommends a saddle height that yields a 30-degree bend in your knee when you are seated with the ball of your foot on the pedal and the pedal is in the 6 o'clock position.

The Greg LeMond Method

Greg says you should multiply your inseam length in centimeters (measured in stocking feet from floor to crotch) by .883. Measure yours by standing with your back against a wall and your feet about 15 centimeters apart. Put a carpenter's square or record album snug against your crotch, exerting the same pressure as your saddle would. One edge should be flat against the wall. Have a friend measure from the top to the floor.

The product of this equation should equal the length from the center of the bottom bracket axle to the top of the saddle (see Figure 9.8). If you have clipless pedals, LeMond recommends subtracting 3 millimeters from this measurement to get your saddle height.

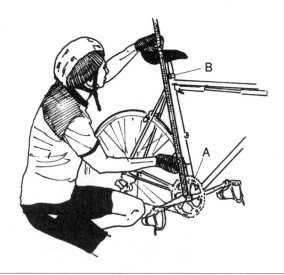

Figure 9.8   Greg LeMond recommends multiplying your inseam by .883 and making the product equal the length from the center of the bottom bracket axle along the seat tube (Point A) to the top of the saddle in line with the seat post (Point B).

The Andy Pruitt Method

Andy is a certified athletic trainer and physician's assistant who has treated many of the top cyclists in the United States. He has experimented with a riding position that he feels puts minimal pressure on the knee and allows for a powerful pedal stroke. His method of setting saddle height is similar to John Howard's and also uses a goineometer. He uses the greater trochanter (hip) to the lateral condyle (bump on the outside of the knee) to the lateral malleolus (bump on the outside of the ankle) as reference points for selecting saddle height (see Figure 9.9). The angle formed from these points should be between 25 and 30 degrees.

By using this seat height, you can reduce knee injuries and also avoid the dead spot at the bottom of the pedal stroke. But you should be careful in determining the anatomical landmarks, because if you do not hit the right places, you can be off by a great deal.

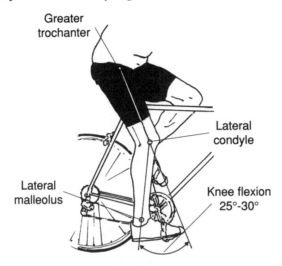

Figure 9.9   Andy Pruitt recommends that the saddle height be such that the angle formed by the three points shown in this figure is between 25 and 30 degrees.

Common Ground

If you complete all the measurements properly, you will notice that all methods yield similar saddle heights. Whatever method you use, make sure that your saddle is level or pointed up slightly at the nose. A horizontal saddle allows you to move back and forth across the saddle to change position as the terrain dictates. And if there is anything that all the opinions on saddle height agree on, it is that you'll have to change your position slowly. If you are currently used to riding at a saddle height that is off by a lot, you should only move the saddle up or down 2 millimeters every 2 weeks.

The Fore/Aft Position of the Saddle

One of the longest-standing recommendations for achieving horizontal saddle position is commonly called KOPS, for "knee over pedal spindle." Complete this check while your bike is mounted on a wind-load simulator and with the top tube leveled with a carpenter's bubble level. Figure 9.10 shows you how. First, get seated comfortably, with the crank arm in the 3 o'clock, or horizontal, position. Locate the bony protrusion below your kneecap. Drop a plumb line from this point; it should bisect the forward pedal's axle. Slide on the saddle until the string and axle line up, then dismount and move the saddle forward or backward along its rails as needed. Repeat this process until your knee lines up with the pedal's axle. Make sure your foot is located in its normal position. Dropping or raising your heel can change the position of your knee. The rails under the saddle allow it to be moved about 2 inches.

After this adjustment, recheck your saddle height. Moving the saddle forward is the same as lowering the saddle slightly; moving the saddle backward raises the saddle. A midsized bicycle frame with a seat-tube angle of 73 or 74 degrees allows for sufficient fore/aft saddle adjustment to accommodate most riders. If you ride a bike with a 75-degree seat-tube angle and have a long thigh, you may not be able to put the seat back far enough.

The position of the knee over the pedal's axle is just a starting point. You will need to personalize your fore/aft position to accommodate your physique and meet your riding needs. A road cyclist will usually ride with the knee 1 or 2 centimeters behind the axle, and a sprinter will ride with the knee 1 or 2 centimeters in front of the axle. A triathlete, too, usually rides in a more forward position, with the knee in front of the pedal's axle. This allows her to get into a more aerodynamic position and lay out over the bike without her knees hitting her chest. And because most triathletes come from a running background and have strong, flexible hamstrings, they feel more comfortable in this position.

Figure 9.10   When your fore/aft seat position is proper, a plumb line dropped from below your kneecap will bisect your pedal axle when you have the crank arm at a 3 o'clock position.

Saddle Tilt

The saddle should be set either level or with a slightly elevated nose. You can check saddle tilt by placing a carpenter's level along the longitudinal axis of the saddle.

Some women prefer the nose of the saddle to be angled slightly downward to prevent pressure on the perineal area. Some men will opt to have the saddle tilted more upward, but this may lead to urologic and neuropathic problems.

Stem Height

The top of the stem should be no more than 5 centimeters below the top of the saddle. Going lower than this may help your aerodynamic position slightly, but it will put more strain on your neck. If your thigh comes in contact with your torso when you ride, it is a sure sign that the stem is too low. Keep in mind that a higher stem will be more comfortable and a lower stem will be more aerodynamic. Do not extend the stem beyond the mark on the side of the stem or you risk breaking it out of the headtube.

Stem Extension

The measurement that most affects upper body position is *reach*, the combination of handlebar extension and top-tube length. In an off-the-shelf bicycle frame, the length of the top tube (measured from the center of the seat tube to the center of the head tube) is proportional to the length of the seat tube and corresponds to the upper body measurements of the average-size cyclist who would need that frame size. As mentioned earlier, only in the last few years have frame manufacturers addressed the needs of female cyclists, who generally have shorter upper bodies and longer legs than men of the same height.

To determine proper stem extension, mount your bike on a wind-load simulator and assume a normal riding position with your hands on the drops of the bars. Have a friend (it's best to have a very *close* friend) drop a plumb line from the end of your nose while you are looking down at a 45-degree angle to the floor surface. The plumb line should fall about 1 inch behind the handlebars (see Figure 9.11). While maintaining the same position, look at the front hub. If the majority of the hub is obscured from view by the handlebars, the stem is of acceptable length.

After you are in shape, taking a long ride may let you know if the stem length is correct or not. If it is too short, you will experience pain in your neck and shoulders. If the extension is too long, you will feel discomfort

Figure 9.11 With your stem properly extended, a plumb line dropped from your nose while you are looking down at a 45-degree angle will fall about 1 inch behind the handlebar.

in the backs of your arms. According to Greg LeMond, your elbow should touch your kneecap, or be within an inch of it, when your hands are on the drops, your elbows are bent at a 65- to 70-degree angle, and your legs are in the 1 o'clock and 7 o'clock pedaling positions.

Stems come in extensions from 4 to 14 centimeters to allow for proper fit. If you find yourself needing a much shorter or longer stem, the top-tube length of your bike is the major problem. Never allow very long or short stems to compensate for a poorly sized frame. Your steering and center of gravity will be compromised, and the bike will not be very comfortable to ride.

The Handlebars

For a road bike, select handlebars that are straight across the top. They should be as wide as the bony protrusions on the top outsides of your shoulders. If your bars are too narrow, they will restrict your breathing; if too wide, they will leave your chest area too open and increase wind drag.

Adjust the bars so that the bottom of the drops is parallel to the ground. A neutral position for the brake levers is achieved when the tips are in line with the bottom of the drops.

Crank-Arm Length

Biomechanists will be the first to tell you that crank arms influence your cadence and the leverage you can exert on the pedals. Longer crank arms are used for pushing large gears at a low cadence, and shorter arms allow for a higher cadence with smaller gears. You would use short crank arms for track sprints and criteriums, and longer crank arms for time-trialing and climbing hills. On your mountain bike you would use longer crank arms for better leverage in climbing.

Check your crank-arm length if you feel your knee is flexing too much at the top of the pedal stroke even though your saddle height may be properly set. You may have to switch to shorter arms. You can change the crank arms for comfort and performance just as you can the stem or saddle. When you change the crank arms, you may need to readjust saddle height.

The first coach or biomechanist to arrive at a formula to determine proper crank-arm length may win a Nobel Prize. For the time being, most people agree that crank-arm length should be proportional to your height and leg length. See Table 9.1 for an idea of the crank-arm length you should try under most riding conditions.

Table 9.1 Finding the Right Crank-Arm Length	
Cyclist's height (inches)	Crank-arm length (millimeters)
Less than 60	160
60-64	165-167.5
65-72	170
72-74	172.5
74-76	175
Over 76	180-185

Aerodynamic Positioning

Anyone who has raced a bicycle in a triathlon or duathlon will have experienced the adverse effects of wind resistance. In the early 1980s, the use of disk wheels and aerodynamic bikes and clothing set a precedent and firmly established the benefits of reducing wind resistance. It was not until the late 1980s and the introduction of the Scott DH handlebars that the next step in aerodynamic efficiency developed: radical changes in position on the bike.

Recently, I attended a seminar sponsored by Performance Bicycle Shop in which Boone Lennon presented his key points on correctly positioning an athlete on a bicycle that has aero bars. Boone is a former ski coach and current bicycle-racing enthusiast who holds two patents on aero-bar design and who, with Scott USA, introduced these bars to the cycling and triathlete mass market. Much of the information Boone relayed to the audience was from extensive wind-tunnel testing done at Texas A&M. He also told of the years he spent field-testing the bars, completing coast-down tests on the roads around his home in Ketchum, Idaho.

In all his work on handlebar development, he never wanted to sacrifice the comfort of the cyclist. His mission was to make athletes more aerodynamic while allowing them to ride more powerfully. He mentioned four areas that you should concentrate on to reduce air resistance through body position: keeping your arms narrow, your back flat, your chin down, and your knees in close to the top tube.

Boone used the analogy of your body being an "open cup" when you ride into the wind with your arms wide apart. By narrowing your arms, you close the opening of the cup and allow for the wind to be directed around your body (see Figure 9.12). Begin by gradually bringing your armrest pads a few centimeters in closer on the handlebars until you can comfortably ride with your forearms touching for long periods of time. This may take you several weeks or months. Once you can ride like this comfortably and powerfully, you have accomplished Boone's first goal of closing the cup.

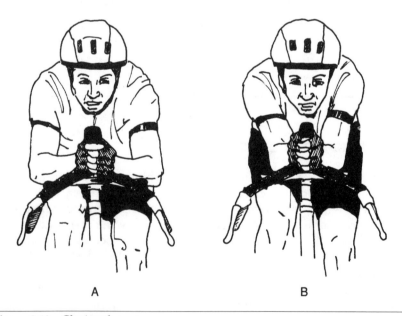

A   B

Figure 9.12   Closing the cup.

Next, work on riding comfortably with a flat back (see Figure 9.13). You can accomplish this by tipping your pelvis forward on the saddle. Make sure your saddle is level and your stem length is long enough to get the proper stretch in your back. This will eliminate the hump—most obvious from a side view—that you see in many cyclists' backs. Do not practice this movement until you have been able to ride with your forearms touching for long periods of time.

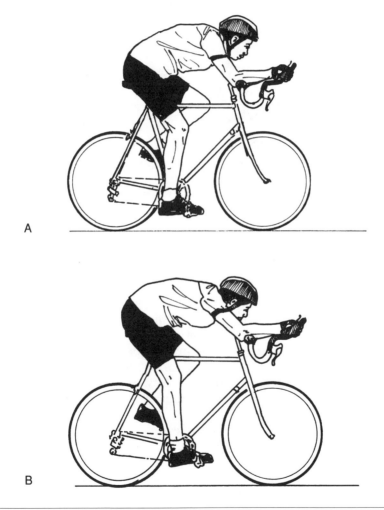

Figure 9.13 To change from riding with a rounded back (a) to a flat back (b), rotate your pelvis forward on the saddle.

Now you need to lower your chin to fill in the gap between your arms (see Figure 9.14). Lowering your chin will also lower your shoulders and make you a more perfect aerodynamic object. Do not drop the chin so low that you cannot safely look down the road. Safety and comfort are your key concerns while time-trialing or riding off the front of the pack.

Figure 9.14   Lower your chin to fill the gap between your shoulders and arms to further close the cup.

Once you have accomplished these changes in upper body position, learn to keep your knees in while pedaling. If your new upper body position causes you to throw out your knees to avoid hitting your arms, you may have to raise the stem or your shoulders slightly. Keeping your knees in while pedaling is just as important as keeping your forearms together, your back flat, and your chin low. Research conducted in the wind tunnel has shown no correlation between pedaling rate and a reduction in wind drag.

During the question-and-answer session at the end of his presentation, Boone mentioned that the tilt of the bars is important in accomplishing one or more of the four steps to positioning yourself comfortably on the bicycle. Most athletes that I have observed in racing keep the tilt of the bars somewhere between 15 and 30 degrees to achieve optimum comfort, performance, and power.

Several seminar participants were concerned about the effect of this aerodynamic position on breathing and oxygen consumption. Recent research completed by Steve Johnson at the University of Utah and published in *Cycling Science* has shown that using aero bars in this position had no measurable physiological cost upon cycling. Fifteen highly trained subjects rode a bicycle ergometer in the laboratory under two different submaximal conditions. The ergometer was fitted either with dropped bars or with clip-on bars.

There was no evidence in the study to suggest that the clip-on bars interfered with breathing mechanics. In addition, there was no significant difference in oxygen consumption when the athletes worked at 80% of maximum during the 10-minute steady-state ride. Therefore, concerns that the severely crouched position required for using an aerodynamic handlebar will interfere with breathing are unfounded.

As with any new equipment, the more practice you have riding with the aero bars, the more familiar and comfortable you will become with their operation. Not using aero bars or clip-ons is sure to put you at a disadvantage in certain events. And they are certainly much cheaper than disk wheels. With practice, you will be able to ride well in the new position, as shown in Figure 9.15.

Figure 9.15 A frontal view of an aerodynamic and biomechanically comfortable riding position.

Riding in the Dirt

Your body position will be different on a mountain bike mainly because of the upright bars. Upright bars hold your upper body more erect, which puts more weight on the saddle and rear wheel. This allows for better traction and enables a seated cyclist to push a larger gear. Since many of today's mountain bikes have the same seat-tube angles as road bicycles, cyclists often use the same saddle height and fore/aft dimensions as on their road bicycles.

The top tube of a mountain bike should be 2 to 4 inches lower than that of your road bike. But if you ride a 24-inch road bike don't assume that a 20- or 22-inch mountain bike will be the right size. Like road bikes, mountain bike sizes are usually determined by seat-tube length, and some models have sloping top tubes that result in extremely short seat tubes. In these cases, smaller frame sizes fit larger cyclists. The clearance between the crotch and top tube should be 3 to 6 inches.

Stem extension is important because you will often be riding out of the saddle, shifting your body. If your knees hit the bars, consider changing to a longer stem with a higher rise. Pro racers usually use low-rise stems, sometimes as low as a 90-degree angle, that are around 135-150 mm for a 5'10" to 6'0" rider.

On a mountain bike, your upper body will in most cases be more extended. As on the road bicycle, the top of the stem should be 1 to 2 inches below the imaginary horizontal line extending from the top of the saddle. A frame that is too small will force you to lean over too far because the handlebars are so far below the saddle. Too large a frame will also stretch you out too far. A comfortable reach on a mountain bike is one that gives you enough room for lots of body English on climbs and descents and allows no overlap of knees and elbows. Too high a position will raise your center of gravity and unevenly distribute your weight between the front and rear wheels.

Optimal Pedaling Cadence

The optimal pedaling cadence depends upon the type of riding you are doing—sprinting, hill-climbing, or time-trialing—and also upon the crank-arm length you are using. Observations of competitive cyclists reveal that cadences during flat riding generally range from 80 to 110 revolutions per minute and that more experienced cyclists usually select higher cadences.

A recent study conducted by Dr. James Hagberg on seven elite cyclists reported that while they rode at 80% of maximum on their own bicycles, their cadences varied from 72 to 102 revolutions per minute, with a mean for the group of 92.

As a general rule, lower cadences emphasize power output and higher cadences emphasize leg speed. Climbing hills requires high power outputs and you will range from 60 to 80 revolutions per minute. In situations requiring speed, such as sprinting, your cadence will go to 120 or higher. Again, an ideal range will be around 90 revolutions per minute.

Not all riders use the same gears and revolutions per minute under the same conditions. For example, Davis Phinney likes to time-trial in a 53 × 14 gear at 90 to 100 revolutions per minute, whereas Mike Engleman likes to push a 53 × 12 gear at 80 to 85 revolutions per minute. Everyone has different riding habits, muscle-fiber types, and levels of experience. Find the combination of gears, revolutions per minute, and crank-arm length that will give you the most performance with the least injury.

The Final Spin

Cycling involves the repeated application of force to the pedals of the bicycle in order to go fast. This pedaling action requires you to put adequate force to the pedals to overcome air resistance, gravity, and friction. Your pedaling action is a repeated circular motion that is restricted by the design of the bicycle and your position on the bike.

The ability to go fast and climb hard while cycling is very important. In addition to strong muscles and proper nutrition, the frame size, gear ratio, pedaling cadence, and your position on the bicycle are crucial to performance. You must consider the bicycle and yourself as one integrated unit.

Even though you may want to develop a position like Lance Armstrong or Miguel Indurain, you must let your own riding style and anatomy dictate your position. Your highest priority should be adjusting your bike and, when necessary, adapting your style to assure pain- and injury-free riding. Improved performance will follow.

© Graham Watson

Cutting the Drag

Aerodynamics cost me the Tour de France.

—*Laurent Fignon*

As a cyclist, friction is not your friend—it slows you down. True, you need some friction. If parts of your drive system did not touch, you would not have contact between the chain and the chainring and you would go nowhere. In this case, a little resistance goes a long way, but it is important to make sure that friction doesn't work against you.

Some excess friction is easy to detect. When your chain grinds along the front derailleur, you know it. You feel it, you hear it, and then you repair the problem. But other frictions are much harder to detect and calibrate. These are known in physics as types of drag, or resistance.

You and your bike, as a single unit, encounter two main points of friction: one, known as wind resistance, is between you and the atmosphere around you; the other, rolling resistance, is between the tires and the road. Like the friction between your chain and chainring, some wind and rolling resistance is good. But you need to know how to manage these resistances so they don't slow you down unnecessarily. This chapter will tell you about newer, more sophisticated ways you can add a little oil to yourself and the bike so that you can cut through the air and push down the road more smoothly and faster than ever before.

Wind Resistance

In sports such as cycling, downhill skiing, and speed skating, strategies have developed to alleviate the effects of wind resistance, or aerodynamic drag, on the forward velocity of the athlete. In cycling, wind resistance can comprise over 90% of the total resistance to motion, so disk wheels, one-piece suits, contoured helmets, clip-on handlebars, and aerodynamic bicycle frames have been developed to minimize resistance.

All cyclists should understand the basics of aerodynamics because it will mean less work for them on the road and faster riding times. At the 1989 Tour de France, after racing 2,100 miles, Greg LeMond won by 8 seconds and introduced the world to clip-on aerodynamic handlebars.

At the 1991 World Championships, Jens Lehman of Germany beat Chris Boardman of Great Britain by 9 seconds in the qualifying rounds of the pursuit. Then, in the 1992 Olympic pursuit final, Boardman caught the reigning champion, an unprecedented feat. In 1993, Boardman set a world hour record on a new Corima bicycle, and his teammate, Graeme Obree, again broke the world pursuit record on a "homemade" aerodynamic bicycle.

Much of the credit for these feats must go to the revolutionary designs of the bicycles. By using aero handlebars, disk and tri-spoke wheels, and low-profile bikes, these cyclists firmly established the benefits of reducing air resistance in competitive cycling.

Before we look at how to reduce air resistance we need to examine some of the established principles of aerodynamics. *Air resistance* is the common term for what is known technically as *aerodynamic drag force*. Aerodynamic drag can be broken down into these categories: surface drag, profile drag, air density, and air speed.

Surface Drag

Surface drag, or skin friction, is determined by the surface area of the cyclist and the smoothness of her surface. If you can keep the air flow around your body smooth (laminar), there is less drag. This has an effect of reducing aerodynamic drag on the cyclist so that she has less resistance to pedal against.

Surface drag will increase as the velocity of the air flow increases (as speed increases), as the amount of surface area parallel to the flow increases (more surface exposed to more air), and as the roughness of the clothing, bike, wheel, and helmet increases. The more open your position on the bike and the rougher the texture of your clothing, the greater the surface drag. You do not travel slowly enough through the air to sustain a laminar air-flow pattern; therefore, profile drag is the main source of drag in cycling.

Profile Drag

Profile drag is the main air-resistance force operating on your body when you are cycling. This type of drag is also known as *form drag*, or *pressure drag*.

As is shown in Figure 10.1, when you ride your bike you act as a barrier to air flow; an area of high pressure is found in front of you, which slows you down. When this happens, a "back flow" occurs over your body, which causes the flow to separate from the surface, and the amount of turbulence increases. This boundary-layer separation causes a turbulent low-pressure area behind you. This area of low pressure is continually being formed as you move through the air. Such a pattern is called *turbulent flow*.

For example, when you move your hand rapidly along the surface of water you are experiencing turbulent flow. The movement of water "downstream" of your moving hand is caused by the motion of your hand relative to the surrounding water.

This drag is known as *pressure drag* because it is the pressure difference between your front side hitting the air and your trailing surfaces that creates a suction-like effect that acts against your forward motion. In addition, the more abrupt the change in shape toward the rear of the body, the greater the magnitude of the suction effect. That is why streamlining the body, helmet, and wheels reduces pressure drag.

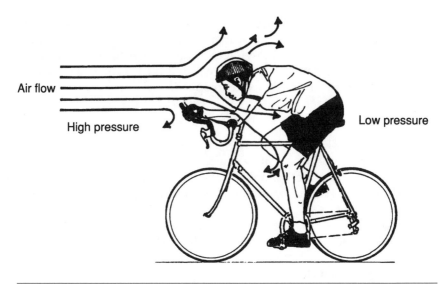

Air flow

High pressure

Low pressure

Figure 10.1   A high-pressure area is found in front of the cyclist, which slows the cyclist.

Profile drag is so named because the profile, the area exposed perpendicular to the approaching air flow, partly determines the magnitude of the drag. Thus a smaller frontal area will experience less drag than a larger frontal area. As we will discuss later in the chapter, you can control several factors that contribute to the size of your frontal area. Reduce your size, put on aero or clip-on handlebars, wear tight-fitting clothes, and keep your knees close to the frame, and you will pick up speed. It does work. Air drag can be reduced in direct proportion to frontal area—cut your frontal area in half and you cut the drag force in half!

Air Density

The reduced air resistance at higher altitudes has been established as a help to a cyclist's performance. Most cycling world records have been set at high altitudes. Francesco Moser went to Mexico City (7,400 feet) for the hour record, and many cyclists travel to the Colorado Springs Velodrome to set fast times.

As you climb above sea level the air pressure falls, the air becomes less dense, and the air resistance is reduced; therefore, it is easier to pedal through it.

Figure 10.2 shows the effect of altitude on bicycle speed. In theory, a cyclist's speed should increase substantially with higher elevations, as shown in the upper segment of the figure. However, actual times recorded in Mexico City seem to be only 3% to 5% higher than times set at sea level rather than the 8% to 9% predicted by the graph. The decrease is due to the lower barometric pressure, which does not move as much oxygen into your lungs to be used for energy production. You have to rely on more anaerobic resources to produce muscular energy. However, in events up to 1 hour and with the use of aerodynamic equipment, the decreased air resistance seems to outweigh the adverse effect on the heart and lungs.

Air Speed

Your riding speed is clearly related to air drag: no movement, no air drag. However, an important aspect of air speed, or velocity, is that drag

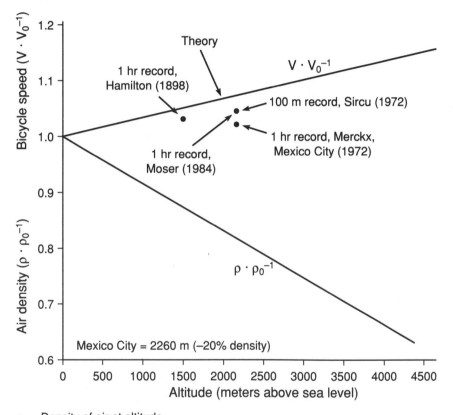

Figure 10.2 The effect of altitude on air density and cycling speed.

Note. From "Mechanical Factors Affecting the Speed of a Cycle" by C. Kyle. In *Science of Cycling* (p. 129) by E.R. Burke (Ed.), 1986, Champaign, IL: Human Kinetics. Copyright 1986 by Edmund Burke. Adapted by permission.

does not increase in direct proportion to speed, but in relation to the square of the velocity. In other words, double your speed and air drag increases fourfold. Twice as many air molecules collide with the surface twice as fast.

Because power = force × velocity, the power you will need to overcome air drag is proportional to the cube of the velocity. The problem with going faster on a bicycle is that if you want to double your speed, your power output will have to increase eight times. For example, doubling your power output while riding at 20 miles per hour will only speed up the bicycle to about 25 miles per hour. So to go faster on a bicycle, you have to either significantly increase your power or decrease your surface or profile drag. As you will see, it is easy to increase your speed by decreasing your air resistance, but it is certainly more expensive than training harder.

Decreasing Wind Resistance

There are three basic methods a cyclist can use to reduce wind resistance—drafting, decreasing the frontal area, and streamlining components. (In some competitions, such as the International Human-Powered Vehicle Championships, you can also add a fairing to your bicycle.)

Drafting

In order to be successful in bicycle racing you must know how to draft. It is also the least expensive method of reducing drag. Remember, the area behind a cyclist is a low-pressure area, so when someone passes you, jump in behind them and ride in their low-density space. This effect is called drafting and is more noticeable the closer you can ride to the cyclist in front of you. You must learn to ride comfortably within 6 to 10 inches of the back wheel in front of you. Table 10.1 shows the decrease in wind resistance as the distance between cyclists decreases. It takes

Table 10.1 The Effect of Drafting	
Wheel gap (feet)	Decrease in wind resistance (%)
0.5	−44
1.0	−42
2.0	−38
3.0	−34

months of practice to ensure that you can ride safely while drafting in a single pace line or in a pack of cyclists.

While drafting, a cyclist can consume from 30% to 40% less energy than those leading the pace line or pack. Research was recently completed by Dr. James Hagberg at the University of Florida that measured the reduced oxygen consumption (shown as energy savings in Figure 10.3) of cyclists who were drafting in various formations on a flat road.

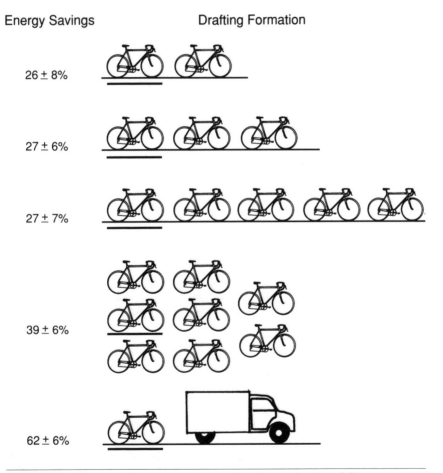

Energy Savings   **Drafting Formation**

26 ± 8%

27 ± 6%

27 ± 7%

39 ± 6%

62 ± 6%

Figure 10.3   Reduction in oxygen consumption due to drafting different numbers and formations of cyclists and a vehicle at 25 mph. The underlined cyclist represents the position of the test subject. All reductions are significant compared to riding alone at 25 mph.

Note. From "The Effect of Drafting and Aerodynamic Equipment on Energy Expenditure During Cycling" by James Hagberg and Steve McCole, 1990, *Cycling Science*, **2**, p. 20. Copyright 1990 by Cycling Science Publications. Adapted by permission.

Drafting at 20 miles per hour, $\dot{V}O_2$max was reduced by 18% as compared to riding alone. At 25 miles per hour, the benefit was considerably greater, saving 26%. You might think that drafting a line of riders would increase the benefit, but the study does not bear this out. Drafting one cyclist or a line of two or four resulted in about the same reduction in $\dot{V}O_2$max at 25 miles per hour.

With a group of eight riders there was a reduction of 39%—significantly more than drafting behind riders in a pace line. This was probably due to the greater frontal area of the leading riders and to the riders on the side deflecting more air. The greatest reduction in energy cost—62%—came from riding behind a truck. In fact, in 1985 John Howard went 152 miles per hour riding a bicycle behind a race car using a special enclosure at Bonneville Salt Flats.

The key to riding in a group is to take turns at the front, allowing yourself time to recover while riding in the draft of the other cyclists. Cyclists in a pace line can travel over 2 to 4 miles per hour faster than a lone rider over the same distance.

Decreasing Frontal Area

You are the real aerodynamic culprit on the bicycle. The human body causes about 70% of the total drag (the bicycle and wheels about 30%), so improvements to your riding position will be the most important factor.

Riding on the drops of the handlebars gives a more aerodynamic shape to the upper body and lowers your frontal area facing the wind. Compared to riding in a touring position, with your hands on the tops of the bars, the crouched racing position lowers wind resistance by more than 20%. This could mean over a 3-minute improvement in a 25-mile time trial.

Recently, work completed at the Texas A&M wind tunnel has shown that clip-on handlebars and other models of aerodynamic bars can reduce wind resistance at the typical racing speed of 25 miles per hour. Compared to "cowhorn" bars, aero bars will save from 1 to 2 minutes in a 25-mile time trial and increase your speed by .5 miles per hour, or more. See Chapter 9 about setting your position on the bike using clip-on bars.

The test showed that as the elbows were pulled progressively inward, the drag decreased. This is because when the elbows are spread, the turbulent wake from the arms spins off into space and energy is lost, but when the elbows are drawn inward, air flow around the body is smoother—in other words, the body is drafting in the slipstream of the arms. It takes time to get accustomed to riding with your elbows in, but faster time trials will be your reward.

Oran Nicks, director of the A&M wind tunnel, said that allowing your upper arms to stick out can really slow you down. "The drag on the two upper arms of a cyclist may closely approximate the amount of drag of the rest of the body's frontal area," said Nicks. The proper positioning for a rider has been detailed in the discussion of the biomechanical elements of cycling in chapter 9. Review pages 179-183 to ensure that you put yourself in position to get the greatest advantage of your aero bars.

Going With the Flow

Another major improvement you can make without greatly increasing your expense is to wear aerodynamically efficient clothing. Loose-fitting shorts and jerseys flutter in the wind and raise wind drag enormously. Covering long hair, wearing aerodynamic clothing, using disk wheels, and cleaning up your components may reduce drag as much as 5% to 10%. Table 10.2 shows how various components can shave time off a 25-mile time trial.

Table 10.2 Time Saved in a 25-Mile Time Trial Resulting From Aerodynamic Changes	
Item	**Time savings (s)**
Spoked aero wheels	39
Aero bicycle frame	42
Aero handlebars	30-60
Aero clothing	14-25
Aero water bottle	14
Aero helmet	20-25
Clipless pedals	9
Aero crank arms and chainrings	6
Two-disk wheels	70

The Smooth-Dressed Cyclist.   As shown in Figure 10.4, a tight, slick skinsuit allows the air to flow smoothly over the body. A Lycra suit can lower wind resistance by as much as 6% compared to a standard cycling jersey. A better fitting outfit can mean saving from 14 to 25 seconds in a 25-mile time trial.

Hairodynamics.   Wind tunnel tests have shown how much hair, in all forms, slows a cyclist down. Long or bushy hair has a disastrously

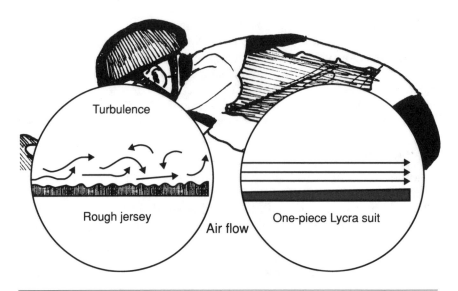

Figure 10.4 Skin material and airflow.

high wind drag. Because it will cover and confine hair, almost any helmet will lower drag. Have you ever seen a bearded cyclist do well? Perhaps we now know why.

Streamlined Helmets and Head Position.   Besides discovering that a cyclist without a helmet has a higher drag, testing has produced two interesting facts: First, the blunt, blocky helmets commonly used in racing today may be light and provide good cooling, but their wind resistance is much higher than a good aero model's. Standard helmets lose more than 1 second per mile to an aero helmet. Therefore, aero helmets should be used in short time trials of up to 1 hour, where cooling is not usually a problem.

Second, there is an optimum head position when wearing an aero helmet. With the head about halfway down (your face at about 45 degrees to the ground), the drag for streamlined helmets is minimal. Because the helmet is parallel to the airflow, and because the tail is off the back and leaves a clear passage for air flowing over the shoulders, the flow is smooth and the apparent aerodynamic position of the helmet is optimal.

Bicycle Frames.   When you are purchasing a bicycle frame, buy the smallest frame size that will give you proper riding position. Small frames weigh less and have lower wind resistance.

For many years now teardrop-shaped aero tubing has been popular with time trialists. Figure 10.5 shows why. In wind tunnel tests, certain

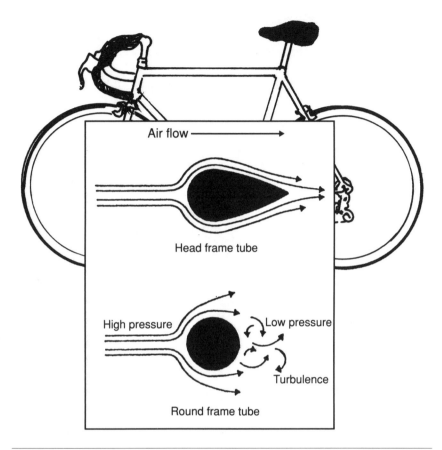

Figure 10.5   Teardrop frame sections reduce wind resistance by as much as 10%.

tubing specifications have proven best. Follow these specifications to select the proper tubing dimensions. If the length-to-width ratio of the tubing cross-section is 1.6:1, the tubing has a drag that is about 70% of standard, round bicycle tubing. If the length-to-width ratio is 2.4:1, the drag is about 38% of standard tubing.

Aero Wheels.   In the past few years at time trials and track events, instead of standard steel-spoke wheels with 28 to 36 spokes, we have seen the rise of disk and three-spoke wheels. Disk and tri-spoke wheels are not new. In 1891, the British publication *Cycling* described the disk wheel as "the greatest invention to affect the modern bicycle."

The main advantage of aero wheels is a reduction in wind drag, especially when wind conditions are calm, and this yields faster times. Here are some aerodynamic facts:

- Lens-shaped disks have a lower drag than flat-disk wheels.
- Smaller wheel diameters have a lower drag.
- Disk wheels or three-spoke composite aerodynamic wheels are better than any standard, round steel-spoke wheels.
- In a mild crosswind, the drag of disk wheels or three-spoke wheels actually decreases due to aerodynamic lift in the direction of the motion generated by the airfoil shape. This means that on a circuit course, with light wind, an aerodynamic wheel will be twice as effective as a standard wheel.
- Narrow tires have a much lower drag than wider tires.
- With standard, round steel-spoke wheels, aero rims are best. With standard flat rims, the turbulent flow over the trailing part of the rim creates an enormous cavity drag, whereas the flow over the trailing edge of an aero rim is smooth and the apparent aerodynamic cross-section is much less.
- With standard steel-spoke wheels, aero-bladed spokes are best. Round spokes produce very high drag. The fewer the spokes in the wheel, the lower the drag.

When you select your wheels, keep three things in mind:

1. Low weight is best.
2. The lower the spoke count, the better, as long as strength is adequate.
3. Most good disk wheels and tri-spoke wheels have about the same air drag.

Head-, Tail-, and Crosswinds.   By now you know—the wind affects both your cycling speed and your attitude. Winds speed up or slow down a cyclist by approximately half the wind speed; thus, a tailwind of 10 miles per hour increases your speed by about 5 miles per hour; a headwind of the same speed will slow you down by about the same speed. However, on an out-and-back time-trial course, your best time will only come on a calm day. A steady wind from any direction will result in a slower time on the course.

Wind tunnel studies show that only those winds that are within the trailing 160 degrees of an imaginary circle drawn around you on a bike will provide assistance; winds from anywhere in the remaining 200 degrees (including head- and crosswinds) will slow you down. Table 10.3 shows the effect on riding speed of riding a 20-mile time trial on an out-and-back course with a direct headwind and tailwind. There's not much you can do about this situation—draft on another cyclist and cherish the calm days.

On an out-and-back course you should try to put the same amount of energy on both legs of the course. Too often cyclists will go too hard into

Table 10.3 The Effect of Wind on Bicycle Speed on a 20-Mile Out-and-Back Course			
	Wind speed (mph)		
	0	**2**	**5**	**10**
Speed with wind (mph)	20.0	21.0	22.6	25.4
Speed against wind (mph)	20.0	19.0	17.5	15.2
Average speed (mph)	20.0	19.95	19.73	19.02
Time (min:s)	60:00	60:09	60:50	63:06

Table courtesy of Chester Kyle, PhD. Printed with permission.

a headwind, expend too much energy, and not have much left for the return. Using a heart rate monitor, you will be able to maintain a steady heart rate on both legs of the ride and can adapt your effort and speed accordingly.

Theoretically, if you use an aero bicycle on a racecourse with cross-winds, your time could be faster. When the wind is at an angle to your direction of travel, the airfoil shape of the wheels and frame develops some lift at right angles to the wind. Recently, Du Pont Corporation tested its tri-spoke wheel and a lens-shaped disk wheel in a wind tunnel and found that both wheels had dramatically lower drag in a wind that was 10 degrees to the plane of the wheels while spinning at 30 miles per hour (equivalent to a 5-mph crosswind at a 30-mph bicycle speed). At this wind angle, the wheels developed a forward thrust that resulted in lower drag.

Weight and Aerodynamics.   You might assume that heavier riders would encounter much greater wind resistance due to their increased surface area. But this isn't so. Although a heavier cyclist will have a larger weight or volume than a lighter cyclist, body surface area does not increase linearly as a function of weight or volume. The bigger you are, the lower your surface-to-volume ratio. On the average, surface area increases as a function of body weight only by a power of about .85. In other words, large people have more volume than small people have, but not that much more surface area.

When larger cyclists go into an aero position, they are able to reduce their frontal areas dramatically. So although they may indeed have larger surface areas than smaller cyclists, in the aero position the frontal areas they present to the wind may not be much greater than that of smaller cyclists. Assuming all other conditions are equal, the larger cyclists may have the advantage because their increased muscle mass can enable them to overcome the wind resistance better than smaller cyclists.

Does this mean bulking up is good? Not necessarily. There is more to riding effectively than overcoming wind resistance; there are biological economies involved too. Take acceleration, for example: Additional weight to yourself or the bike will increase inertia and therefore the time it takes you to get up to speed from a dead stop. This is time a track cyclist cannot afford.

Another good example is hill-climbing. If you look at the maximal oxygen consumption values of elite athletes, it is not unusual to find smaller cyclists with $\dot{V}O_2$max values of over 80 milliliters of oxygen per kilogram of body weight per minute, while larger cyclists will have values around 75 (with certain notable exceptions such as Miguel Indurain). Since the energy required to climb a hill depends on body weight, the cyclist with the highest aerobic capacity relative to body weight has the advantage. It's true that larger cyclists may have an advantage at high speeds on the flats, but as soon as air resistance is less important, every cyclist can at least hold his or her own.

What about the weight of specialized equipment? Chester Kyle, a bicycle aerodynamics expert, did research for the U.S. Cycling Team that showed that adding 6 to 7 pounds to a bicycle had little effect on the outcome of a 25-mile time trial on a flat course. So if the equipment you add to your bicycle is designed specifically to reduce aerodynamic drag, then the trade-off is in your favor, especially if you ride on flat or rolling courses. If a disk or tri-spoke wheel or aero handlebar is slightly heavier than nonaero equipment, choose the aero equipment every time. The savings from the decreased wind resistance outstrips the negative effect of a little extra weight.

Decreasing Rolling Resistance

Now that you know several ways to reduce wind resistance, let's shift gears and see how rolling resistance slows you down. If you understand the factors involved in rolling resistance, you will be able to choose properly fitted and sized low-profile tires for your wheels.

Tires and Rolling Resistance

The greater the area of tire contact with the road, the greater the rolling resistance and the more power you will have to put into the bicycle to propel it. The area of contact depends on the width of the tire, the tire's air pressure, and the weight of the rider and bicycle. A narrow-profile

Effect of Weight on the Energy Cost of Bicycling

For years cyclists have been spending hundreds of dollars to reduce the weight of their bicycles. Even Andy Hampsten switches from his Shimano dual-control lever to a down-tube shifter for his big chainring to reduce the overall weight of his bicycle. The logic is that a lighter bike will have faster acceleration, have lower rolling resistance, and require less effort on a climb. In simple mechanical terms, it takes more energy to average the same speed with additional weight. It's valid thinking, provided that frame, crank arm, and wheel stiffness can be maintained with a lighter machine. Here are some tips and information to consider if you are going to choose lightweight components and bikes to improve your performance.

The ability to accelerate quickly—whether starting, coming out of turns, or chasing down another rider—is critically important to racing cyclists. Adding weight to a bicycle will reduce the rate of acceleration, but how much it will do so depends in part on where the weight is located. Reducing so-called rotating weight, for example, is generally more important to performance than taking the same amount of weight off the frame or another static component.

Additional weight slows you down when you are climbing. The energy you need to move a weight up a hill increases in proportion to the weight being moved—in other words, the weight of you and your bicycle. Less weight on the bicycle means less weight to drag up the hill.

In addition, extra weight causes a greater deformation of the sidewalls and tire tread, thus increasing the rolling resistance. Rolling resistance increases in direct proportion to the weight that the wheel supports and is equal to about .3% to .5% of the load on the wheel. It can be reduced by carrying lighter loads on the wheel and using larger diameter wheels with smoother and thinner treads and stronger sidewalls.

Having light rotating components is even more important. To accelerate a wheel or pedal-and-shoe system, you need the kinetic energy of rotation as well as the kinetic energy of linear motion. For example, if the weight is mostly concentrated in the wheel's rim and tire, you will need almost twice the energy to

(continued)

Effect of Weight   *(continued)*

accelerate as for a nonrotating weight. In other words, 1 pound added to a wheel or pedal-and-shoe system is equivalent to nearly 2 pounds on the bicycle frame.

Work I completed with Ned Frederick of Exerter Research has shown that the addition of 250 grams to a pedal-and-shoe system, or 500 grams total for both feet (about the difference between the lightest and heaviest pedal-and-shoe systems on the market), would require an additional power output of 1.3% of rotational power at constant speeds on a level road. Climbing and accelerating would add about another .4%. The effect on rolling resistance would be about .07%. This means that the net effect of all factors of a realistic increase of 250 grams on each leg would be to increase the power required by a cyclist by approximately 1.5% to 1.7%. The increase could be significant in a long road race of 100 to 125 miles, with several hills and a sprint at the end. We estimated that 1.3% more oxygen would be needed for 200 watts of work (approximately 24 to 25 kilometers per hour) when an additional 125 grams is added to each pedal-and-shoe system (250 grams total).

The number of companies selling titanium replacement components is staggering. Cyclists are looking for ways to reduce energy cost or are foregoing purchasing new bikes in favor of lightening the bicycles they already own. Titanium parts can cost significantly more than standard components—from as little as $.35 to over $1 per gram. Changing from a traditional tubo style saddle, weighing over 375 grams, to a WaveFlo Elite, weighing a mere 210 grams, costs $.35 per gram. Switching from a standard steel-bottom bracket (210 to 270 grams) to a 139-gram Sampson Statics bottom bracket will cost you about $1.04 per gram. Upgrading from a 600-gram clipless pedal-and-cleat system to the Speedplay X/1 pedal-and-cleat system (224 grams) will cost you $1.33 per gram. Similar "savings" can be found in skewers, stems, seatposts, tires, rims, hubs, spokes, and bolts. The cost is high, but remember, for every pound of weight saved, that next hill will not seem as difficult to climb.

Increased weight retards cycling performance far less than aerodynamic drag does. Thus, for example, aerodynamic handlebars and disk wheels (which increase weight but reduce wind drag) in a 100-mile competition may be more beneficial than an ultra-light frame and wheels. Fortunately, lightweight disk and tri-spoke wheels can be built with the same shape and rigidity as the heavy disk wheels of a few years ago. There is no reason for a heavier frame or components unless stability and handling cannot be maintained otherwise.

tire with a high air pressure will have little surface area in contact with the road, and its rolling resistance will be 25% to 35% less than that of a low-pressure touring tire.

A good tubular tire for racing can weigh as little as 4.5 to 5 ounces (130 to 140 grams) and hold up to 220 pounds of pressure (15 atmospheres). These tires are very narrow (16 to 18 millimeters), have a smooth thread, and are constructed with thin tubes and sidewalls. They are made of nylon, silk, or Kevlar.

Unlike wind resistance, which increases at the square of the velocity of the bicycle and rider, the rolling resistance of bicycle tires is nearly constant regardless of speed. Thus, as your speed increases, rolling resistance becomes less important than wind resistance.

Another factor to consider is the diameter of the wheel. As wheel size decreases, the tire must deform progressively more to support you and the bike; consequently, smaller wheels have a higher rolling resistance. This effect will be increased on rough roads, because the wheel will require a larger propulsive force to get over the bumps than would a larger wheel. But if you select a high-quality tire with a lighter, smaller disk wheel, you may save time, because the reduction in wind resistance will outweigh the increased rolling resistance—as long as the road is not too rough.

In addition, remember these points when trying to decrease rolling resistance:

- Correctly match the tire and rim size. Incorrectly matched tires and rims will increase rolling resistance. Even a few millimeters can make a big difference.
- Glue your tubular tire properly. An improperly glued tubular tire will cause constant moving of the tire on the rim and will increase rolling resistance.
- A tire thread that is smooth and thin will have less rolling resistance.

Weight and Rolling Resistance

Most cyclists only think about the weight factor when they are climbing a hill. But the weight of the bicycle and yourself can also affect rolling resistance and acceleration. The one place where extra weight is an advantage is on the downhills.

Increased weight on the tire will increase rolling resistance. Rolling resistance increases in direct proportion to the weight that is supported by the wheel and is equal to about .3% to .5% of the weight on the wheel. A light, narrow tire with high air pressure and a light load will have far less resistance than a standard touring tire on a racing bike.

Remember, rolling resistance is not affected by speed. The drag caused by wind resistance begins to exceed rolling resistance once your speed reaches about 10 miles per hour.

The Final Spin

In this chapter we discussed many aerodynamic and mechanical factors that can improve your performance. Let's review some key points that you, using a conventional bicycle, can do to improve your performance aerodynamically.

1. Streamline your body. Wear a one-piece suit, an aerodynamic helmet, and shoe covers. An aerodynamic helmet can reduce your cycling time by about 15 seconds in a 25-mile time trial.
2. Clean up your bike. Use aero tubing and components. Conceal brake cables. Use disk wheels with narrow-profile tires.
3. Learn how to draft, or ride closely behind other cyclists. This technique may reduce energy cost by up to 27% if you ride at distances closer than 6 inches to the wheel in front of you. When possible, ride in the middle of a group; this may reduce oxygen cost as much as 40%.
4. Reduce your frontal area. Use aero bars and learn how to ride comfortably in a time-trial position for long periods of time.

It is the engine within your body and the skills you gain through training that are most important to a winning performance. But if the race is close, aerodynamic equipment and position may make the difference.

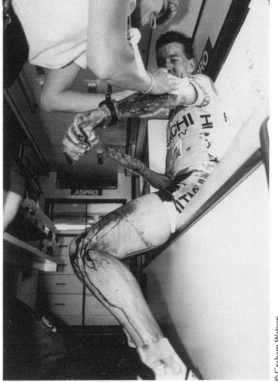

© Graham Watson

Addressing Your Aches and Injuries

I have had many injuries in my career, most of them the result of a spectacular crash. But those kinds of injuries usually heal quickly. It's the sneaky ones that you have to watch for.

—*Davis Phinney*

Few cyclists get through their careers without falling off their bikes and getting "road rash." They also risk fractures, contusions, sprains, and a variety of overuse injuries, though many of these injuries are preventable through skillful riding, correct position on the bike, and bicycle maintenance.

Some cyclists are challenged by personal conditions such as asthma or diabetes. All of us fall prey to illnesses, such as colds and flus, which we may or may not be able to ride through. And we all encounter environmental conditions that can be hazardous to our health.

This chapter will focus first on injuries. Bicycling injuries can be classified by the mechanisms that caused them. Some are caused by crashing, others by overuse and errors in training. We will explore the injuries that you'll most likely experience and how they may be prevented and treated. Later, we will talk about the possibilities of riding through some illnesses and adverse environmental conditions.

Crash-Related Injuries

Two studies in the medical literature have reported on the type and number of injuries experienced by competitive cyclists while racing and training. Both papers point to abrasions as the number-one injury experienced by cyclists.

One study reported on the over 600 participants in the Ore-Ida Women's Challenge bicycle stage race from 1984 to 1991. Of all the injuries experienced by the cyclists, over 72% that occurred in the race were abrasions. Drs. Michael Gibson and Richard King, physicians for the race, reported contusions and lacerations as the second and third most experienced injuries in the race. Most of the athletes returned to competition the day after being treated in the mobile clinic after the race.

In the early 1980s, Thomas Bohlman reported that most of the superficial injuries he observed were abrasions and that 65% of the abrasions were minor and occurred to the hip, elbow, and knee—in fact, 20% of all abrasions were to the hip, the first impact point in most injuries. The abrasions occurred in falls caused mostly by flat tires or colliding with other cyclists.

Both studies reported that the incidence of head injuries were reduced with the use of approved helmets. Each year in the Ore-Ida Challenge, crashes resulted in many broken helmets, but only two serious head injuries occurred in those 8 years of the race. Although Bohlman's study was completed before approved Snell and/or American National Standards Institute (ANSI) helmets were required, he still showed that a "hard shell" helmet may have helped prevent head injuries.

Road Rash

You're on a fast descent and as you corner, your wheels slip out from under you. Several layers of skin are left on the asphalt. Abrasions, the most common cycling injury, are wounds that break the skin's protective barrier, damaging the soft tissue underneath and opening the way for invading bacteria.

If not taken care of properly, what may seem an insignificant injury can lead to infection and fever. These complications from abrasions, the result of improper and delayed wound care and management, can result in several days off your bike. All abrasions, even the most superficial, must be considered potential contaminations and must be cleansed and dressed properly.

First-Aid for Road Rash. Numerous products and treatments are available to protect you from infection, promote healing, and permit you to resume cycling and exercise as soon as possible after an accident. This wound-care regimen outlines how to use the several products available at your local drugstore to care for abrasions.

1. Clean the wound thoroughly. Several products are available to supplement or substitute for soap and water. Hydrogen peroxide, an old standby, not only cleans but also kills germs. Any visible foreign particles should be cleaned from the wound.
2. Apply dressings in order to

   - protect the wound from germs and infection,
   - provide a moist environment to speed healing,
   - provide pressure and compression to the wound (this limits or reduces swelling while increasing drainage),
   - protect the wound from further injury that might cause pain or disrupt the healing process, and
   - prevent movement of the wound that might interfere with healing, especially on arms and legs.

Many athletes use a topical antibiotic ointment and a nonadhering dressing. These ointments are a shotgun approach to the prevention of infection in abrasions. They contain two or three different antibiotics, each effective against a different range of bacteria, to make sure nothing grows in the wound except skin.

The antibiotic ointment should be covered with a nonadhering dressing and held in place by tape or a "fishnet" sleeve. This sleeve (a tubular netting) will hold the dressing in place and still allow the extremities free range of movement. The netting also will not cause excessive heat buildup in hot weather. If these products are not carried by your local drugstore, inquire at a medical supply company for them.

High-Tech Dressing for Abrasions.   Welcome to the world of high-tech first-aid and semipermeable dressings, made of hydrogel (a 96% water substance) wrapped in a porous plastic. These dressings are available under the brand names Second Skin, DuoDerm, Tegaderm, Bioclusive, and Op-Site. They encourage a moist wound environment in which scab development is exhibited and epidermal (skin) cells form rapidly. Several clinical studies have shown that when these products are applied to a clean wound and changes in dressing are made at 24-hour intervals or as needed, most abrasions will heal in 4 to 8 days.

As with using antibiotic ointments, you should monitor the wound and change the dressing when it appears to be dirty or no longer adheres properly. Once again, tape or fishnet can be used to hold the semipermeable dressing in place. Removal should be done carefully to eliminate potential reinjury of the newly formed skin. The wound can be rinsed with saline or clean, cool water, but it is not necessary to remove all traces of the dressing material.

These procedures should suffice in most cases, but if a fever develops and the wound feels warm to the touch, or the borders turn pinkish or red, consult a physician to check for infection. By using proper cleaning and wound management you can take care of the most common injury in cycling.

Body Damage

If injury results from a hard fall, you may want to reduce potential swelling by cooling the injured area as quickly as possible. Applying a cold compress immediately can reduce swelling and inflammation, minimize pain, and reduce bleeding under the skin, which causes bruising. For best results, cold must be applied before swelling occurs. If you can get the ice on quickly, it can make a big difference. Most of us do not carry ice to events, and if we do, it has usually melted by the time we need it for emergencies. Now there is help, however—instant cold packs are available from several manufacturers.

Cold packs contain an inner bag of blue liquid that, when broken and mixed with the water crystals, sets up a chemical reaction to produce instant cold. So you can carry this in your race-day accessories bag or waist pack with your other first-aid equipment and have the equivalent of an ice pack, even when you are miles from an ice cooler.

The ice pack should be applied after a wound is cleaned and dressed and the dressing held in place with a compression or stretch-type bandage (this type of wrap will provide compression, which will reduce the swelling).

Practical Guidelines
for Combating Crash-Related Injuries

Not knowing how to elude dangerous situations and making tactical errors are leading factors in cycling accidents. Exhaustion, leading to poor concentration and slow reflexes, also plays an important role. This particularly applies to riding in large packs. Here are some points to remember to help prevent serious crash-related injuries.

1. Experienced cyclists practice tumbling exercises in the off-season. When they fall, they try to roll with the fall, protecting the head with the arms, so the impact will be taken on the back and shoulders.
2. Always wear gloves while cycling to protect the palms of your hands when you fall with your hands outstretched.
3. Except in extremely hot weather, wear two layers of clothing on your upper body. In a fall, the outer layer will slide over the inner layer, protecting your skin from greater abrasions by dissipating some of the friction.

Riding in a pack, knowing how to fall, keeping your bicycle in top mechanical condition, and—most importantly—wearing your helmet will reduce the frequency and severity of crash-related injuries. The notion that the effort spent preventing injuries is more rewarding than the energy spent curing them makes good sense, and not just for cyclists.

Why Wear a Helmet?

More and more cyclists are wisely buying bicycle helmets to protect their most valuable asset—their brains. If you are one of the few still not convinced you need a helmet, take a look at Table 11.1.

Even careful cyclists crash—every 4,500 miles on the average. Nobody expects to fall, but in time, you will crash too. When you do, it is essential to have proper head protection, because 75% of the over 1,400 annual deaths from bicycle accidents in the United States are due to head injury. Road rash and broken bones heal; major injuries to the brain may not. There are other benefits to wearing a helmet:

-   *Visibility*. You are easier to see with a colorful headpiece on, especially at dusk, in rain or fog, or after dark. Putting retro-reflective trim tape on the helmet or wearing a neon helmet cover makes you even more visible.
-   *Image*. When you wear a helmet, motorists will expect you to ride correctly, because you will look like you know what you are doing.

Table 11.1   Do You Really Need a Helmet? Consider These Facts:

1. When you crash, you are likely to land on your shoulders and head, because in most circumstances, the top tube and handlebars will trap your legs. Many people think they will be able to tuck their heads and roll, but unless you practice this maneuver a lot, do not expect to do it instinctively.
2. A drop of only 1 or 2 feet at very slow speeds can cause serious brain damage. Broken bones will heal; a scrambled brain will not. Your brain, the most important part of your body, is very sensitive to impact even at slow speeds.
3. You *will* crash on your bicycle. The odds are that it will happen, and the more you ride your bike, the sooner it will happen.
4. Helmets are needed even in quiet, rural areas: Car-bike collisions cause only 12% of all casualties to cyclists; other dangers are still present on every ride you take.
5. On any ride you take you may catch a wheel in a crack, skid on gravel, hit a pothole or drain grate, or collide with another bike, vehicle, or dog.

- *Climate Protection.* A helmet will help keep your head dry in rain or snow. If you do have to cycle in bad weather, a helmet will make your riding much more enjoyable.
- *Emergency Data.* Write your name, address, phone number, and any medical condition on a piece of tape inside your helmet. This will save you from transferring this information from jersey pocket to jersey pocket.

Pick a helmet that looks good on you. If you don't like the way it fits, the color, or the shape, you probably will not wear it. With the variety of available colors, shapes, and designs—even Lycra covers to match your clothing—there is no reason for not wearing a helmet. No cyclist I know has ever regretted buying a helmet, but several crash victims I know have regretted not having one on.

Hot Heads

Many cyclists wonder if wearing helmets can lead to overheating. Several years ago Dr. Carl Gisolfi conducted a study at the University of Iowa to answer this question. Cyclists rode a bicycle ergometer at about 70% of their maximums in an environmental chamber for 2 hours. In two trials, the cyclists wore either no helmet or a hard-shell helmet in over

Helmets for Heady Cyclists

Evidently, a lot of people are still unaware of the protective abilities of the helmets available on today's market and of what makes a helmet good. A bicycle helmet is designed to prevent penetration and to absorb the impact of a fall. Most of the helmets with smooth outer shells provide the added advantage of distributing the impact over their entire surface rather than allowing an intense blow to impact at a single spot. Underneath, an expanded polystyrene (Styrofoam) liner absorbs and reduces the impact distributed by the shell. The impact is absorbed as the inner liner is crushed and, in the case of a really severe impact, as the outer shell is crushed as well.

In 1986, a small company named Giro Sports Design took the market by surprise and manufactured a helmet that weighed 7.5 ounces and passed both ANSI and Snell standards. It eliminated the hard shell from the helmet, and at first, these helmets had the potential to break apart on impact and required a Lycra cover to hold them together after impact.

Recently, some manufacturers have added features to improve the impact performance of their helmets while still maintaining the soft shells. Several companies use a layer of nylon mesh molded into the foam to keep the helmet from coming apart during a crash. Giro helmets and Bell helmets offer an internal reinforcement ring molded into the foam to serve the same function. And some companies use a dual-density process that puts higher density foam outside the helmet and a lower density foam inside.

A new type of helmet has entered the market. These helmets use an outer microshell that is lighter and thinner than the polycarbonate or plastic material of the standard hard-shell helmet. They offer the advantages of the hard shell in a lightweight format. All major helmet manufacturers offer microshell helmets. They feel the 7- to 9.5-ounce helmet has greater overall integrity than the pure soft-shell helmet.

The true test of a helmet is how much impact it can absorb and, thereby, keep from the head. The level of impact is measured in "g" forces and is determined by placing an instrumented head form, the size and weight of the human head, inside the helmet and dropping it on an anvil from a specified height. The most the

(continued)

Helmets   *(continued)*

human head can stand is 400 gs for a very short period of time. The higher the drop and the lower the number of g's transmitted to the head, the better the helmet.

Currently there are two standards used in the United States to qualify the effectiveness of helmets in impact tests. The American National Standards Institute's (ANSI) Z 90.4 standard requires that a helmet dropped on both round and flat anvils from 1 meter not exceed 300 g's. The second and tougher standard, known as the Snell standard, requires a drop from 1.2 meters on the round anvil and from 2 meters on the flat anvil to yield the same g results on impact. Meeting the Snell standard usually requires a thicker or firmer Styrofoam liner. A helmet that does not have an ANSI or Snell sticker attached to the inside does not pass the standards and offers only an illusion of safety.

Protection also depends on a snug fit and secure straps. Most helmets come with sizing pads of various thicknesses, but many don't have adequate buckles and straps. Again, check for an ANSI or Snell sticker in your helmet. Other things being close to equal, you might do well to choose a helmet based on whether you can make it fit comfortably and snugly and whether the straps and buckle seem strong.

Adjusting the straps is critical and not that easy. When the helmet is properly positioned on your head, you should not be able to take it off or displace it without unfastening the buckle. Just making the chin straps snug won't always prevent the helmet from rolling forward on your head. The rear straps must also be adjusted properly. About half of your forehead should be showing, and the chin strap should be back toward your Adam's apple.

90-degree Fahrenheit temperatures. Head, skin, and rectal temperatures were recorded at regular intervals. Results showed no statistical differences in external or internal body heat, heart rate, or sweat production between the two rides. The participants described the exercise as similar to a 50-mile race. None of them felt the helmets were causing them to overheat.

But even after this information was made public, many cyclists still questioned the data, because they believed that riding under real road conditions would yield different results. Research conducted for Giro by Professor Bonnoit, director of the Laboratory of Biomechanical Applications at the University of Medicine in Marseille, France, answered cyclists who wanted data showing the effects of riding on the road with and without a hard-shell helmet.

Dr. Bonnoit's research showed a Giro Air Attack helmet to be cooler than the traditional hairnet helmet by as much as 14 degrees Fahrenheit. These results were derived from trials performed by two cyclists climbing Mount Ventoux, one of the hardest and most exposed climbs in the Tour de France. Data were gathered on 2 consecutive days in June of 1991. On Day 1, Cyclist A wore an Air Attack, and Cyclist B wore a hairnet helmet. On Day 2, Cyclist A wore the hairnet helmet; Cyclist B, the Air Attack. Sensors were attached to each cyclist at six locations on the head to measure temperature both where the head was exposed to air flow and where the head was covered by the helmet.

Bonnoit and his team believe the amazing cooling effect of the Air Attack has two components. First, its expanded polystyrene foam acts as an insulator, protecting the head from the heat of the sun. Second, its unique ventilation system pulls air through the helmet and over the head, cooling the head down four times faster than a hairnet helmet. "With an expanded polystyrene helmet, you have a unique combination of insulation and ventilation that we believe is not available with a hairnet helmet, cap, or bare head," says Professor Bonnoit. "The helmet's ability to keep body temperature lower in hot conditions is remarkable."

Remember though, you must train in your helmet in order to acclimate yourself to the heat. Otherwise you'll experience discomfort during races or long tours. You must adapt to the helmet in training, not just put it on for an event.

Overuse Injuries

Crashing results in some gory, dramatic, traumatic, and painful injuries. No matter what, you can't prepare for every accident—that's why they're called accidents. But there is a second type of injury whose prevention is almost totally under your control. These are injuries that result from training and riding poorly or training and riding too much. Saddle sores, painful joints, muscle soreness, and burnout result from the use and abuse that serious cyclists commonly inflict upon themselves. These injuries creep up on you much more slowly than that irresponsible cyclist who causes the peleton to crash, but these delayed-onset injuries may be as painful as crash-related mishaps and, worse, can keep you off the bike every bit as long.

Injuries may be a fact of life for you as a serious cyclist, but that doesn't mean you have to put up with more than your fair share of them. Being in condition, maintaining a correct position on the bike, and wearing protective clothing will prevent many overuse injuries and illnesses.

Saddle Soreness

In the 1990 Tour de France, Greg LeMond was forced to adjust his riding style (and not enter any races after the Tour) because of saddle sores. What is a saddle sore? It's a crotch infection that usually starts as a small pimple. In most cases, a saddle sore's life span is just a few days. But during this time it may become hard, red, inflamed, and painful. In some cases, the infection doesn't disappear; it spreads to adjacent tissue and creates larger sores, boils, or cysts that affect more tissue and may even require surgery. It can happen to the best of cyclists. In 1991, Jean Francois Bernard had to drop out of the Tour de France and then had to have surgery to remove a cyst.

To prevent saddle sores, the part of your anatomy that everything in cycling "hinges on," the groin area, needs to be kept clean and as free from friction as possible. Saddle sores usually occur from irritation or chafing of the hair follicles. The predominant bacterial infection, staphylococcus, is forced into the skin by pressure or irritation from the saddle, and a saddle sore is born.

Because chafing and sweating are major causes of saddle sores, every effort should be made to minimize them. First, dress right. To control chafing and cushion your posterior, wear chamois- or synthetic-lined cycling shorts without underwear. Keep the leather chamois material soft by rubbing in a washable lubricant such as A&D Ointment or Noxzema Skin Cream before every ride. Wash the shorts often. In fact, buy two or more pairs so that you always have a fresh pair.

These days many companies offer more high-tech and synthetic liners. You will hear terms such as Suedemark II (Hind), Microsuede (Cannondale), and Ultrasuede (Pearl Izumi), among others. Combined with other fabrics (for example, terry or polypropylene) they create a viable combination of performance, durability, and ease of care. Pearl Izumi and Hind are two companies that also offer shorts designed especially for women, with better fit and chamois design.

Second, wash regularly with an antibacterial soap. Steward Pharmaceutical's Hibiclens and Purdue Frederic's Betadine Surgical Scrub work well and are available at drugstores without a prescription. Regular use of these products will reduce bacterial growth and the chance of infection. Ordinary soap will not work as well, because it does not contain any antibacterial agents. And after your showers use talcum powder or baby powder to control moisture.

Third, experiment with different saddles. There are many saddle brands and configurations on the market: gel, leather, and nylon. Find one that fits you best—one that is wide enough to let the bones of your rear end (ischial tuberocities) make proper contact with the rear of the saddle, but is not too wide. A wide saddle will cause chafing, which could lead to bacterial infection. A good saddle should be stable enough to keep your body still, yet flexible enough to absorb large road shocks.

If early symptoms of saddle sores occur, such as redness or soreness, consider changing your saddle. You may have to try several types to find one that is comfortable for you. As with running shoes, some brands of saddles will fit you better than others. Sitting farther back on the saddle will distribute more surface area over the saddle, and lowering your handlebars a little will help reduce the pressure on your seat by shifting more weight to your arms and hands.

Fourth, ride smart. Stand up on the bike periodically and stretch out the posterior muscles for 15 to 20 seconds every half hour. It's also wise to rise out of the saddle to go over railroad tracks and rough patches.

If all else fails and you still develop a saddle sore, don't cover it with salves or ointments because they have a tendency to keep the bacteria alive. Use the antiseptic, Hibiclens, mentioned before. And take a few days off the bike.

If quick treatment doesn't result in a quick cure, consult your physician or a dermatologist. They may recommend a broad-base oral antibiotic, such as erythromycin, and topical antibiotics. Recently, some cyclists have experimented with Acutane (available through prescription only), which is a synthetic form of vitamin A and has proven effective in the treatment of saddle sores and boils. But if you are pregnant, you should avoid Acutane.

Like all great cyclists, you will have to deal with saddle sores sometime, but cleanliness, proper clothing and equipment, and skin care may be all that is needed to keep you in the race, and not on the sidelines sitting uncomfortably in a comfortable chair.

Neck Soreness

Despite its therapeutic value, cycling is hard on the muscles of the neck. The primary muscle used to support the neck and head during cycling is the trapezius. Several other muscles give minor support and help turn and tilt the head; among them are the sternocleidomastoid and levator scapulae.

These muscles get sore because you have to hold your neck in an extended position for long periods. Numerous contestants in the annual transcontinental Race Across America have had to drop out because of, or have had their times affected by, unbearable neck pain. In fact, several years ago, race winner Paul Solon was not able to complete the race in less than 8 days because he lost over 9 hours of riding time due to a painful neck that made it impossible for him to see down the road.

His support crew remedied the situation by devising a Rube Goldberg–type harness: Cloth was wrapped around his forehead and behind his ears and was attached to a bungie cord that ran down his back and fastened to a belt around his waist. During the last few days of the race, and with numerous stops to adjust the harness, Solon crossed the line in New York City in 8 days, 8 hours, and 45 minutes. This set a new record, breaking the old one by over 1 hour.

Most of us will never reach this point of fatigue in our long-distance riding. If you practice proper conditioning, the right position on the bike, and various stretching exercises, you should not have such neck problems.

It is always wise to check your bike to see if there are any adjustments you can make to avoid developing a sore neck.

The position of the handlebars and length of the stem are key to establishing head and neck position and comfort while riding. If the stem is too long, you will probably have to flex your neck upward at an extreme angle to see the road ahead. Riding mile after mile in this overextended position will quickly lead to fatigue in your neck muscles, then to severe local pain, and possibly to headaches. Changing to a shorter stem, raising the stem, and switching to handlebars with less drop are all things you can do to correct your position.

Your position is correct if, when you are riding, your hands are in the drops of the bars and your view of the front wheel axle is blocked by the handlebars. If the wheel axle appears to be in front of the handlebars, you need a shorter stem. If the axle appears to fall behind the bars, you need a longer stem. I have heard other people recommend that the saddle of the bike be moved forward or back to correct this position, but I caution you against this adjustment: It will change the angle of your knee over the pedal axle and throw off your pedal stroke. Your best bet is to purchase the proper stem length. In extreme cases, if your torso and arm length cannot be accommodated to the frame you are currently riding, you may have to consider purchasing a new frame.

Never keep your head in a static position for an extended period of riding, and don't scrunch your shoulders up and pull your head down into your shoulder cavity. Lots of cyclists have this turtle look.

You should tilt your head from side to side on occasion. This will help to relax the trapezius and stretch out the muscles on either side of the neck. When you come to an occasional stop on your rides, say for a stop sign or stoplight, let your head drop down to your chest, then rotate it around in circles; you will feel the tension disappear. Repeat the rotation in the opposite direction. You might also try rubbing your neck with your hands to relieve some of the tension. Relax. Let the blood flow to your neck muscles.

Remember to ride with your elbows flexed during long stages or on rough terrain. Riding with locked arms will transmit the road shock through your arms into your neck and upper back and cause pain and fatigue. Tensing your arms and upper body will not add anything to your performance but will lead to soreness and actually cost you more energy. Your arms should be relaxed, not stiff and tight. Learning to relax your upper body and arms takes some practice. When you ride hard, try not to tense your upper body, and use only your legs. Changing hand positions on the bars frequently, wearing padded gloves, and riding with the elbows flexed will help absorb road shock.

One of the limiting factors of lowering your upper body into the more aerodynamic position required by aero and clip-on handlebars has to do with your ability to flex your neck so that you can see the road properly. In most cases, when you switch to aero bars you will have to switch to a new stem too. These bars require more vertical stem extension to maintain proper back flexion and weight transfer. To obtain maximum flexibility for the more aerodynamic position you will have to lower the stem over a period of time as you adjust to the position. This may take several weeks of lowering the stem about 1 millimeter a week.

Finally, the key to keeping your neck healthy in cold weather is to keep the neck warm. This will prevent sore throats and breathing problems. A turtleneck undershirt or a high-necked warm-up or jersey will do a fine job of stopping the wind and keeping in the warmth. Cyclists often wonder if it is possible to damage their lungs by breathing in cold air. The truth is that even during cold weather, exercise will still markedly increase your body temperature. The extra heat will warm the air that you breathe. For example, air taken in at –40 degrees Fahrenheit will be warmed more than 100 degrees before it reaches your lungs.

If you find that breathing cold air makes you feel uncomfortable, wear a face mask that fits over your mouth and nose. Spenco and 3-M make masks that are porous enough but still help you maintain heat and moisture. Try to maintain breathing through your nose *and* your mouth. Although air is warmed more through your nose than through your mouth, your nose alone will not permit enough air through to supply your oxygen needs during cycling.

Back Pain

Your workouts were going great until you decided to train for your first long stage race. You had been putting in between 100 and 150 miles per week. This mileage made you feel good, kept your weight down, and gave you defined calves and rock-hard quads. When you decided to train for the stage race, though, things started to fall apart.

Maybe you were too eager, or maybe it was the excessive mileage or the hard intervals that led to your injury. Could it have been the hill work or improper position on the bike? It started as a dull ache in your lower back, but not in any one place you could put your finger on exactly. Soon, riding your bike any distance was painful, and it began to bother you even as you sat at your desk.

Most of the low-back discomfort you experienced is not serious and reflects only minor injury, caused by overexertion or improper position on the bike. Pain occurs when specific nerve endings are abnormally stimulated to send messages up the spinal cord to the brain. Because the bones, discs, ligaments, and muscles of your back are supplied by many nerve endings, there are various and often interrelated conditions that can cause back pain. Frequently, the muscles, receiving your brain's message of pain, try to protect your back and go into spasm to hold your back immobile and quiet. In addition to the most common causes— improper position and physical overuse—the stress, fatigue, and anxieties of daily life can significantly increase low-back pain.

Before we go too far, let's make sure you understand that cycling is good exercise for your back when you ride correctly. The exercise of cycling supplies blood and nutrients to the muscles, discs, and ligaments of the back. But, as with all exercise, it must be performed properly and in moderation.

Although the muscles of the back may not be directly involved in pedaling, they help stabilize your body on the bike and increase the energy transfer from the hip and leg muscles to the pedals. The primary muscle groups of the lower back and trunk that affect cycling are the latissimus dorsi, erector spinae, and the external oblique muscles. The muscles of the upper back used in cycling are the trapezius, teres major and minor, and the infraspinatus.

In order to get the most from these muscle groups, you must be set up properly on the bike. Proper position will ensure that you use the large muscles of your trunk to your advantage.

Most back problems arise from riding in a position that is too low or from excessive time with your hands on the drops of the bars. Dropped handlebars give you the advantage of being able to switch hand positions during long rides. Change positions between the drops, brake levers, and the tops every few miles or as the terrain warrants. Most of the time your hands should be on the tops of the bars. Changing hand positions will allow you to use your back muscles differently, stretch your muscles, and vary the flexion of your back while you are riding.

Take advantage of your dropped handlebars in order to gain the most power and leverage from your back muscles. During a long climb, always ride seated and with your hands on the tops of the bars, a position that facilitates breathing under a heavy workload. Slide slightly back in the saddle and use your lower and upper back muscles to put more power into each pedal stroke, which will also allow you to use larger gears. Periodically, on the longer and steeper climbs, get out of the saddle, wrap your hands around the brake hoods, and use your arms, body weight, and back muscles to turn the pedals over. This will allow you to use the back muscles a little bit differently and to stretch them out so they do not become too stiff or fatigued on the long climb. Even on flat ground, getting out of the saddle occasionally relieves stiffness and lets you stretch the back and leg muscles.

There are other simple precautions that will reduce your risk of back pain caused by cycling. Be sure you do not make any abrupt changes in your training program, your position, your equipment, or the terrain you train on. Increase your mileage, speed, and gearing gradually. If you add a hilly route to your program, take it easy the first few times, and let your body get used to the stresses of hill-climbing. Let your back muscles gradually adapt to their increased workload. The same goes for time trialing: Increase your distance and intensity gradually.

Make stretching a part of your program, and add specific exercises to your routine if you experience pain or stiffness in your lower back. Tight back muscles limit your range of motion and make you more prone to pulls and strains. Strengthen your abdominal muscles; weak abdominals allow the lower back to curve inward, increasing the strain on the muscles, ligaments, and discs of the lower back. By strengthening and stretching your torso—back and front—you will improve your overall fitness and performance.

If you experience back pain that does not subside after stretching or correcting your bike position, slow down and take 1 or 2 weeks off the bike. It is time to seek the advice and care of a sports medicine specialist. Most specialists will first prescribe a program of rest, stretching, and abdominal exercises. If the suspected cause of the back pain is bone-related—such as compression, spondylolysis, spondylolisthesis, or a herniated disc—more extensive and prolonged methods of treatment will be prescribed.

Finally, before riding in cold or cool weather, make sure your jersey or warm-up top is long enough in the back to cover you fully. Keeping your lower back area warm will make you less susceptible to muscle or ligament strains. As is true of most cycling injuries, preventing back injuries is preferable to experiencing and treating them and is certainly more conducive to a longer and less painful cycling career.

Muscle Soreness

"My legs and shoulders feel so heavy I have a hard time lifting them. I'm going to take the day off." These are common words after early season intervals or a hard session in the weight room. Why? What makes muscles sore and stiff? How could your body let you down like this? You, who worked out in the gym several hours each week and had plenty of miles in your legs, and who up to this point believed your body could take any punishment, should not feel any pain.

Whatever you did, you did too much, too soon. Now it's the day after, and you have athletic hangover. You are experiencing muscle soreness.

Causes of your postexercise soreness may vary from the overuse of large muscle groups to minor strains in your individual muscle fibers. Despite what your high school coach may have told you, the culprit is not lactic acid. Lactic acid buildup has been blamed for prolonged muscle fatigue and discomfort, but this concept is not widely accepted today.

Lactic acid is produced during intense exercise when the oxygen demands of the muscle fibers increase beyond what the blood is capable of delivering. To produce the energy it needs, the body begins another process, which works in the absence of oxygen. Lactic acid, a by-product of this process, locks up your muscles and, because it is an acid, causes them to experience that burning sensation.

But lactic acid is completely washed out of your muscles within 30 to 60 minutes after you finish riding. Muscle soreness does not show up until 24 to 36 hours later, so scientists have been racking their brains to come up with another explanation. The most popular theory today is that when you overdo your cycling, skiing, or weight workouts, you cause microtrauma to the muscle fibers. You do localized damage to the muscle-fiber membranes and contracile elements.

Over the 24 hours, the damaged muscle becomes swollen and sore. Chemical irritants are released from the damaged muscle fibers, and they stimulate pain receptors in the muscle. In addition, your workout has increased the blood flow to the worked muscle, causing it to swell and exert enough pressure to stimulate pain receptors. Instead of having free-moving muscle fibers the next morning, you have fibers that are fatigued and swollen and have microscopic tears.

Whatever the precise mechanism, current scientific research points toward muscle damage as the culprit of muscle soreness. The nerves in your muscles perceive this abnormal state and send messages of pain to your brain when you start to move around the next morning. By moving the sore muscles, you gradually begin to restore them to a normal state, but you will not be able to exercise to your full potential because the damaged muscles have lost some strength.

Typical recommendations for short-term treatments include stretching, applying sports balms or creams, submersing in a hot tub, or spending time in a sauna. Some athletes also use aspirin and anti-inflammatory medication to reduce the pain and swelling.

The cure for chronic muscle soreness is relatively simple: If you gradually increase the strength and endurance of your muscles, and if you stretch and warm up properly before engaging in activity, your muscles will not get as sore. Cycling, running, and swimming call upon muscles that are not used regularly in your daily life. It all comes down to specificity of training, in which your muscles, tendons, and ligaments adapt to a particular sport, activity, or movement pattern over a period of time.

In addition, as we grow older our muscles and surrounding tissues have less elasticity, so we tend to feel soreness and tightness more quickly than we did in high school. An individual who stays in shape throughout the year should be able to exercise with minimal muscular soreness—even when he reaches his 30s and 40s. After a very hard day on the bike or in the weight room, he may feel somewhat stiff, but after a little stretching and warm-up activity this feeling should go away.

Sore muscles are usually damaged muscles. As with any injury, sore muscles must be given time to heal. This may mean a few days of easy cycling or other light activity. Then you can begin to push harder again. But don't go too hard or too fast, because you'll wind up back on the sidelines again. Remember, the best way to prevent or reduce muscle damage is prior physical conditioning.

Knee Pain

Knee pain is one of the most common overuse injuries cyclists experience. Stephen Roche and Bernard Hinault are just two of the cyclists who have recently come close to having their careers end because of knee problems.

Jim Holmes, MD, and Andy Pruitt, PA, ATC, who have treated some of the top cyclists in the world, reported at the 1991 International Olympic Medical Conference that anterior knee problems—specifically, chondromalacia and patella tendinitis—were the most common problems found in 63% of the 134 cyclists in their study. Medial knee injuries were diagnosed in 21% of the cyclists and accounted for the second-largest type of overuse injury.

They reported that training modification, rest, ice, massage, and bicycle-position correction effectively improved symptoms in 75% of those treated. Second, their work showed that most injuries occurred predominantly in the preseason and race season: the time of year when your mileage is high, you are pushing large gears, and you may not wear cold-weather clothing when you should.

Thomas Dickson, MD, team physician for the U.S. Cycling Team at several world championships, states that "many cyclists often make the mistake of keeping their saddles too low and, secondly, many people ride in too high a gear. By riding along in a high gear with a low saddle position, the cyclist is unnecessarily increasing the force across the kneecap at the top of the pedal stroke." On the other hand, a saddle that is too high causes excessive extension of the knee and undue pressure on the knee area. Ride only gears that you are comfortable with, and be sure you have properly fit the bike to your measurements, as discussed in chapter 9.

How the foot is positioned on the pedal can also affect the pressure on the knee. The use of clipless pedals, which allow the foot to "float" a few degrees during the pedal stroke, reduces stress on the knee's ligaments. But remember to have someone experienced check your initial cleat alignment on the pedal. Visit your local bike shop and use a rotational adjustment device (RAD) to adjust your cleats properly (for more information, see chapter 9).

Wearing warm clothing during cold weather also helps protect the knees. Wear tights when the temperature is below 60 degrees Fahrenheit. In inclement weather, wear tights that have a wind-proof material over the front of the legs. And during the spring or while riding in the mountains, when and where the weather can change rapidly, carry leg warmers with you on the bike.

Hot Feet

If you experience "hot feet," that numbness or burning sensation in the balls of your feet, there are several remedies to consider. First, check to make sure the forefoot of the shoe is wide enough to accommodate your foot. You may also consider inserting a thin replacement insole in your shoe. Spenco makes an excellent replacement insole that is available at most bicycle and sporting goods shops. If you still have problems, you might try using a leather-soled shoe with an insole; this combination attenuates road shock better than nylon or lexan.

The type of shoe closure you decide upon may also add to your cycling comfort. You have a choice of Velcro closures, laces, or a combination of both. Recently, ski-binding-type closures have been added to several brands of shoes. Velcro closures are popular among triathletes because Velcro makes the shoes easier to get in and out of in the transition area. Their other advantage is that the tension can be easily adjusted during long rides, which is important when your feet swell after about 50 miles of riding on a hot day.

Sore Hands

The ulnar nerve is the major nerve of the lower arm. Descending along the inside of the forearm, it enters the hand on the palm side. Stress on this nerve causes numbness in your hand, weakness in your grip, and loss of muscular control in your fourth and fifth fingers.

Every time you ride a bike, road or trail vibrations are transmitted through the bike to your body. Wearing no gloves or worn-out gloves, using inferior bar grips, riding rough trails, and riding in an incorrect position can lead to ulnar neuropathy, or deadening of the ulnar nerve. Adjusting the handlebars to allow proper weight distribution, using quality handlebar grips, and wearing padded gloves will help prevent or decrease pain and discomfort. But ignoring continued pressure and vibration in the palms of your hands can lead to permanent nerve damage.

Until recently, if a cyclist needed some cushioning to alleviate sore hands, she looked for a pair of gloves with a thicker layer of foam padding or added more handlebar padding to her bike. This may have contributed to loss of road feel and interfered with shifting and braking. But now several manufacturers have stepped forward with the use of viscoelastic polymers, or "gels," offering cycling gloves with gel pads in the palms.

The viscoelastic polymers absorb shocks and vibrations that are transferred through the handlebars to the hands, elbows, and shoulders. These materials add a protective layer of life-like synthetic tissue that absorbs and evenly disperses handlebar pressures. In addition, gels will not compact over time, as foams do, and lose their ability to attenuate trail shock.

Burnout

The phenomenon of overtraining—also known as staleness, burnout, or fatigue—is very real. Considering the length of the cycling season, family responsibilities, and the demands placed on today's athletes in school, cyclists have good reason to watch out for staleness and symptoms of overtraining.

When you train, it is an essential and difficult task to find your optimum training thresholds and not exceed the limits of your stress and adaptation capacities. Because of the scope of this topic, we will not attempt to cover all the factors and possible mechanisms thought to contribute to overtraining. But we will look at evidence that implicates specific physiological and psychological variables that have been shown to be related to the deterioration of athletic performance due to overtraining.

In *The Lore of Running*, Dr. Tim Noakes gives examples of several nationally ranked athletes with symptoms of overtraining. One athlete exhibited the classic physical and psychological signs when his morning pulse had increased by 10 beats and he complained that he was lethargic, was sleeping poorly, and had less enthusiasm for training and, particularly, competition. He expressed concern that his legs felt sore and heavy and that the feeling had lasted for several training sessions. Another distance runner reported that 3 weeks after a marathon he was still sleeping poorly, had a persistent sore throat, and had low energy levels. These two athletes were exhibiting some of the classic signs and symptoms of overtraining (see Table 11.2). Both were in urgent need of complete rest from hard training.

The symptoms of overtraining may be seen in the athlete who is eager to excel and begins to train frequently and intensely. At first the athlete improves, but after a while his times become stationary and below his set goals. Anxious to pass the dead point, the athlete begins to train even harder. Instead of improving, his times become worse, and he begins to feel inadequate and frustrated. Besides declines in performance, some changes in personality and behavior can be detected. The athlete has developed to a state of staleness.

A good example of this happened during the summer of 1986, when Janelle Parks, a member of the U.S. National Team, was having a hard time finishing races and completing training sessions prior to the World Championships. For a while, she thought that it would be best to train

Table 11.2 Physical and Psychological Characteristics of Staleness	
Physical changes	**Emotional and behavioral changes**
Muscle soreness	Irritability
Gradual weight loss	Loss of enthusiasm
A drawn look	Lack of appetite
Swelling of the lymph nodes	Depression
Increased morning heart rate	Anxiety
Heavy legs	Desire to quit training
Constipation or diarrhea	Sleep disturbances
Inability to complete training	Loss of self-confidence
Fatigue	Inability to concentrate
Flu-like symptoms	

harder and put in more miles on the road. Her performance continued to decline. The coaching staff was able to convince her to take about 5 days off the bike and rest. She returned to cycling refreshed. Several weeks later she finished second in the women's World Championship road race.

Physiological Indicators for Monitoring Overtraining. In the early 1980s, Dick Brown, who at the time was an administrator and physiologist at Athletics West (a world-class running club), conducted a study to try to identify potential indicators of overtraining among athletes. Of the several dozen indicators monitored, three were found to be helpful to athletes in their daily training and could be recorded in their training diaries without expensive monitoring equipment. These were morning body weight, morning heart rate, and hours of sleep.

Brown's research found that if an athlete's morning heart rate was 10% or higher, if he received 10% less sleep, or if his weight was down 3% or more, then his body was telling him that it had not recovered from ths previous hard workout or that some form of illness was plaguing him. Brown's research points out that an athlete should cut back on that day's workout if she has two abnormal indicators and should take the day off and nap if she registers in the red on all three indicators.

If the signs of staleness or overtraining are present, you may have to suspend training for several days or decrease the intensity and duration of the sessions. If strong signs or symptoms prevail, it is possible you will have to spend days or weeks at a decreased level of training before you recover and can return to hard training.

Preventing Overtraining. What can be done to prevent overtraining? Take the following measures into account:

1. Sleep at least 8 hours a night when you are training hard.
2. Eat a balanced diet that includes all the basic nutrients.
3. Do at least 8 to 10 weeks of endurance work to build up a good base. Do not increase the frequency, duration, or intensity of the training sessions too quickly.
4. Gradually build up the quantity and quality of your training so that you are prepared both physically and mentally for its increasing volume.
5. Many coaches recommend taking a 15- to 30-minute nap before the afternoon workout.
6. When you are training hard, the intensity of your work should correspond to your individual level of fitness and experience, not someone else's.
7. Know yourself and how you react to stress, and continually review your mental training log to monitor your stress and training goals.

8. Use a training diary, and record morning pulse rate, body weight, sleep patterns, medical problems, and all your training sessions on a daily basis.
9. Schedule days of rest into your training program on a periodic basis. They will make you stronger.

Every discussion of overtraining usually ends with the same, and rather indefinite, definitive statement: Too little stress, physical or psychological, does not bring about desired changes; too much stress is harmful. But by being aware of your body's warning signals and by knowing the stages of adaptation, you can progress safely through training and steadily improve your fitness.

Environmental Conditions

Cycling is an outdoor sport. That's probably one of the things that draws you to it: Breaking away from your house, your school, or your office can bring you a great sense of freedom. Taking that twist road as fast as you can or climbing that hill is hot, demanding work. Still, you love it.

Let's face it, though: Sometimes the great outdoors can be a great pain. As fun as it is, there are challenges other than the road to overcome: heat and humidity, air pollution, and the thin air found at high altitudes.

Heat and Humidity

As the rains of spring fade into the hot, hazy days of summer, cyclists must adjust to riding in the heat. Excess heat can trouble any cyclist, beginner or experienced stage-race rider, causing problems from simple tiredness to heat exhaustion.

During cycling, heat produced by the working muscles exceeds heat released by the body, and body temperature rises. The rise in body temperature causes an increase in sweating and blood flow to the skin. Heat is removed by the evaporation of sweat from the skin.

The most efficient way to lose heat during cycling is primarily through sweating and with some convective heat loss. Convective heat loss is increased as the air temperature drops. On a long ride, a cyclist may incur sweat losses of 1/2 to 2 pounds per hour. Even under moderate weather conditions (65 to 79 degrees Fahrenheit, little cloud cover, and moderate humidity) there is the threat of heat stress. Water loss of this extent puts severe demands on the circulatory system, which is approximately 70% water. When water is removed from the blood, its capacity to carry nutrients to the working muscles, as well as its ability to distribute heat to the skin to be vaporized as sweat, is reduced. When the cooling mechanism fails because of dehydration, the result is heat exhaustion or heat stroke.

Heat exhaustion is characterized by peripheral circulatory collapse. The cyclist becomes weak and fatigued and may faint. Headache and nausea are other symptoms. When heat exhaustion occurs, stop riding immediately and move to a cool and shaded area. If possible, begin drinking fluids and have someone put cold wet towels over your body. Seek medical help if your condition does not improve fairly rapidly or if your symptoms get worse.

Heat stroke is caused by failure of the sweating mechanism. It is characterized by a rapidly increasing body temperature. The skin is dry, the body temperature is over 105 degrees Fahrenheit, and the pulse is rapid and weak. The cyclist may be unconscious.

Treatment is immediate emergency care. Lower the body temperature to below 102 degrees as soon as possible using cold water. If the victim is conscious, give him cold fluids. Immediately take the victim to the hospital, and keep wetting all body surfaces on the way.

Ingesting fluids while cycling in the heat can help lower body temperature. Research completed on cyclists shows that rectal (core) temperatures were 2 degrees lower when cyclists drank fluids than when they did not. One cyclist's internal temperature reached 105.5 when he ran out of fluid, but leveled off at 103 when he drank fluids, during a 2-hour ride at 75% of maximum in an environmental chamber.

Many cyclists will go on a 50- to 100-mile ride on a hot day with only two water bottles. In a ride of this distance, a cyclist may lose from 7 to 10 pounds of water weight if she rides hard on a very hot day. Even if the cyclist drinks two bottles (approximately 40 ounces), this will only replace about 2-1/2 pounds of fluid. The advantages of drinking plenty of fluids are lower core temperature and delay of stress on the circulatory system, allowing the body to perform at its maximum.

In addition to drinking fluids, cyclists can acclimate to excessive heat and humidity by cycling at a moderate pace in a hot environment. Aim to ride between 1 and 1-1/2 hours per day for 5 to 15 days before taking a long ride, entering a tour, or racing in hot and humid weather. The cyclist who has acclimated to the heat will be able to perform better because she has a lower internal temperature and heart rate, a better regulation of body temperature, and fewer heat-stress symptoms than a cyclist who has not. Exposure to heat without exercise results in only slight acclimatization. So it is important for a cyclist who works out in air-conditioned places but is going to have to race in the heat—or for a cyclist who is heading to a warmer climate for the winter—to get some hot-weather training in as often as possible.

There are a number of other tricks you can use to prevent overheating. During periods of extreme heat and humidity, ride during the coolest part of the day whenever possible. This may mean rising early and riding before you go to work or school. Second, if you are sensitive to heat, the hotter the day, the slower and shorter you should ride. Third, regardless of hydration and acclimatization, a cyclist can add to heat stress by wearing improper clothing. A light-colored jersey will help reflect the sun's rays, not absorb them like a dark jersey. A loose jersey of a breathable fabric will allow more sweat to evaporate. Never wear a long-sleeve jersey or tights in hot weather.

Fourth, keep track of your body weight; don't allow yourself to get into a state of chronic dehydration. This is especially important if you're training or riding a tour of several days in length in the summer. Weigh yourself each morning; if you are down 2 or 3 pounds from the day before, you have not rehydrated yourself properly. You should make an effort to drink plenty of fluids at meals and in the evening during hot weather.

Finally, reconsider what fluids you drink during cycling. As described in chapter 8, fluids ingested during cycling should contain 5% to 10% carbohydrate and small amounts of electrolytes. Such drinks will provide a source of fuel for the working muscles and will facilitate the absorption of water and glucose from the intestine. Find a sports drink on the market that tastes good to you when you are cycling and use it on rides lasting over 1 hour. You will be surprised how it will improve your performance and make the ride more enjoyable.

Although the summer sun can melt the asphalt, the properly prepared cyclist, armed with common sense and plenty of fluids, can ride all summer long without overheating.

Air Pollution

It was warm, but not very hot—a great day for a time trial. The sky was clear and the winds were light. Then after several hours of riding you began experiencing shortness of breath, coughing spells, and a nagging headache.

What you did not realize was that the race site was near several industries and the course followed an eight-lane highway, both of which contributed to the high levels of carbon monoxide and ozone in the atmosphere. At the finish, your time was significantly slower than normal, and several other cyclists said they had experienced similar symptoms.

Athletes' lungs are at special risk from airborne contaminants because their increased rate and depth of respiration during exercise results in their respiratory tracts being exposed to high amounts of pollutants. Also, the necessity of breathing through the mouth bypasses the scrubbing action of the nasal passages. There are many different chemicals that pollute our urban environment, but we will concentrate here on ozone and carbon monoxide.

Ozone.   Ozone, a common and typical constituent of the urban environment, is the most toxic contaminant and causes the greatest decreases in athletic performance. It is a powerful oxidizing agent and can constrict air passages, thus leading to a lower capacity for forced expiration. Ozone is produced photochemically via the action of ultraviolet radiation on unburned gasoline vapors and other gases. Once created, it remains in the area for a long time. This form of ozone is not to be confused with (our friend) the ozone layer, one of the outer layers of the atmosphere that surrounds the earth.

Current research on ozone's effect on athletes confirms that heavy exercise drastically increases the toxicity. Work completed a few years ago by Henry Gong, MD, at the Human Performance Laboratory at the University of California at Davis found that exercising in simulated ozone concentrations equivalent to an average-to-bad day in a large city (.30 parts per million) greatly reduced performance. Almost half the subjects who engaged in heavy exercise could not complete the 60-minute tests, and all said they could not perform normally under these conditions. Many complained of wheezing, shortness of breath, headaches, and nausea.

Cyclists who train in high-ozone areas should consider training in the early morning or evening, because ozone concentrations tend to increase rapidly after 8 a.m., peak early in the afternoon (about 1 p.m.), and then decrease to near background levels by 7 p.m.

No one can predict an athlete's sensitivity to ozone, but it has been shown that sensitivity diminishes with repeated exposure. This suggests an adaptive response in the lungs as cells damaged by exposure are replaced by those more resistant. At the Institute of Environmental Stress, University of California at Santa Barbara, a study by Barbara Drinkwater measured the effects of ozone exposure on young men for 2 hours a day for 1 week. The men's sensitivity was greatest on the 2nd consecutive day of exposure. By the 5th day, they no longer responded to the ozone. In effect, they adapted, and the greater the initial sensitivity, the longer it took for the adaptation to occur.

Despite the adaptive response, cyclists would gain little by attempting to acclimate themselves to ozone pollution. Some athletes take a long time to adapt, and others never adapt at all. And we don't know if it's a healthy adaptation, similar to adapting to heat or altitude. Research coming out of the University of California at Los Angeles Medical School shows that long-term exposure may lead to lung fibrosis and emphysema.

Carbon Monoxide.   Carbon monoxide is another air pollutant found in large cities. It is emitted through car exhaust, industrial waste, and cigarette smoke. Its chief danger is that it squeezes oxygen out of the circulatory process. As carbon monoxide enters the bloodstream via the lungs, it readily combines with the hemoglobin in the blood—200 times faster than oxygen does!—effectively cutting down the body's oxygen supply. Even at low concentrations of 5% of the volume of air taken into the lungs, carbon monoxide has been shown to produce headaches, dizziness, confusion, and increased body temperature.

For a study conducted on athletic performance after exposure to auto exhaust, a team of swimmers was driven around the Los Angeles area for an hour before a meet while a control group remained at poolside. The control group did measurably and consistently better in competition. The implications to cyclists should be clear. More than one athlete has found himself "gassed out" by cars, buses, and motorcycles while she was training or racing.

Here are a few guidelines to remember to help minimize the risks and discomfort of carbon monoxide pollution:

1. If possible, avoid training on or by roads during the peak traffic periods, generally, 6 to 9 a.m. and 4 to 8 p.m.
2. During the winter, if you have to train along roads, and if you have a choice between morning and afternoon training, choose the afternoon. In the morning, wind speeds are generally light and pollutants are not as easily dispersed as they are later in the day.
3. Avoid roads any time there is high truck usage.
4. Ride as far right of the road as possible without compromising your safety. A few feet can make a significant difference.

You need to be just as concerned about the level of pollution in the air as you are about the temperature and the number of hills on the course. It is one more vital way to prevent exhaustion.

Altitude

Above 6,000 feet, breathing is the limiting factor to performance. When you travel to the mountains, atmospheric pressure decreases and the air is thinner, so there's less oxygen available. You will notice that your breathing is faster and deeper, your heart rate is elevated, and at times you feel short of breath. These are the normal and helpful results of your body's attempt to get more oxygen to the working muscles.

You may also have a headache, a touch of nausea, or feel tired. About 15% of all cyclists have such symptoms, which usually go away in 24 to 48 hours. As your body works harder to get oxygen, you will lose more fluid than usual from the deeper breathing and from sweating—although you won't often notice this. It is important to maintain your body's fluids, so drink two or more times the water or juices you would at sea level. Alcohol and caffeine have an extra impact at altitude, so consume them in moderation.

At this altitude the sun has more burning power, and a bad sunburn can spoil your race, so use a protective sunscreen. It can also get cold very quickly at altitude, so while you're out training, in addition to extra fluids and sunscreen, be sure to carry a light jacket, tights, gloves, and a hat. Hypothermia (low body temperature) can come on rapidly if you are caught out in a rainstorm without proper protection at 6,000-plus feet—even during the summer.

Sleeping problems are the number one complaint people have when they arrive at altitude. The lack of oxygen affects both sleep and arousal patterns, so your sleep tends to be lighter and you wake up a lot during the night. You also may experience a dry mouth while you're sleeping, so you may want to keep a glass of water by your bed at night.

So how can you prepare for cycling at altitude? We know that the longer you can train at altitude, the better prepared you will be to race at altitude. Your respiratory distress will go down, your body will begin to produce more red blood cells to help carry oxygen, and more changes will begin to take place at the cellular level. The whole effect is a more rapid and efficient movement of oxygen from the lungs to the tissues. The net effect of this acclimatization to high altitude is a gradual improvement in performance.

Two weeks to acclimate is best, but 7 to 10 days will do for some cyclists. A more realistic choice for some people is several weekend visits to altitude. This can be feasible if there are mountains not too far from where you live. Try to get into the 6,000- to 9,000-foot range. Your best bet is getting in several visits to altitude and then coming out 7 to 10 days before the race.

If such acclimatization is not possible, then literally fly to your event as late as possible the day before the race, compete, and leave before the effects of altitude can take place.

Here are some additional tips to follow throughout your training at altitude and during your final stay before a race:

1. Don't waste your first days loafing around. Light exercise stimulates breathing and circulation and speeds adjustment.
2. Even if you are having trouble sleeping, try to get plenty of rest.
3. Use a humidifier. Bring one with you, or rent one while you are there.
4. Eat smaller but more frequent meals, because digestion can be more difficult at altitude. Eat plenty of carbohydrates, which you need for energy and recovery.
5. Take deeper breaths as often as possible.

6. Drink as much water as you can, but avoid alcohol for the first 2 or 3 days.
7. Stop for short rest periods if your heart rate exceeds your target range for extended periods of time.
8. Carry and drink more water during training than your thirst dictates. When you run, drink a little every 5 or 10 minutes.
9. In the final days before the race, consume 60% to 70% of your calories in carbohydrates. This will ensure that your muscles are loaded with glycogen for race day.

Keeping these training tips in mind, here are some additional things to remember on race day:

1. Set out at a pace that does not allow for undue lactic acid accumulation. If your respiratory rate appears faster or your depth of breathing more labored than usual, chances are the pace is too intense.
2. Make sure you accept fluids and food at the feed zones. Do not allow yourself to become dehydrated.
3. Carry extra clothing; in the mountains the weather changes rapidly, the wind can dramatically reduce temperatures, and hypothermia can set in quickly.

With a better understanding of your responses to altitude and a well-thought-out training program, you can have a very enjoyable experience training or competing at altitude.

When You Change Environments: Cycling Away From Home

You have trained long and hard to reach your level of fitness. You have started traveling to races in various parts of the country and plan a trip to race internationally during the early season. Did you know that your fine edge can be quickly lost after traveling across as little as one time zone or that eating improperly in a foreign country can spell immediate disaster?

Two of the most common concerns of traveling (OK, besides airline meals) are jet lag and traveler's diarrhea. A cyclist who understands the problems of extended travel and how to avoid travel-related minor illnesses will be able to perform more effectively.

What Is Jet Lag?

Most plants and animals, including humans, have become synchronized with the 24-hour light-and-dark cycle. This is known as the circadian rhythm, from the Latin *circa dies*, meaning "about a day." Because our body rhythms are synchronized with this cycle, we sleep, work, and perform more effectively at certain times of the day than at others. Body temperature steadily drops early in the morning while we're sleeping and rises in the afternoon. Similarly, blood pressure and hormonal functions fluctuate according to a 24-hour cycle.

When the light-and-dark cycle is changed, the body rhythms become desynchronized, and an athlete may experience problems with sleep, digestion, alertness, performance, recovery, and temperament. In females, menstrual pain and dysfunction may occur.

Upsets in the body's circadian rhythm will occur after traveling quickly through several time zones. Generally, jet lag follows this pattern:

- 1 to 2 time zones crossed: little or no effect on you
- 3 to 6 time zones crossed: noticeable effect
- 7 to 10 time zones crossed: considerable effect
- 11 to 15 time zones crossed: marked effect

How to Travel

The following guidelines can be used to reduce the effects of extended air travel and the resulting changes in circadian rhythm:

1. Some cyclists like to take a very long ride just prior to a trip, knowing that they might be spending 1 or 2 days in transit and, hence, not be able to ride. That's a mistake. A trip through a number of time zones is a workout in itself. If it will be morning when you arrive at your destination, try to sleep on the plane; if it will be evening, try to avoid sleeping on the plane.

2. Try to change your sleeping schedule before the trip. For example, if you will be traveling to where the waking hours come earlier than you are used to, you should go to bed earlier and get up earlier for several days. In this way you will adapt somewhat to the time schedule at your destination. Before traveling to a time zone where the waking hours come later than you are used to, retire later and rise later.

3. Eat lightly during the trip, but drink plenty of fluids like juice and water to avoid dehydration. Avoid alcohol and caffeine.

4. Mild isometric exercises and walking around the cabin during the flight may relieve stiffness and boredom and help lessen fatigue.

5. If possible, schedule your arrival for the evening hours. Otherwise, a light ride after you arrive may help you get to sleep.

6. During the first few days don't let the excitement of your new surroundings cause you to work too hard. Take it easy, or you may get worn down and increase your chances of becoming sick.

7. Prior to the trip, learn about the environment you'll be entering. Prepare for the weather conditions, customs, food, transportation, and so on. This may reduce some of the stress.

Adapting Your Diet

A major factor that influences your degree of impairment from jet lag is diet: the type of food you eat and the timing of your meals. Certain foods appear to help the body adjust more quickly to changes in circadian rhythms, and properly timing food intake has also been shown to facilitate adaptation following transmeridian flight.

According to Dr. Charles Ehret, one of the leading authorities on diet and jet lag, "Two of the major keys in combating jet lag lie in the storage organs for energy reserves of the body, including the muscles and the liver, and the body's natural production of glycogen, which, in a very real sense, is the fuel of the body." Alternating light and heavy meals before a flight continually empties the body's supply of glycogen and then replenishes it, allowing a person's circadian rhythms to quickly shift to a new time zone.

If You're Going South

The condition of acute diarrhea has been most extensively studied in Americans visiting Mexico, where about 60% of travelers are affected. Known as "tourista" and "Montezuma's revenge" in Mexico, traveler's diarrhea can be just as common in the Mediterranean and Europe. Cyclists visiting the Soviet Union, where it's commonly known as "trotsky's," have also suffered it.

Contributory causes of the disease include changes in living habits, unusual foods or drinks, and viral or bacterial infections. But the major cause is the bacteria E. coli (Escherichia coli), which stimulates the intestine to hypersecrete fluid and electrolytes. E. coli can be picked up when you drink from mountain streams.

There are several ways to help prevent traveler's diarrhea. Drink only bottled water and use it for ice cubes, coffee, and brushing your teeth. Peel your fruits and avoid leafy vegetables. And stay away from dairy products that have not been pasteurized.

Recently some physicians have been administering the antibiotic doxcycline (trade name, Vibramycin). Although this and other antibiotics reduce the incidence of diarrhea, there is concern that extended use of this drug might induce resistance to bacteria. It can also cause skin rashes in some people when they are exposed to strong sunlight.

Bismuth subsalicylate, known by its trade name of Pepto-Bismol, has also been used to treat and prevent traveler's diarrhea. Its greatest benefit is that it is nearly nontoxic. In a recent study, preventive oral doses of Pepto-Bismol (2 ounces taken several times a day) reduced the incidence of diarrhea by 50%. Whether the inconvenience of such a large dose is worth a 50% chance is a personal decision. In any case, the compound is safe and can also be used to help treat the disease once it has occurred.

If you get traveler's diarrhea, go on a liquid diet that includes fruit juices that are rich in potassium, and add a pinch of salt. As symptoms subside, bland foods such as bananas, rice, toast, and eggs can be added. Dairy foods should be avoided.

It may be wise to pack a bottle of diarrhea medicine when you travel to other countries, just in case. Remember, if you use antibiotics or other medication (like Lomotil) for the prevention or relief of traveler's diarrhea, they should only be taken with a physician's advice.

Medical Problems Away From Home

If you get sick or injured on a trip, for heaven's sake, see a doctor if at all possible. Try to find out what it is—for example, cold, flu, or virus—and try to determine the recovery period.

Here are some books and other resources that will give you background information on medical care and services in foreign countries:

- *Travel Healthy* (1986) by Harold M. Silverman. Avon Books, New York, NY.
- *Traveler's Medical Manual* (1985) by Angelo T. Scotti with Thomas A. Moore. Berkeley Publishing Group, New York, NY.
- *Health Guide for the International on the Trip* (1978) and *Planning Your Trip* (1988) from International Travel and Your Health, Office of Epidemiology, New Mexico Health and Environment, Santa Fe, NM.

In general, healthy traveling is no longer a contradiction in terms. You can travel, enjoy your trip and cycling experiences, and return home without undue stress or illness. Just incorporate planning and prevention into your itinerary.

Personal Conditions

As if it weren't enough that you must guard against injuries and adverse environmental conditions, there are a number of non-cycling-related medical conditions, from the common cold to a chronic disease, that you may have to cope with. We'll consider some of these in the remainder of this chapter.

Colds

Though it is relatively mild, the common cold is one of the most ubiquitous hazards known to humankind. It afflicts nearly everyone many times, and some more than others. Despite our occasional delusions of invincibility, even cyclists are susceptible to colds.

Viruses are the cause of the common cold. Incapable of living on their own, these small particles need the human body to survive. Viruses invade their host—you—through the lining of the nose and throat. At some point you may feel temporarily worse, suffering headaches and muscle aches, but these more severe symptoms are usually caused by a brief run of the virus through the body. Rarely does your temperature stay elevated for long.

Be a Loner.   The primary factor that makes a person susceptible to colds, and something we usually have little control over, is exposure. Exposure to a cold virus can occur simply by touching the hand of an infected person or any other contaminated surface. This is why individuals who live or work in crowded conditions are more susceptible to colds.

Contrary to popular wisdom, there is absolutely no evidence that cold weather, dampness, or changes in temperature will lead to colds. The only reason for not cycling on a cold, damp day is that it is unpleasant.

Coping With a Cold.   The onset of a cold is usually announced by dryness or burning in the nose; then a watery nasal discharge appears. This is the point when treatments of nasal sprays, antihistamines, and decongestants usually begin. Despite relieving the symptoms, these drugs do nothing to the viral cause, nor do they prevent further complications. In fact, most of the time they make you feel tired and lethargic.

The most effective treatment for a cold is to liquefy and warm your mucus so that it will flow more freely and carry with it more of the virus as it leaves your body. One method of doing this is to take a shower or lie in a bath and breathe in warm, wet air. Drinking warm fluids will also help.

Adequate humidity in your living and working areas is quite important in cold prevention and treatment. To keep the relative humidity from dropping below 35%, a home humidifier is a good preventive investment. Cycling outdoors in the winter can aggravate dry airways because of the low humidity associated with lower temperatures. Wearing a face mask and drinking fluids will alleviate this problem.

Running Its Course.   A cold should not curtail your training. If a cold strikes, increase your fluid intake, turn the humidifier on, and take aspirin to relieve your aches and pains. Unless there are complications, you should be able to maintain your cycling program.

When symptoms progress to involve more body functions, special precautions are advised. Increased muscular pain, ear infections, a sore throat, and colored mucus are signals that complications have arisen. Medical assistance is required, and antibiotics will have to be used to fight the secondary bacterial infections. Now you must curtail your training and rest.

Fever associated with these bacterial infections is your body's defense of increasing your metabolism so that your body will produce more antibodies to kill invading germs. Fever may also be beneficial because many germs that attack humans grow best at the body's normal temperature of 98.6 degrees Fahrenheit. They do not multiply at higher temperatures. Fever is the body's way of telling you that it is fighting bacterial infection, and you're better off resting, not cycling.

As soon as your temperature returns to normal, it is all right to resume your cycling program. However, you may be surprised to discover how quickly you lost your endurance. Studies on endurance athletes show that after 10 days of not exercising, they lose about 10% of their endurance. The results may be more devastating after a cold associated with fever. A study conducted in Sweden showed that colds associated with muscle aches and pains kept athletes from regaining their full capabilities for over several weeks. It took this long for certain chemicals necessary for energy production to return to normal levels in the muscles.

Once the symptoms of the cold or infection subside, recovery is an individual matter. Remember, as long as no fever is present, it appears safe to cycle through a cold, taking care to ride within the limits of your energy and capability to stay warm. Gentle exercise tends to break up the congestion quicker than complete rest does. But keep the pace down to prevent coughing.

Colds with fever, and the flu, require more delicate care. A period of convalescence—first rest, then a gradual return to a full schedule—is a must. Don't ride with a fever. After that, as a rule take 2 days easy for each day of fever. For example, 4 days of fever and symptoms would mean an additional 8 days of recovery. Extended cycling that causes fatigue should be avoided or recurrence is a distinct possibility.

The Asthmatic Cyclist

What is it like to ride with asthma? Alexi Grewal, Olympic road champion, once described it as trying to breathe through a straw while riding. Grewal is among the 10% to 15% of the population that suffers from asthma, 60% to 90% of whom are susceptible to exercise-induced asthma (EIA) attacks.

Exactly how exercise leads to an asthma attack is not firmly established, but breathing a lot of cool, dry air seems to be the most common trigger. Incoming air must be warmed and moistened before it reaches the alveoli, the minute air sacs deep in the lungs where oxygen and carbon dioxide are exchanged. Cool, dry air saps the bronchi of heat and moisture, triggering broncospasms (narrowing of the breathing passages), which restrict air flow to the alveoli.

One of the best courses of action for cyclists who experience EIA is to warm up properly and gradually increase riding effort or speed. Asthmatic athletes who use a good warm-up or increase the workload gradually are less likely to induce EIA than those who rapidly increase their level of work. Often cyclists who experience EIA will ride with a balaclava or a mask to moisten the air when the temperature is below 50° Fahrenheit.

There are some medications that are legal for athletes to use for asthma. One of the more popular asthma medications is albuteral. Effective in relieving the symptoms after they begin, albuteral provides protection from EIA in 80% to 95% of the athletes who use it before exercise. When it is administered with a special inhaler 10 to 20 minutes before a ride albuteral helps prevent broncospasms from occurring. Another medication, cromolyn sodium, is slightly less effective but has the fewest complaints of side effects.

Some foods, air pollutants, pollens, and other allergens can trigger asthma. Because asthma is a chronic disease, there's no instant remedy. But by continually managing their illness through medication, proper warm-up, and relaxation techniques, asthmatic cyclists can keep their competitive edge.

The Diabetic Cyclist

Recent findings in diabetic care have solved the problems that used to hinder people who have diabetes from becoming active in cycling. But there are still too many diabetics who are a lot less active than they would like to be only because they do not understand how to cope with the disease. If you have diabetes, not only can you become an active and successful athlete, but cycling can even help you control the condition. To perform at your best safely, however, you need to understand how exercise and diabetes interact and how to adjust your exercise program to allow for the physiological changes training and competition will cause.

Basically, there are two types of diabetics. Type II, or late-onset, diabetes means there is enough insulin in the blood to pass sugar into the muscle cells where it is converted to energy. Insulin is a hormone in the body used to help transport glucose from the blood into the cells. In Type

II diabetes, however, the cells do not respond adequately to the hormone, and blood sugar levels remain high. This form of diabetes usually occurs in middle-age people who are overweight and inactive, and it can be dramatically improved through diet and exercise.

In Type I diabetes, the pancreas doesn't produce enough insulin to help transport the glucose into the muscle cells. This form of diabetes usually occurs in younger people, before the late 20s, and injections of insulin and a controlled diet must be followed to compensate for the body's lack of insulin. In either type, if diabetes is left untreated, the results are high levels of blood glucose, which can cause heart, kidney, and vision problems.

The three major influences on blood glucose levels are insulin, diet, and exercise. In nondiabetics, the pancreas automatically releases the proper amount of insulin needed at any given moment to regulate blood glucose. The diabetic, on the other hand, lacks this built-in mechanism and must control his body's delicate balance. Because insulin, diet, and exercise affect one another, exercise cannot be changed without a corresponding change in insulin or diet, and diet cannot be altered unless insulin therapy is changed. Further adjustments must be made to account for illness, emotional stress, menstruation, and infection, all of which affect insulin levels.

What happens when a diabetic becomes a cyclist? Although exercise cannot cure diabetes or end insulin injections, it does help lower blood glucose and can lessen the amount of insulin needed daily. Exercise has an insulin-like effect on the muscles in that it increases the permeability of the muscle membranes. By doing this, it also reduces the amount of insulin required. Over the long run, being active lowers the amount of glucose in the blood, which is the main objective of controlling diabetes.

Increasing the level of activity and exercise for an individual with diabetes requires careful planning and scheduling. To compensate for the glucose-lowering effects of exercise, a diabetic athlete must go into a ride with a normal or slightly elevated blood glucose level. This is easily achieved by eating a carbohydrate snack about 30 minutes before exercising.

Remember, the key to controlling diabetes is maintaining a consistent balance between exercise and energy output, food intake and insulin. A spur-of-the-moment ride or run may sound like fun, but if you have diabetes, you cannot modify your exercise routine without also modifying your medicine and/or diet. This kind of planning takes practice. Keep an accurate training diary in order to plan meals and the amount of insulin needed for the type of training session or race you have planned.

Diabetics who require insulin injections must plan carefully in advance so that they are not cycling miles away from their homes when insulin levels are peaking in the blood. The combined effect of insulin and exercise may allow too much glucose to enter the cells and result in low levels of blood glucose (hypoglycemia). If you have diabetes, carry carbohydrates in the form of candy or a sports drink with you on the bike in case of an emergency (weakness, headache, dizziness, confusion). To prevent hypoglycemia you will need to either decrease your insulin dosage or eat more food prior to your workout.

One technique that many diabetic athletes use is to eat immediately before and after exercise. The food you eat before the workout provides the glucose during the session. Then eat immediately after the workout and again a few hours later. Hypoglycemia episodes are not uncommon 3 to 4 hours after a hard workout or race, probably due to the muscles' need to replenish glycogen stores and their increased demand for glucose. Remember, exercise also increases the insulin sensitivity, making the diabetic athlete even more susceptible to postexercise hypoglycemia.

Where the insulin is injected is also important. If you inject insulin into an active cycling muscle, like the thigh or buttock, increased blood flow to the working muscle will cause the insulin to be absorbed quickly, which will lower blood glucose too quickly. Before you make any changes in insulin dosage or diet, please consult your physician.

Make sure you inform your training partners and coach of your condition. Your companions should also be informed of what to do in an emergency. If you are out on the road, your coach or partners should know the symptoms of hypoglycemia and hyperglycemia. Hyperglycemia (high blood glucose) may occur if you have not taken enough insulin or have consumed too much carbohydrate. Above all else, train with another person, carry carbohydrates with you at all times, and wear a medical-alert tag identifying your condition.

Women's Health Issues and Cycling

Before 1984, female cyclists were not participants in the Olympic Games. The limitation on women's road racing was defended on the grounds that long-distance sports (such as cycling and running) might be harmful to women's health. But research and position statements by the American College of Sports Medicine have done much to dispel the idea that endurance exercise is harmful for the healthy, trained female athlete.

Since 1984 other endurance events for women—such as the 70-kilometer team time trial, the 3,000-meter individual pursuit, and the 30-kilometer points race—have been added to the World Championships and/or Olympic Games.

Scientific studies show that men and women adapt to exercise training in a similar manner. Female road cyclists have high maximal oxygen consumptions and low relative fat content. The challenge of heat stress in long-distance cycling and the changes in oxygen pressure at altitude seem to be well tolerated by women. And the limited amount of studies available suggest that women have the same rate of orthopedic injuries. Still, women have to contend with some health issues that men never have to face.

Menstrual Patterns in Female Cyclists. Strenuous cycling can have an impact on just about every part of the body, including the female reproductive system. When women suddenly increase their levels of cycling activity, they often detect changes in the heaviness of their menstrual flows and in the amount of menstrual discomfort. Some women stop menstruating altogether (amenorrhea) or may have irregular menstrual cycles (oligomenorrhea).

According to Charlotte Sanborn and Wiltz Wangner, Jr., athletic amenorrhea is most common in girls and young women who engage in heavy physical training. Among cyclists, amenorrhea is most common among females who are putting in long miles and who are dieting to lose weight or maintain very lean physiques. There is also some evidence that being driven toward stressful patterns of achievement may also lead to irregular menstrual patterns ("The Female Athlete and the Menstrual Cycle," pp. 111-30 in *Sport Science Perspectives for Women*, J. Puhl, C.H. Brown, & R.O. Voy, eds).

If a woman is experiencing menstrual irregularity, it is important to rule out possible medical disorders and pregnancy. Many female cyclists assume that irregular menses are a normal result of hard training and are no cause for concern. Indeed, in most cases a short period without menstruation will cause no lasting negative health risks, but you want to make sure that you do not have a more serious problem. You should never assume that amenorrhea is either due to or related to cycling.

After a physician has ruled out a medical disorder, she may simply want to monitor you periodically during your training. Many times, the menstrual cycle will return to normal when training is decreased (as in the off-season).

However, recent research indicates that females who go for long periods of time without normal menstruation have some cause for concern. Amenorrhea and oligomenorrhea often indicate that levels of the hormone estrogen are low. Estrogen is important not only for normal reproductive function but also for controlling bone density. Research has shown that amenorrheic athletes have a much higher incidence of stress fractures, tendinitis, and muscle strains.

Studies of female athletes have shown that some have the bone densities of women in their 50s and 60s: They are exhibiting the symptoms of osteoporosis. Women who are training and dieting to be healthy and fit are in fact aging rapidly. When bone density decreases in the spinal column, these cyclists may be more susceptible to chronic back problems.

Bone loss may be slowed or prevented by calcium supplementation and/or estrogen or progesterone replacement. The American Academy of Pediatrics recommends prescribing low-dose oral contraceptives (less than 50 micrograms of estrogen per day) to protect against skeletal demineralization in amenorrheic girls over age 16. As with any medication, however, the harmful side effects must be weighed against the benefits of another treatment with less severe side effects. The key is to seek out medical care at the first signs of menstrual irregularity.

Cycling During Pregnancy.   Not many years ago, pregnant women were told to take it easy. Today, women are hearing that regular exercise during pregnancy is healthy for both the mother and the child.

As we know, everyone responds differently to exercise, and this includes pregnant women. Factors that influence individual response to exercise are body composition, age, body weight, environmental conditions, and physical condition.

As the pregnancy progresses, changes in endocrine, cardiovascular, and respiratory functioning will affect a woman's response to exercise. Cardiac output (blood pumped by the heart per minute) and blood volume will increase by 30% to 45% during pregnancy. Resting heart rate will also be higher, though arterial blood pressure tends to remain stable.

Many women are concerned about fetal responses to activity. They wonder if there will be a reduction in blood flow to the uterus during cycling. Research has shown that during moderate exercise there may be a slight decrease in overall uterine blood flow, but blood flow appears to be redistributed favoring the placental flow.

Many female cyclists choose to continue their training programs during pregnancy but have to modify the duration and intensity of exercise. Some programs may need to be modified as pregnancy progresses. Mountain biking will have to be eliminated, road training will have to be cut to shorter distances, and eventually a pregnant woman may have to switch to stationary cycling.

Cycling is a good non-weight-bearing activity. Many women find riding stationary bikes safer than riding on the road, especially when changes in their center of gravity affect their balance. Swimming is also an excellent non-weight-bearing activity.

Weight training may be continued during pregnancy, provided that the goal is strength maintenance and that proper breathing technique is practiced.

Avoid water skiing, horseback riding, scuba diving, and the like; stick to low-impact activities such as cycling. If it hurts while you're doing it or later in the evening or the next day, don't do it.

Follow these exercise precautions during pregnancy:

- Your core temperature should not exceed 101 degrees Fahrenheit. Check your temperature rectally early in your pregnancy after a standard workout and use this measure to help you guide workout intensity.
- Avoid saunas and hot tubs.
- Follow the American College of Obstetricians and Gynecologists' recommendation that you keep your heart rate below 140 beats per minute during exercise.
- Proper hydration and good nutrition are essential. Drink plenty of water during exercise, and establish sound eating habits.
- Discontinue exercise if any unusual symptoms occur, and consult your physician.

Cycling After Pregnancy.   Listen to your body, which will tell you when to resume exercise after delivery. If you had a normal delivery, you can probably resume exercising as soon as you can do so without pain. But a return to high-intensity cycling should be avoided prior to the postpartum examination because your muscles have not yet returned to your prepregnancy state and your chances of injury are greater. If you are breast feeding, you can exercise provided you have adequate breast support and maintain hydration. Include activities like cycling and walking in your program.

Many female athletes feel that they are stronger and actually improve their performance after pregnancy. It has even been postulated that the stresses of labor and delivery somehow make a woman tougher and better able to compete.

The Final Spin

It's safe to say that every year the competitive cyclist will become injured or ill at least a few times. Your best bet for treating the injury or illness is to be conservative and return to training cautiously. The competitive cyclist will find the line between overtraining and undertraining a fine one. Too much mileage and intensity may lead to injury and illness, too little to underachieving. Often this is what makes the difference between winning and losing at all levels of competition.

The cyclist who repeatedly loses training time will be in worse condition than the conservative and healthy cyclist. An important part of training is learning to prevent injuries and illnesses and knowing how and when to return to training.

Preventing injury and illness means eliminating their causes and reacting to the early warning signs. Most problems can be prevented, but once one occurs you must treat the cause, treat the injury, and rehabilitate your body in order to return to competitive fitness.

Appendix

The Cyclist's Directory:
Organizations and Services Worth Knowing About

These are organizations that offer services to both competitive and serious recreational cyclists. Contact these organizations for information on competition, training, coaching, and other benefits offered to their members.

U.S. Cycling Federation. 1750 East Boulder, Colorado Springs, CO 80909. (719) 578-4581. Governs bicycle road and track racing in the United States.

National Off-Road Bicycle Association. 1750 East Boulder, Colorado Springs, CO 80909. (719) 578-4717. Plans off-road events and governs off-road racing in the United States.

League of American Wheelmen. 190 West Ostend Street, Suite 120, Baltimore, MD 21230. (410) 539-3399. Sponsors annual rides and lobbies for cyclists' rights.

Triathlon Federation. P.O. Box 15820, Colorado Springs, CO 80935-5820. (719) 597-9090. Governs triathlons and duathlons in the United States.

International Human Powered Vehicle Association. P.O. Box 51225, Indianapolis, IN 46251-0255. (317) 876-9478. Promotes human-powered vehicle development and sponsors rallies and races.

Canadian Cycling Association. 1600 James Naismith Drive, Suite 810, Gloucester, ON K1B 5N4, Canada. (613) 748-5629. Governs amateur and professional racing in Canada and offers information on touring and provincial associations.

British Cycling Federation. 36 Rockingham Road, Kettering, Northants NN16 8HG, Great Britain. (0044-536) 412211. Governs amateur and professional cycling and touring in Great Britain.

Australian Cycling Federation. 689 Broadway, Sidney, NSW 2007, Australia. (0061-2) 2818688. Governs professional and amateur racing in Australia.

New Zealand Cycling Federation. P.O. Box 35-048, Christchurch, New Zealand. (0064-3) 385-1422. National organization for professional and amateur cycling in New Zealand.

Index

About the Author

Ed Burke has written or edited eight books on cycling and is renowned for translating the latest scientific research into practical applications for cyclists. He was a staff member of the 1980 and 1984 U.S. Olympic cycling teams and is coordinator of sports science and technology for the national cycling team. Ed holds a doctorate in exercise physiology from The Ohio State University and is an associate professor in the Department of Biology at the University of Colorado. He lives in Colorado Springs with his wife, Kathleen.

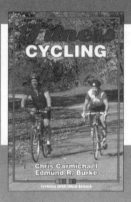